The Third Sector As A Renewable Resource for Europe

Bernard Enjolras • Lester M. Salamon
Karl Henrik Sivesind • Annette Zimmer

The Third Sector As A Renewable Resource for Europe

Concepts, Impacts, Challenges and Opportunities

Bernard Enjolras
Institute for Social Research (ISF)
Oslo, Norway

Karl Henrik Sivesind
Institute for Social Research
Oslo, Norway

Lester M. Salamon
John Hopkins University
Baltimore, MD, USA

Annette Zimmer
Institut für Politikwissenschaft
Westfälische Wilhelms-Universität
Münster, Germany

ISBN 978-3-030-10063-6   ISBN 978-3-319-71473-8 (eBook)
https://doi.org/10.1007/978-3-319-71473-8

© The Editor(s) (if applicable) and The Author(s) 2018. This book is an open access publication
Softcover re-print of the Hardcover 1st edition 2018
Open Access This book is licensed under the terms of the Creative Commons Attribution 4.0 International License (http://creativecommons.org/licenses/by/4.0/), which permits use, sharing, adaptation, distribution and reproduction in any medium or format, as long as you give appropriate credit to the original author(s) and the source, provide a link to the Creative Commons license and indicate if changes were made.
The images or other third party material in this book are included in the book's Creative Commons license, unless indicated otherwise in a credit line to the material. If material is not included in the book's Creative Commons license and your intended use is not permitted by statutory regulation or exceeds the permitted use, you will need to obtain permission directly from the copyright holder.
The use of general descriptive names, registered names, trademarks, service marks, etc. in this publication does not imply, even in the absence of a specific statement, that such names are exempt from the relevant protective laws and regulations and therefore free for general use.
The publisher, the authors and the editors are safe to assume that the advice and information in this book are believed to be true and accurate at the date of publication. Neither the publisher nor the authors or the editors give a warranty, express or implied, with respect to the material contained herein or for any errors or omissions that may have been made. The publisher remains neutral with regard to jurisdictional claims in published maps and institutional affiliations.

Cover illustration: Getty/moodboard

Printed on acid-free paper

This Palgrave Macmillan imprint is published by the registered company Springer International Publishing AG part of Springer Nature.
The registered company address is: Gewerbestrasse 11, 6330 Cham, Switzerland

Acknowledgments

This book synthetizes the findings of the Third Sector Impact (TSI) project funded by the European Union's Seventh Framework Program (FP7) for research, technological development and demonstration (grant agreement no. 613034). The project consortium included Ruth Simsa (Vienna University of Economics and Business), Bernard Enjolras, Karl Henrik Sivesind and Signe Bock-Segaard (Institute for Social research, Oslo), Lester M. Salamon and Wojciech Sokolowski (Johns Hopkins University, School of Advanced International Studies (SAIS) Bologna Center), Jeremy Kendall (University of Kent, School of Social Policy, Sociology and Social Research), Annette Zimmer and Benedikt Pahl (Westfälische Wilhelms-Universität Münster, Department of Political Science), John Mohan (Third Sector Research Centre—The University of Birmingham), Taco Brandsen and Ulla Pape (Radboud University Nijmegen, Department of Political Science and Public Administration), Rocio Nogales and Jenny Eschweiler (EMES European Research Network), Nadine Richez-Battesti and Francesca Petrella (Aix-Marseille University—The Institute of Labour Economics and Industrial Sociology (LEST—CNRS), Rafael Chaves (The University of Valencia (Spain)), Gojko Bežovan (University of Zagreb, Institute for Social Policy), Ewa Leś (Warsaw University) and Renzo Razzano and Ksenija Fonović (SPES—Associazione Promozione e Solidarietà).

This book builds upon the project's 14 working papers and 8 national reports, all of which are available on the website of the TSI project: http://thirdsectorimpact.eu. Bernard Enjolras served as overall coordinator of the project, whereas the substantive work of the project was divided into four work-packages, each of which was directed by a separate individual and involved multiple members of the project consortium. Thus, Lester M. Salamon led the work-packages on "Concepts and definitions" and on "Size and scope of the third sector in Europe," Karl Henrik Sivesind led the work-package on "Impact of the third sector," and Annette Zimmer led the work-package on "Barriers to third sector development and policy-recommendations."

The project also benefited greatly from the inputs of an advisory board composed of Edith Archambault, Emeritus Professor at the University of Paris 1 Pantheon-Sorbonne (France); Antonella Noya, Senior Policy Analyst and Manager of the OECD/LEED forum on social innovation at the OECD (Paris); Thomas Boje, Professor at Roskilde University (Denmark); Enrico Giovannini, President of Istat Italian National Institute of Statistics and Pavol Frič, Research Director at the Center for Social and Economic Strategy, Charles University of Prague (Czech Republic). In addition, the project also received important help from the dozens of national and European stakeholders who took part in the series of stakeholder seminars and workshops at the national and European levels that formed an important part of the project's work, and from two special working seminars focused on the conceptualization of the third sector that engaged the input of leading academic experts on the third sector, including Jacques Defourny (University of Liege), Kirsten Grønbjerg (Indiana University Bloomington), Lucas Meijs (Erasmus University Rotterdam), Marthe Nyssens (Catholic University of Louvain) and Naoto Yamauchi (Osaka University).

We express our deepest thanks to all the participants in the TSI project who, in different capacities—consortium members, advisers, discussants, stakeholders—contributed enormously to the analyses that are presented here.

Contents

1. **Introduction** — 1
   Bernard Enjolras

2. **Beyond Nonprofits: In Search of the Third Sector** — 7
   Lester M. Salamon and Wojciech Sokolowski
   1. The Challenge — 10
      1.1 A Diverse and Contested Terrain — 10
      1.2 A Sector Hidden in Plain Sight — 12
      1.3 Why Address this Challenge? The Case for Better Conceptualization and Data — 13
   2. Overcoming the Challenges: The Approach — 15
      2.1 Establishing the Criteria for an Acceptable Conceptualization — 15
      2.2 The Concept of a "Common Core" — 16
      2.3 Retention of Component Identities — 17
      2.4 Building on Existing Progress — 17
      2.5 A Bottom-up Strategy — 19
   3. Key Findings and Implications — 20
      3.1 Enormous Diversity — 20
      3.2 Considerable Underlying Consensus — 24

4	Toward a Consensus Operational Conception of the TSE Sector	31
	4.1 Institutional Components	31
	4.2 Informal and Individual Components	42
5	Conclusion and Next Steps	45

3 The Size and Composition of the European Third Sector   49
Lester M. Salamon and Wojciech Sokolowski

1	The Contours of the European TSE Sector: The Aggregate View	54
	1.1 An Enormous Economic Engine	54
	1.2 Volunteer Engagement	54
	1.3 What does the European TSE Sector Do?	56
	1.4 Revenue Structure	57
	1.5 Institutional Structure	58
	1.6 Longitudinal Changes	61
2	A Diverse Sector: Regional Variations	61
	2.1 Regional Variations in Overall TSE Sector Scale	63
	2.2 Regional Variations in the Institutional Composition of the TSE Sector Workforce	64
	2.3 Regional Variations in European TSE Sector Functions and Revenue Patterns	65
	2.4 Summary	67
3	Explaining Cross-national Variations in TSE Sector Dimensions	67

Appendix 1: Estimates of TSE Sector FTE workforce in EU and Norway, by Component, 2014   76
Appendix 2: Methodology for Estimating the Size of the Third Sector in Europe   78
   Nonprofit Institutions (NPIs)   78
   Cooperatives and Mutual Societies   80
   Social Enterprises   83
   Direct Volunteering   84
   Estimation of the TSE Sector Size   85

    Estimation of Service and Expressive Shares
       of the Workforce   86
    Estimation of TSE Sector Revenue Shares   86
    Summary of Sources of Data on TSE Sector Average
       Annual Employment Changes by Country   87

4   The Roles and Impacts of the Third Sector in Europe   95
Bernard Enjolras and Karl Henrik Sivesind

  1 Impact Areas   97
  2 Selected Evidence of TSIs   100
    2.1 Some Methodological Challenges   100
    2.2 Impact on Civic Engagement, Empowerment,
         Advocacy and Community Building   101
    2.3 Impact on Well-being and Quality of Life   107
    2.4 Impact on Human Resources   110
    2.5 Impact on Social Innovation   112
  3 Can the TSE Sector Expand Civil Liberties and the
     Public Sphere?   114
  4 Does the European Third Sector make a Socioeconomic
     Impact?   117

5   Barriers to Third Sector Development   125
Annette Zimmer and Benedikt Pahl

  1 Introduction: A Success Story and a Clouded Horizon   125
  2 Third Sector Impact Country Clusters   128
  3 Third Sector Environment   131
    3.1 Societal and Economic Trends   131
    3.2 European Union as a Key Actor?   132
  4 Barriers to Third Sector Development   136
    4.1 Common Barriers   136
    4.2 Regional Diversity and Regime-specific Barriers
         to TSO Development   141

			Appendix	154
			Stakeholder Survey	154

6 The Road Ahead: A Policy Agenda for the Third Sector in Europe   161
Bernard Enjolras

1	Three Scenarios			162
2	The Civic Economy Strategy: A Policy Agenda for Europe			163
	2.1	Improving the Legitimacy and Visibility of the Third Sector in Europe		163
	2.2	Improving Third Sector Finances and Government-Third Sector Partnership		169
3	Fostering Foundations' Supportive Role of the Third Sector in Europe			172
4	Improving the Attractiveness of TSOs			172
	4.1	Renewing the Third Sector's Values		173
	4.2	Increase the Attractiveness of TSOs as Employers		173
	4.3	Increase the Attractiveness of TSOs for Volunteers		174
	4.4	Increase the Attractiveness of TSOs for Honorary Board Members		174
5	Conclusion			175

References   177

Index   195

List of Contributors

Bernard Enjolras is Research Professor and Director of the Center for Research on Civil Society and Voluntary Sector in Norway.

Lester M. Salamon is Professor at the Johns Hopkins University, Baltimore, Maryland, USA, and Director of the Johns Hopkins Center for Civil Society Studies.

Karl Henrik Sivesind is Research Professor at the Institute for Social Research, Norway.

Annette Zimmer is Professor of Social Policy and Comparative Politics and lead researcher for Third Sector Impact work at Münster University, Germany.

Benedikt Pahl is a research assistant for the Third Sector Impact at Münster University, Germany.

Wojciech Sokolowski is Senior Research Associate at Johns Hopkins University, Baltimore, Maryland, USA.

List of Figures

Fig. 2.1	Conceptualizing the third sector: a graphic representation	29
Fig. 2.2	Criteria for determining significant limit on surplus distribution for TSE in-scope institutional units	37
Fig. 3.1	Size of the European TSE workforce versus employment in major industries in 29 European countries, 2014	55
Fig. 3.2	Composition of European TSE workforce, FTE Paid versus Volunteer Workers in 29 European countries, 2014	55
Fig. 3.3	European TSE sector workforce activity, by function in 29 countries, 2014	57
Fig. 3.4	European TSE sector revenue structure in 29 countries, 2014	58
Fig. 3.5	Institutional structure of the European TSE Sector in 29 countries, 2014	60
Fig. 3.6	Average annual change in employment in selected European countries, NPIs vs. Total economy	62
Fig. 3.7	European TSE sector workforce as a percent of total employment, by region, 2014	64
Fig. 3.8	Institutional composition of EU TSE sector workforce, by region, 2014	65
Fig. 3.9	European NPI workforce, by function, by region, 20 EU countries	66
Fig. 3.10	NPI revenue structure, by region, in 20 EU countries	66
Fig. 4.1	Political engagement by relative size of third sector workforce (20 EU countries)	102

Fig. 4.2	Social trust by the relative size of the third sector workforce (20 EU countries)	103
Fig. 4.3	Macro impact explanatory model	105
Fig. 4.4	Self-reported health by relative size of third sector workforce (20 EU countries)	108
Fig. 4.5	Self-reported wellbeing by third sector workforce (20 EU countries)	109
Fig. 5.1	Financial Barrier: Lack of Public Funding. Source: Zimmer and Pahl (2016: 10)	137
Fig. 5.2	Human Resource Barrier: Difficulties Recruiting Volunteers. Source: Zimmer and Pahl (2016: 6)	138
Fig. 5.3	Human Resource Barrier: Difficulties Recruiting Board Members. Source: Zimmer and Pahl (2016: 7)	139
Fig. 5.4	External Relations Barrier: Increasing Bureaucracy. Source: Zimmer and Pahl (2016: 8)	139
Fig. 5.5	External Relations Barrier: Low Pay of Employees. Source: Zimmer and Pahl (2016: 11)	140

List of Tables

Table 3.1	Regional grouping of EU countries plus Norway	63
Table 4.1	Linear regression of social trust index, political engagement index, self-reported well-being and self- reported health by country	106
Table 4.2	Linear regression of self-reported well-being and self-reported health by country	109
Table 5.1	Grouping of TSI Countries by Pattern of Third Sector Development	128

1

Introduction

Bernard Enjolras

More than a decade ago, Jacques Delors, former President of the European Commission, reflecting on how he sought to promote the third sector in his position as the head of the European Commission, emphasized the "poor recognition of the third sector" at the European Union level (Delors 2004: 211). More than ten years later, recognition of the third sector in Europe is still poor.

Indeed, the third sector in Europe lacks a clear identity and there is no clear-shared understanding across Europe and within the European Union regarding what exactly the third sector is and what its role is in the European public space. A main reason for this lack of common identity is that the manifold self-organized citizen-based initiatives that make up the third sector are not sufficiently aware of being part of a sector sharing common attributes, values and what economists call a common "objective function" or underlying objectives, regardless of their specific field of activity.

B. Enjolras (✉)
Institute for Social Research (ISF), Oslo, Norway
e-mail: bernard.enjolras@socialresearch.no

This lack of recognition, common identity and awareness has consequences for the visibility and political legitimacy of the third sector at both the national and European levels, and is both a symptom and a cause of the knowledge gaps that afflict this sector. Although official statistical procedures have been developed at the international level to generate systematic comparative data on key features of the scale, scope and impact of at least one of the main components of the third sector—that is, nonprofit institutions—and volunteering, Europe's statistical agencies have been slow to adopt these procedures and, therefore, slow to assess the contributions of even these major components of the third sector to Europe's economy and society. Additionally, in spite of the importance of the third sector in Europe, limited awareness exists about the barriers that hinder the operation and impact of third sector organizations (TSOs) or about the steps that could be taken to eliminate or reduce them.

The project out of which this report emerged—the EU FP7-funded Third Sector Impact Project—mobilized the collaborative efforts of 12 European research institutions along with dozens of stakeholders and external advisors in an ambitious effort to fill these knowledge gaps.

In order to make headway on this task, it was first necessary to clarify the concept of the third sector in its European manifestations. As noted in Chap. 2 of this book, like other social science concepts before it, such as "democracy," "the state" or the "business sector," the concept of a third sector is a contested one, with numerous competing terms and definitions in circulation and serious questions in some quarters about whether it is even possible to think of this collection of entities and activities as a definable sector at all (Dekker 2004; Evers and Laville 2004). One reason for the confusion surrounding this concept is the enormous diversity of entities potentially embraced by it, and the wide variety of terms used to depict it. Included here are organizations variously referred to as voluntary organizations, nonprofit organizations, nonprofit institutions (NPIs), nongovernmental organizations (NGOs), associations, civil society, social economy, solidarity organizations, cooperatives, mutuals, foundations, civil society and, more recently social enterprises (Salamon et al. 2004). Despite this diversity, our project managed to formulate a consensus conceptualization of a fairly broad common core of the third sector in its European manifestations and to win significant buy-in to this conceptualization on the part of a fairly broad array of European academics and third sector stakeholders.

The conceptualization of the third sector is not a goal in itself, of course, but a necessary step toward gaining better knowledge of its scope, scale and special characteristics. This requires attention to multiple dimensions, however. Financial measures are important, but cannot be relied upon exclusively, since one of the distinctive features of this sector is that much of its activity is undertaken for other than purely remunerative or financial objectives. Similarly, simple measures of the number of entities can be misleading since organizations in this sector vary massively in scale and complexity and some of the most important activity of this sector occurs outside of formal organizations. More suitable measures may therefore focus on the human resources that this sector engages, both as paid staff and as volunteers. And the focus must go beyond third sector aggregates to take account of important variations among countries and fields of activity. In each of these ways, our project made significant progress, developing a first empirical estimate of the scope and size of the European third sector as identified in our consensus conceptualization, and documenting as well the variations evident among different European regions and third sector components.

In line with the emphasis in the recent, widely read Stiglitz report (2009) on broadening our systems for measuring societal activity beyond simple economic measures to encompass multiple dimensions of wellbeing, the designers of the call that led to this project specified that our goal should go beyond measuring the size of the third sector and should encompass as well an assessment of this sector's political, social and economic impacts. Because the project did not have the resources to undertake new empirical research on this topic, our focus here was to lay the groundwork for such research by analyzing the work that has so far done on various dimensions of third sector impact (TSI), to summarize what is known and to point the way to the more thorough and systematic approach that is needed.

In addition to clarifying the concept of the third sector, gauging the scope and scale of this sector, and assessing what is known about the sector's broader social and political impact, this project also sought to determine whether there are barriers that might be impeding the impact that the sector could have and to suggest ways to reduce any barriers that might exist. As will become clear in the body of the report, our research uncovered two broad sets of barriers: first, those essentially internal to the sector's organizations relating to the recruitment and training of personnel and intra-organizational dynamics; and second, those external to the sector's organizations relating to the political, economic, legal and social environment within which the sector's organizations and volunteer personnel operate. In both arenas, our research discovered enormous strains resulting from market pressures, changing government policies as well as broader cultural and demographic transformations. Fortunately, some organizations have found resilient ways to cope with these challenges, but some of these pose real risks to the historic functions of this sector.

In a time of social and economic distress and enormous pressures on governmental budgets, the third sector and volunteering represent a unique "renewable resource" for social and economic problem- solving and civic engagement in Europe, not as an alternative to government, but as a full-fledged partner in the effort to promote European progress. At such a time and in such a context, a better understanding of the third sector and the role it can play in the future of Europe is all the more crucial. Providing that understanding in a straightforward and accessible way is the goal that this short volume seeks to achieve. To do so, the three chapters that follow lay the groundwork for this task by explaining what the third sector is; estimating this sector's size, scope and regional variation; and assessing, as far as possible given the available data, its socioeconomic impact. The last two chapters then focus on the future of the third sector in Europe—its challenges and opportunities, the developmental trends and barriers it is facing, the strategies organizations are pursuing and the strategy that sector actors and governments can usefully pursue in response.

References

Dekker, P. (2004). The Netherlands. From private initiatives to non-profit hybrids and back? In A. Evers & J.-L. Laville (Eds.), *The third sector in Europe* (pp. 144–165). Cheltenham: Edward Elgar.

Delors, J. (2004). The European Union and the third sector. In A. Evers & J. L. Laville (Eds.), *The third sector in Europe* (pp. 206–215). Cheltenham: Edward Elgar.

Evers, A., & Laville, J.-L. (Eds.). (2004). *The third sector in Europe*. Cheltenham: Edward Elgar.

Salamon, L. M., Sokolowski, S. W., & Associates (Eds.). (2004). *Global civil society: Dimensions of the nonprofit sector* (Vol. II). Bloomfield, CT: Kumarian Press.

Stiglitz, J. E., Sen, A., & Fitoussi, J.-P. (2009). Report by the commission on the measurement of economic performance and social progress. Retrieved from www.stiglitz-sen-fitoussi.fr

Open Access This chapter is distributed under the terms of the Creative Commons Attribution 4.0 International License (http://creativecommons.org/licenses/by/4.0/), which permits use, duplication, adaptation, distribution and reproduction in any medium or format, as long as you give appropriate credit to the original author(s) and the source, a link is provided to the Creative Commons license and any changes made are indicated.

The images or other third party material in this chapter are included in the work's Creative Commons license, unless indicated otherwise in the credit line; if such material is not included in the work's Creative Commons license and the respective action is not permitted by statutory regulation, users will need to obtain permission from the license holder to duplicate, adapt or reproduce the material.

2

Beyond Nonprofits: In Search of the Third Sector

Lester M. Salamon and Wojciech Sokolowski

In calling for a study of the scope, scale and impact of the third sector in Europe, the authors of the tender that led to the present book wisely emphasized that "stock-taking presupposes conceptual clarification," and set the project out on a search for a consensus conceptualization of the uncharted social space beyond the market, the state and the household thought to encompass the third sector. While there was some agreement about what this sector was not, however, there was no clear agreement about what it included, or what it should be called. An earlier first step toward clarifying the boundaries and content of this twilight zone focused on what is widely considered to be at its core—the set of institutions and associated behaviors known variously as associations, foundations, charitable giving and volunteering; or collectively as nonprofit, voluntary, voluntary and community, or civil society organizations and the volunteer

---

L. M. Salamon (✉) • W. Sokolowski
John Hopkins University, Baltimore, MD, USA
e-mail: lsalamon@jhu.edu

activity that they help to mobilize (Salamon et al. 2004, 2011). Even this was a herculean conceptual task, however, given the bewildering diversity and incoherence of the underlying realities this concept embraced. But no sooner did a consensus form around how to define this core than a chorus of critics surfaced calling attention to an even wider network, not only of institutions and individual behaviors, but also of sentiments and values they claimed had legitimate claims to be considered parts of the third sector domain, at least in Europe if not the entire world (Evers and Laville 2004). And now, perhaps not surprisingly, a know-nothing perspective has surfaced in some quarters challenging the entire objective of conceptualizing and mapping this twilight zone on grounds that it is certain to serve chiefly the nefarious and anti-democratic objectives of state actors and therefore cause actual harm and offer little benefit to the institutions and individual behaviors included or those who benefit from their activities (Nickel and Eikenberry 2016: 392–408).

Against this background, the task to be undertaken in this chapter—to take the next steps in clarifying the composition and boundaries of the twilight zone of institutions, activities and behaviors that lies beyond the market, the state and the family—may appear to be a fool's errand, unlikely to succeed and likely to tarnish the reputations of its authors and cause harm to its putative beneficiaries even if it does achieve its goal. While we certainly concede that conceptualizing and mapping what we here term the "third," or the civil society, sector can serve the control objectives of states, we believe equally strongly that they are at least as likely to empower, legitimize, popularize and validate the behaviors and institutions that operate in this social space and potentially lead to public policies supportive of these institutions and behaviors, rather than only harmful ones.

More than that, we believe that clear and understandable conceptual equipment remains one of the sorest needs in the social sciences, and nowhere more than in the somewhat embryonic field of third sector studies. Indeed, as one of us has written in another context: "The use of conceptual models or typologies in thinking is not a matter of choice: it is the *sine qua non* of all understanding" (Salamon 1970: 85). Political scientist Karl Deutsch made this point powerfully in his *Nerves of Government*, when he wrote: "we all use models in our thinking all the time, even though we may not stop to notice it. When we say that we 'understand' a situation, political or otherwise, we say, in effect, that we have in our mind an abstract model, vague or specific, that permits us to parallel or predict such changes in that situation of interest to us" (Deutsch 1962: 12). It is for this reason that Deutsch argues that "progress in the effectiveness of symbols and symbol systems is thus basic progress in the technology of thinking and in the development of human powers of insight and action" (Deutsch 1962: 10).

Anyone who has followed the development of understanding of the third sector in all of its manifestations must recognize this need for "basic progress in the technology of thinking" in this field. Accordingly, this chapter describes an effort undertaken by a team of scholars to take the next step in conceptualizing this broad sphere of social activity. More specifically, it presents a consensus definition of what for the sake of convenience we refer to as "the third sector" and that later in this chapter we will propose referring to as the TSE sector for reasons that will become clear there.

This conceptualization took advantage of the widespread bottom-up investigation carried out in more than 40 countries scattered widely across the world in the process that led to the conceptualization of the "nonprofit sector" in the Johns Hopkins Comparative Nonprofit Sector Project, but supplemented this with a similar bottom-up investigation carried out in the context of this project in a broad cross-section of European countries—north, south, east and west—to tap understandings of the broader concept of a "third sector" and its various regional cognates, such as social economy, civil society and social entrepreneurship. Building on these bottom-up processes, a consensus conceptualization was hammered out through a vigorous set of discussions among representatives of 11 research institutes, and then further reviewed by the project's advisory board, sector stakeholders and participants in two academic conferences. The goal was to provide as broad a consensus conceptualization as possible, and one that could provide a basis for systematic comparisons among European countries and between them and countries in other parts of the world, and that could be institutionalized in existing official statistical systems and used to generate reliable data on this sector on a regular basis.

To introduce this proposed conceptualization, the discussion here falls into five sections. Section 1, which follows, describes the basic challenge that stands in the way of developing a coherent, common conceptualization of the third sector that can work in a wide assortment of countries and regions, and explains why it might be important for this sector to overcome these challenges. Section 2 then outlines the strategy we employed to find our way around these challenges with the help of a team of colleagues. In Sect. 3, we summarize the major conclusions that emerged from the fact-finding and discussion processes undertaken in pursuit of this strategy. In Sect. 4, we present the key elements of the much-broadened consensus definition of the third sector that resulted, focusing first on the institutional components of this sector and then on the individual activity components. The final section outlines the next steps that will be needed to move toward the development of basic data on the third sector so conceptualized—both in Europe and more broadly—and the progress that has been made in this direction as of this writing.

1 The Challenge

1.1 A Diverse and Contested Terrain

The starting point for our conceptualization work was naturally the existing diversity of views over whether something that could appropriately be called the "third sector" actually exists in different parts of the world and, if so, what it contains. Even a cursory review of the literature makes it clear that the "third sector," and its various cognates, is probably one of the most perplexing concepts in modern political and social discourse. It encompasses a tremendous diversity of institutions that only relatively recently have been perceived in public or scholarly discourse as a distinct sector, and even then only with grave misgivings given the apparent blurring of boundaries among its supposed components.

Some observers adopt a very broad definition that, in addition to organizations, includes the actions of individuals and societal value systems (Heinrich 2005). Others prefer more narrow definitions, focusing, for example, on "nongovernmental" or "nonprofit" or "charitable" organizations. Other definitions fix the boundaries of this sector on the basis of such factors as the source of organizational income, the treatment of organizational operating surpluses, who the organizations serve, how they are treated in tax laws, what values they embody, how they are governed, what their legal status is, how extensively they rely on volunteers, or what their objectives are (Salamon and Anheier 1997a, b; Salamon 2010; Evers and Laville 2004; Alcock and Kendall 2011; Cohen and Arato 1994; Edwards 2011; Habermas 1989). These conceptualizations also identify this sector using different terms—including civil society sector, nonprofit sector, voluntary sector, charitable sector, third sector and, more recently, social economy, social enterprise and many more (Teasdale 2010).

Underlying these different perspectives is the fact that conceptualization of the third sector is a contested terrain, a battlefield where different and often opposing views vie for ownership of the concept and its ideological, cultural, and political connotations (Chandhoke 2001; Defourny et al. 1999; Fowler 2002). Diverse and often conflicting interest groups—from left-wing social movements to conservative think tanks—claim proprietorship of the third sector concept because of the emotively desirable connotations it evokes, such as public purpose, freedom of association, altruism, civic initiative, spontaneity or informality. Regional pride also figures into the definitional tangle. When scholars in one major project focused on "nonprofit institutions" as the core of the third sector, colleagues in Europe accused it of regional bias and pointed to cooperatives and mutual associations as also appropriate for inclusion, notwithstanding the fact that it was often difficult to distinguish many of these latter institutions from regular profit-distributing corporations. Many popular perceptions of third sector activities appear to share an underlying ideological position that places a premium on individual entrepreneurship and autonomy, and opposes encroachment on that autonomy by state authorities, while others see this sector as a source of citizen empowerment (Howell and Pearce 2001; Seligman 1992). The third sector thus becomes the carrier of a wildly diverse set of ideological values—an expression of individual freedom, a buffer against state power, a vehicle for citizen promotion of progressive policies, a partner of government in the delivery of needed services and a convenient excuse for cutting government budgets.

1.2 A Sector Hidden in Plain Sight

One reflection of this conceptual confusion is the treatment of third sector institutions in the basic international statistical systems, such as the System of National Accounts (SNA), which guides the collection of economic statistics internationally, and the International Labour Organization (ILO) standards for labor force surveys, which guide the collection of data on employment and work. Although considerable data is actually assembled on third sector institutions, such institutions have long been largely invisible in these existing official statistical systems. This is so because the concepts used to organize these statistical data have not, until very recently, recognized even nonprofit institutions, let alone other potential third sector institutions, as a class around which data should be reported. Rather, in the System of National Accounts, these institutions are allocated to the corporations, government or "nonprofit institutions serving households" sectors based on whether they (a) produce goods or services for sale in the market, (b) are controlled by government[1] or (c) are financed wholly or mostly by charitable contributions from households. Since many potential third sector institutions, such as nonprofits, cooperatives, mutuals and social enterprises, do produce goods and services that are often purchased in the market or on government contracts (e.g. health care, education, day care), they get assigned to the corporation's sector in national economic statistics, where they lose their identity as third sector entities. Other NPIs judged to be "controlled by" government get allocated to the government sector in economic statistics. The only nonprofit institutions that have been visible in these statistics are thus the so-called nonprofit institutions serving households (NPISH), which are not market producers, not controlled by government, and thus either purely voluntary or supported only by charitable gifts. But this turns out to be a very limited slice of third sector institutions.[2]

---

[1] The language used in the SNA includes entities that may be institutionally separate from government but are "controlled by government," where "controlled by" is defined as more than receipt of government funding.

[2] For more information on institutional sectoring, see 2008 SNA Chap. 4. Although a 2008 revision of the SNA provided an explicit recommendation that statistical agencies separately identify at least the nonprofit components of the various institutional sectors into which NPIs are allocated

When it comes to volunteer work, the situation has been even more problematic. Although the System of National Accounts makes provision for inclusion in basic economic statistics of volunteering done through organizations, it values that volunteer work at the actual cost to employers, which, for all practical purposes, is zero. In the case of direct volunteering, that is, volunteering done directly for other individuals or nonfamily households, the value of this volunteering is counted only if it leads to the production of goods that can be valued at the market cost of comparable products. But direct volunteering that produces services is treated as "household production for own use" and is consequently considered to be "outside the production boundary of the economy" and therefore not counted at all. While quite robust labor force surveys are regularly conducted in virtually all countries, they have historically not asked about volunteer work, and the handful of countries that do ask about such work—through labor force or other specialized surveys—have done so using significantly different definitions and questions, making comparisons across countries—and often even over time within countries—almost impossible. Similarly, time-use surveys (TUSs) ask for both kinds of volunteering defined in accord with the SNA conceptualization outlined above. To date, some 65 countries have implemented TUSs. The problem is that results are often reported at such a high aggregation level that volunteering is not visible in the reporting.

1.3 Why Address this Challenge? The Case for Better Conceptualization and Data

To be sure, as some critics have noted, there are certainly risks in having governments, or any other entity, in possession of data on third sector institutions and volunteer effort (Nickel and Eikenberry 2016). But aside from the fact that in most countries much of such data is already in government hands as a by-product of registration, incorporation or taxation requirements, making such data public can also bring important benefits

---

and to report on them separately from other units (SNA 2008, para. 4.35), this recommendation has not been adopted by Eurostat in the European System of Accounts, which governs the assembly of economic statistics in Europe.

to third sector organizations (TSOs), volunteering and philanthropy. For example, such data can:

- Boost the credibility of the third sector by demonstrating its considerable scale and activity. As it turns out, that scale and breadth of activity are orders of magnitude greater than is widely recognized, justifying greater attention to this sector and its needs;
- Expand the political clout of third sector institutions by equipping them to represent themselves more effectively in policy debates, and thereby help them secure additional resources to support their work;
- Validate the work of third sector institutions and volunteers, thereby attracting more qualified personnel, expanded contributions and more committed volunteers;
- Enhance the legitimacy of the third sector in the eyes of citizens, the business community and government;
- Deepen sector consciousness and cooperation by making the whole of the sector visible to its practitioners and stakeholders for the first time; and
- Facilitate the ability of the third sector to lay claim to a meaningful role in the design and implementation of policies of particular concern to it, including those involved in the implementation of the recently adopted UN Sustainable Development Goals and embodied in the UN's 2030 Development Agenda.

At the end of the day, the old aphorism that "what isn't counted doesn't count" seems to hold. At the very least, other industries and sectors act in ways that seem to confirm the truth of this aphorism. They are therefore zealous in their demand for reliable data about their economic and other impacts. When existing official data sources fail to provide this, they mobilize to insist on it. This was the recent experience, for example, with the tourism industry, which, like the third sector, finds its various components—airlines, cruise ships, hotels, theme parks, national parks, restaurants and many more—split apart among sectors and industries in existing statistical systems, making them invisible *in toto*. To correct this, the tourism industry mobilized itself to pressure the official overseers of the System of National Accounts to produce a special handbook calling for the creation of regular *Tourism Satellite Accounts* by national statistical agencies and then mustered financial support to encourage the implementation of this handbook in countries around the world, precisely the objective that has already been successfully pursued for the nonprofit institution component of the third sector, and now, through the present report, is being proposed for a broader "third or social economy" sector, the TSE sector for short, embracing not only nonprofit institutions, but also social economy, social enterprise and civil society and volunteering elements.

2   Overcoming the Challenges: The Approach

To overcome the challenges in the way of formulating a meaningful conceptualization of the third sector and thereby allow this sector to secure the benefits that this can produce, we utilized a five-part strategy.

2.1   Establishing the Criteria for an Acceptable Conceptualization

As a first step in this process, decisions had to be made about the type of definition at which the conceptualization work was aiming. This was necessary because different types of definitions may be suitable for different purposes. In our case, the hope was that we could formulate a definition capable of supporting empirical measurement of the sector so defined. This meant that a basic philosophical conceptualization would not suffice. Rather, we needed one that could identify operational proxies that could translate the philosophical concepts into observable, operational terms capable of being verified in concrete reality. This led us to five key criteria that our target conceptualization had to embody:

- *Sufficient breadth and sensitivity* to encompass as much of the enormous diversity of this sector and of its regional manifestations as possible, initially in Europe, but ultimately globally.

- *Sufficient clarity* to differentiate third sector entities and activities from five other societal components or activities widely acknowledged to lie outside the third sector: (a) government agencies, (b) private for-profit businesses, (c) families or tribes, (d) household work and (e) leisure activities. Defining features or legal categories that embraced entities or activities with too close an overlap with these other components or activities thus had to be avoided.
- *Comparability*, to highlight similarities and differences among countries and regions. This meant adopting a definition that could be applied in the broadest possible array of countries and regions. This is a fundamental precept of comparative work. The alternative would be equivalent to using different-sized measuring rods to measure tall people and short people so that everyone would come out seeming to be the same basic height.
- *Operationalizability*, to permit meaningful and objective empirical measurement and avoid counterproductive tautologies or concepts that involved subjective judgments rather than objectively observable, operational characteristics. Although underlying conceptual or philosophical concepts would be needed to characterize the in-scope components, operational proxies for them would have to be found in order to facilitate actual identification and measurement
- *Institutionalizability*, to facilitate incorporation of the measurement of the third sector into official national statistical systems so that reliable data on this sector can be generated on a regular basis as is done with other major components of societal life.

2.2 The Concept of a "Common Core"

In order to adhere to the comparability criterion, the project had to settle on a conceptualization that could be applied in a broad range of countries, including the Global South and not only the industrialized North. To achieve such comparability in the face of the great diversity of concepts and underlying realities, the work outlined here set as its goal not the articulation of an all-encompassing "definition," but rather the identification of the broadest possible "common core" of the third sector. Central to the concept of a "common core" is the notion that particular countries may have elements in their conceptions of the third sector that extend beyond the common core. This makes it possible to identify a workable common conceptualization of the third sector without displacing other local or regional concepts around which research, data-gathering, policy development and other notions can be organized. Countries or regions can thus use the common core for cross-national comparative purposes and still report on a broader concept in country reports, so long as care is taken to label the different versions appropriately.

2.3 Retention of Component Identities

Consistent with the concept of a modular approach centered on a common-core conceptualization of the third sector is the need to preserve the component identities of the types of institutions and behaviors ultimately identified as belonging to the third sector. This approach opens the door to documenting the significant variations in the composition of the third sector in different locales and avoids lumping quite different collections of institutions and behaviors together in one misleadingly undifferentiated conglomeration.

2.4 Building on Existing Progress

Fortunately, our work was not completely "at sea" in setting out to conceptualize the third sector. Some important progress had already been made in clearly differentiating one set of likely third sector institutions—that is, *associations, foundations and other nonprofit institutions (NPIs)*—and one broad set of likely third sector individual activities—that is, *volunteer work*—in the official international statistical system.

2.4.1 Institutional Components

So far as the first is concerned, the United Nations Statistics Division in 2003 issued a *Handbook on Nonprofit Institutions in the System of National Accounts* (UNSD 2003) that incorporated an operational definition of

NPIs into the guidance system for international economic statistics and called on statistical agencies to produce so-called satellite accounts that would better portray this one important potential component of the third sector in official national economic statistics. According to this UN *NPI Handbook*, such nonprofit institutions could be identified and differentiated from other societal actors on the basis of five defining structural or operational features. In particular, they were:

- *Organizations*, that is, formal or informal entities with some meaningful degree of structure and permanence, whether legally constituted and registered or not;
- *Nonprofit-distributing*, that is, governed by binding arrangements prohibiting distribution of any surplus, or profit, generated to their stakeholders or investors;
- *Self-governing*, that is, able to control their own general policies and transactions;
- *Private*, that is, institutionally separate from government and therefore able to cease operations on their own authority; and
- *Noncompulsory*, that is, involving some meaningful degree of uncoerced individual consent to participate in their activities.

2.4.2 Individual-Action Component

Likewise, the International Labour Organization, in 2011, issued a *Manual on the Measurement of Volunteer Work* (International Labour Organization 2011) that established an internationally sanctioned definition of this form of work, which is one form of individual activity widely considered to be a component of the third sector. Specifically, volunteer work is defined as "unpaid non-compulsory work; that is, time individuals give without pay to activities performed either through an organization or directly for others outside their own family."[3]

---

[3] The original version of the ILO *Manual* stipulated that the volunteer work must be only for persons outside the volunteer's "household," but this exclusion was broadened in a 2013 ILO regulation to outside the volunteer's "family," although no guidance has been provided on how to define "family" for this purpose. This change has the effect of narrowing somewhat the definition of volunteer work.

The institutional units and activities identified by both definitions are clearly separated from for-profit businesses, government agencies and household activities. These definitions thus served as useful starting points from which to set out on a search for defining elements of a broader third sector concept. This search began in Europe because of research findings in that region suggesting that these initial components were not sufficient to embrace the full common core of the third sector concept in this vast and diverse region, but attention was paid to other possible components in other parts of the world as well.

2.5 A Bottom-up Strategy

Finally, to build a common-core, consensus conceptualization of the third sector broad enough to encompass all relevant types of institutions and behaviors in-scope of this sector, yet operational and clear enough to distinguish in-scope entities from ones that bear stronger resemblance to the other sectors, we devised a bottom-up strategy carried out as part of the larger FP7/TSI research project aimed at defining and measuring the third sector in Europe. With the aid of the research partners in this larger project and an agreed-upon research protocol, we reviewed existing literature and conducted interviews to identify national and regional conceptualizations of the third sector and its component parts in five sets of European regions,[4] assessed them against a potential consensus definition of the third sector flowing out of broader work and literature, and then analyzed the resulting observations to find whether common understandings could be discerned in these conceptualizations and manifestations.

This methodological approach was carried out in a collaborative and consultative manner allowing the project's partners to present and discuss

---

[4] For the purpose of this project, detailed literature review and consultation was undertaken separately in five regions of Europe: the Nordic region, embracing Norway, Denmark, and Sweden; Northern Europe, embracing the Netherlands, Belgium, Germany, and Austria; Anglo-Saxon U.K. and Ireland; Southern Europe, embracing France, Spain, Italy, and Portugal; and Central and Eastern Europe, including Poland, Hungary, Slovakia, Croatia, Slovenia, Romania, Bulgaria, and the Czech Republic. Simultaneously, similar inquiries were launched into the relevant characteristics of several possible institutional and individual manifestations of the third sector. For more information on the Third Sector Impact Project (TSI), see the project website: www.thirdsectorimpact.eu.

their unique regional perspectives and concerns at every stage of the investigation, and working to reconcile them with the overarching objective of developing a consensus conceptualization of the third sector that could be effectively applied both to the different regions of Europe, and more generally as well. Every proposed conceptual component was thoroughly reviewed by all project partners and tested against both the agreed criteria and the known realities on the ground. The results were then reviewed in a series of practitioner workshops and academic seminars, which served to help refine wording and clarify concepts. The upshot was a broad consensus on key features of the resulting conceptualization and operational features.

3 Key Findings and Implications

Two major conclusions flowed from this bottom-up review process.

3.1 Enormous Diversity

In the first place, this review confirmed the initial impressions of enormous diversity in the way the term "third sector" is used, and in the range of organizational and individual activity it could be conceived to embrace even within Europe, let alone in the world at large. Indeed, the range of variation was quite striking.

At one end of the spectrum is the UK, which holds to the concept of "public charities," as recently articulated in the Charities Act of 2011, but with its real roots in the Elizabethan Poor Law of 1601. This concept is rather narrow and, though broadened a bit in recent legislation and policy debate, remains confined to a historically evolved concept of charity (Kendall and Thomas 1996; Alcock and Kendall 2011; Garton 2009; Six 6 and Leat 1997). To be seen as having charitable purposes in law, the objects specified in organizations' governing instruments must relate to a list of 12 particular purposes specified in the Charities Act of 2011, and be demonstrably for the public benefit. Not all nonprofit organizations (NPO) are considered charities in the UK, though broader concepts such as "third sector," "civil society," "voluntary and community sector," "volunteering" and "social economy" are sometimes used for policy purposes, but have no legal basis and no clear definitions (UK Office of the Third Sector 2006). The term "social economy" was not widely recognized in the UK until the 1990s (Amin et al. 2002) and is not widely used. In recent years, a robust "social enterprise" sub-sector has emerged, consisting of entities that use market-type activities to serve social purposes, but these take a variety of legal forms. In short, there is no commonly accepted concept of a third sector in the UK, and the plethora of terms and concepts in use raises questions about whether a coherent conceptualization of the third sector is possible, even in a single country, let alone across national borders. At the very least, different definitions may be appropriate for different purposes.

By contrast, in France and Belgium—as well as throughout Southern Europe (Portugal, Spain, Italy and Greece) and in parts of Eastern Europe, the Francophone part of Canada, and throughout Latin America—the concept of "social economy" has gained widespread attention.[5] In contrast to conceptions prevailing elsewhere in Europe—which underscore organizational features like charitable purpose, volunteer involvement or a nonprofit distribution constraint—the social economy conception focuses on social features, such as the expression of social solidarity and democratic internal governance. In its broad formulations, the concept of social economy embraces not only the voluntary, charitable, or nonprofit sectors, but also cooperatives and mutuals that produce for the market, and newly created "social cooperatives" that are even more clearly socially oriented.[6] Since many cooperatives and mutuals have grown into enor-

---

[5] In its Latin American manifestations, the term "social and solidarity economy" is used more widely. See, for example, Mogrovejo, Mora, and Vanhuynegem (2012).

[6] The Social Economy concept has also been recognized in political and legal circles, both national and European. Thus, for example, the European Economic and Social Committee issued an Opinion on 1 October 2009 on "Diverse Forms of Enterprise," and the European Parliament issued a Report of 26 January 2009 on Social Economy. In December 2015, the Council of the European Union issued a "Conclusion" identifying the social economy as "a key driver of social and economic development in Europe" and encouraged "Eurostat and national statistical authorities" to "consider developing and implementing satellite accounts in their respective statistics aimed at establishing the effective contribution of the social economy to economic growth and social cohesion" (General Secretariat of the Council of the European Union 2015). To date, however, Eurostat, the European Statistical Agency, has not incorporated the concept of the "social econ-

mous commercial institutions, the social economy concept thus blurs the line between market-based, for-profit entities and the nonprofit—or nonprofit-distributing—entities that are central to many northern European and Anglo-Saxon conceptions of what forms the heart of the third sector.

Yet another conception of what constitutes the third sector can be found in Central and Eastern Europe, where the broad overarching concept of "civil society" is widely used in public discourse. Civil society consists of formal organizations and informal community-based structures as well as individual actions taken for the benefit of other people, including improvement of the community or natural environment, participation in elections or demonstrations, informal or direct volunteering and general political participation.[7] More narrow terms—third sector or nonprofit sector—are used to denote the set of organizations with different legal forms, including associations, foundations, cooperatives, mutual companies, labor unions, business associations, professional associations and religious organizations. The use of various terms changed during the political transformation following the dissolution of the Soviet bloc. The term "nonprofit sector" was very popular in the beginning of the transformation. However, accession to the EU introduced the concept of social economy in this region as well. Recently, the very broad and inclusive term "third sector" has been gaining popularity. It includes all kinds of civil society activities that have permanent or formal structure, including cooperatives and mutuals that allow profit distribution.

Other countries fall on a spectrum among these various alternatives. Some countries hew close to the "British" end of the spectrum, focusing on structured organizations that adhere to a nondistribution of profit constraint. This is the case, for example, in Germany and Austria, where the term "nonprofit organization (NPO)" is common, though the con-

---

omy" into its statistical system, nor has the United Nations Statistical Division recognized such a grouping as a distinct sector around which data should be organized. Rather, cooperatives and mutuals are considered "market producers" and, as such, are grouped with for-profit companies in the corporation sector of national accounts.

[7] For discussion of the "civil society" concept, see Edwards (2009); Pollack (2004); Zimmer and Priller (2007); Chambers and Kymlicka (2002); Edwards (2011); Seligman (1992); Cohen and Arato (1994).

cept of "civil society" has also gained some traction in these countries. However, the values expressed by various actors in this latter sphere are frequently contested (Chambers and Kopstein 2001; Heins 2002; Teune 2008). And this term does not normally extend to the service-providing NPOs mentioned above. The boundaries between civil society and the NPO sector are often blurred, and "civil society," "third sector" and "NPO sector" are often used synonymously (Simsa 2013), while research under the title of civil society is frequently limited to references to NPOs. In recent years, the term "social entrepreneurs" has gained importance—meaning innovative approaches to mainly social problems, with high market orientation, not necessarily nonprofit, not necessarily involving voluntary elements, and where financial gains can be at least as important as social mission. Cooperatives and mutuals, because they can distribute profit, would not be included in the concept of a third sector in Austria or Germany, though these institutions do exist as parts of the commercial sector. In the Netherlands as well there is also no single overarching concept of the third sector, but three mid-range conceptualizations—*particulier initiatief* (private initiatives); *maatschappelijk middenveld* (societal midfield); and *maatschappelijk ondernemerschap* (social entrepreneurship)—are used instead. These correspond roughly to nonprofit associations providing various services, advocacy groups and social ventures.

Likewise, there is no a single overarching concept of the third sector in the Nordic countries. Instead, different historically evolved types of institutions are commonly identified—voluntary associations, ideal organizations, idea-based organizations, self-owning institutions, foundations, social enterprises, cooperatives, mutual insurance companies and banks and housing cooperatives. Some of these have a legal basis while others do not. For-profit producer, sales or purchasing cooperatives, consumer cooperatives and housing cooperatives have important roles in certain markets in Scandinavia. Cooperatives in the Nordic countries typically distribute profit at a fixed rate according to each member's stake. The cooperative form expanded in the inter-war period in an attempt to reduce the economic crisis, but Norway did not establish a law on cooperatives until 2008. Sweden has a category of "economic associations" (*ekonomiska föreningar*) and has recently developed the cooperative form in areas where the government until recently has been the main supplier.

However, "social economy" is not widely used and most cooperatives are viewed as profit-distributing institutions. The Nordic countries stand out, however, with respect to the emphasis they place on volunteer work in culture, sports and recreation.

One other institutional element identified in several countries as potential components of the third sector are so-called social enterprises. As noted, these are enterprises that use market mechanisms to serve social purposes. Examples include catering firms that sell their products on the market but choose to employ mostly disadvantaged workers (e.g. persons with previous drug habits or arrest records), using the business to help rehabilitate these workers and prepare them for full-time employment (Nicholls 2006; Bornstein 2004). Special legal forms, such as "Community Interest Companies" in the UK and "Benefit Corporations," or "B-Corps" in the USA, have been created for such enterprises in some countries, but not all such enterprises have chosen to seek such legal status, preferring to organize under laws that apply to NPOs or to organize as regular for-profit businesses (Lane 2011; and cicassociation.org.uk/about/what-is-a-cic).

3.2 Considerable Underlying Consensus

Despite the considerable disparities in conceptualizations of the social space connoted by the concept of a "third sector" even in this continent, it is good to remember that the third sector is not the only societal sector that has faced the challenge of dealing with diversity in finding a suitable conceptualization of itself. Certainly, the business sector has every bit as much diversity as the third sector, with multiple legal structures, radically different lines of activity, gross variations in scale, complex interactions with government funding and regulatory regimes and widely divergent tax treatments. Yet, scholars, policymakers and statisticians have found reasonable ways to conceptualize this complex array of institutions and distinguish it from other societal components, and popular usage has bought into this formulation.

And fortunately, as it turns out, a somewhat surprising degree of consensus also surfaced in the responses to our field guide search for clarification of the elusive concept of the third sector in its European manifestations, and it seems possible to imagine this consensus applying more broadly as well. The discussion below outlines four important components of this consensus.

3.2.1 Wide Agreement on Three Underlying Common Conceptual Features

Most importantly, while there was disagreement about the precise institutions or behaviors that the concept of the third sector might embrace, the review surfaced a considerable degree of consensus about some of the underlying ideas that the concept of a third sector evoked in Europe (and very likely beyond it). Three of these can be easily identified. They connect the third sector concept, by whatever term used for it, to three key underlying ideas:

1. *Privateness*—that is, forms of individual or collective action that are outside the sphere or control of government;
2. *Public purpose*—that is, undertaken primarily to create public goods, something of value primarily to the broader community or to persons other than oneself or one's family, and not primarily for financial gain; exhibiting some element of solidarity with others; and
3. *Free choice*—that is, pursued without compulsion.

3.2.2 NPIs are in

Second, there was general agreement that whatever else it embraces, the concept of the third sector certainly embraces the set of institutions defined in the United Nations *Handbook on Nonprofit Institutions in the System of National Accounts* as NPIs, or nonprofit institutions. As spelled out in that *NPI Handbook*, these are *institutions* or organizations, whether formally or legally constituted or not, that are *private and not controlled by government, self-governing, nonprofit-distributing* (viewed as a proxy for public purpose), and engaging people *without compulsion*. The defining elements of this component of the third sector have been tested already in more than 40 countries and incorporated into the latest (2008) edition of the methodological guidelines for the official System of National Accounts that guides the work of statistical agencies across the world. Several partners in the TSI Project reverted to this basic set of institutions in defining the core of the third sector concept.

3.2.3   More than NPIs: Cooperatives and Mutuals

While there was widespread agreement that nonprofit institutions are appropriately considered part of the "common core" of the third sector concept, there was also considerable agreement that they could not be considered to constitute the whole of it.[8] Rather, other types of institutions also needed to be considered. Most obvious were the cooperatives and mutuals that form the heart of the social economy conception so prominent in Southern Europe, but that are present in other parts of the continent and in other regions as well.

The problem here, however, was that some types of cooperatives and mutuals have grown to the point where they are hard to distinguish operationally from for-profit businesses, particularly if some type of limitation on the distribution of profit is taken as a proxy for the pursuit of public purpose, as suggested above and as used effectively in the identification of in-scope NPIs. This applies particularly to such organizations operating in the insurance and financial industries, but extends to some production cooperatives as well. Because of this, there was considerable resistance to embracing all cooperatives and mutuals within the common core concept of the TSE sector in Europe. What is more, there is little sign that it would be possible to convince statistical authorities to include these heavily commercial cooperatives and mutuals as parts of a construct eligible for being carved out of the corporations sector and incorporated into a TSE, satellite account.

---

[8] This perspective is also echoed in a variety of other accounts. See, for example, Van Til (1988); Evers and Laville (2004); Chambers and Kymlicka (2002); Defourny (2001: 4).

3.2.4 More than NPIs: Social Enterprises

A similar situation surrounds the relatively recent concept of "social enterprises." This type of enterprise that mixes social purpose with market methods has recently gained considerable prominence in a number of European countries, such as the UK, France and the countries of Central and Eastern Europe, as well as in parts of Latin America, Asia and Africa. More even than cooperatives and mutuals, however, these entities raise difficult definitional challenges since they seek market returns and are often organized under laws that apply equally to for-profit businesses. In some countries, such as the UK, to be sure, special legal categories have been established for such entities to acknowledge their mixture of social and commercial objectives and activities, as noted earlier. In Italy, for example, a special class of "social cooperatives" has been established for enterprises that operate market production facilities but are required to employ a minimum of 30 percent of their workers from among persons who exhibit one of a list of legally defined forms of disadvantage. In other countries, as well, the cooperative form is also used for such enterprises while elsewhere they organize as NPOs.

There was general agreement that at least some cooperatives, mutuals and social enterprises belong within a concept of a TSE sector. But the fundamental problem facing the inclusion of these entities is the question of how to differentiate the units that should be properly included from those that ought to be excluded due to the fact that they are in fact fundamentally functioning like for-profit businesses and therefore legitimately considered part of the corporations sector in national accounts statistics. This required us to translate the concept of "public purpose" into operational terms that could perform this differentiation function and thus yield a consensus operational definition of the TSE sector amalgam that is consistent with our philosophical principles.

3.2.5 More than Institutions: The Individual Component

The prominence of two other key concepts within the body of thought associated with the "third sector" in Europe made it clear that confining the concept of the third sector to any particular set of institutions would not do full justice to the TSE sector concept in Europe (or elsewhere): (a) first, the concept of "civil society"—with its emphasis on individual citizen action, involvement in social movements, and the so-called public sphere, especially in Central and Eastern Europe; and (b) second, the emphasis on voluntarism as an important component of the third sector concept in the Nordic countries, the UK, and Italy. Accordingly, it was important to include individual activities of citizens within our conceptualization of the third sector. But clearly not all citizen actions could be included. Here, again, distinctions were needed to differentiate activities citizens engage in for their own enjoyment or as part of their family life from those carried out on behalf of others.

The task here was greatly simplified, however, by the existence of the International Labour Organization *Manual on the Measurement of Volunteer Work*, which offered an operational definition of volunteer work that includes many of the activities that could easily be interpreted as manifestations of civil society, including participation in demonstrations, other forms of political action, as well as other activities undertaken without pay for the benefit of one's community, or other persons beyond one's household or family.

3.2.6 Conclusion: Portraying the Third Sector Conceptually

Four more-or-less distinct clusters of entities or activities thus emerged from our bottom-up review process as potential candidates for inclusion within our consensus conceptualization of the third sector in whole or in part: (i) NPOs, (ii) mutuals and cooperatives, (iii) social enterprises and (iv) human actions, such as volunteering and participation in demonstrations and social movements that are undertaken without pay.[9]

However, not all of the entities in each of these clusters seem appropriate to include within a concept of the third sector. This is so because many of them too significantly overlap with other institutional sectors,

---

[9] It should be noted that the individual activity undertaken to or through TSE sector institutions is recorded as work associated with these institutions, whereas the direct individual activity that meets the project's definition is associated with the household sector.

Beyond Nonprofits: In Search of the Third Sector

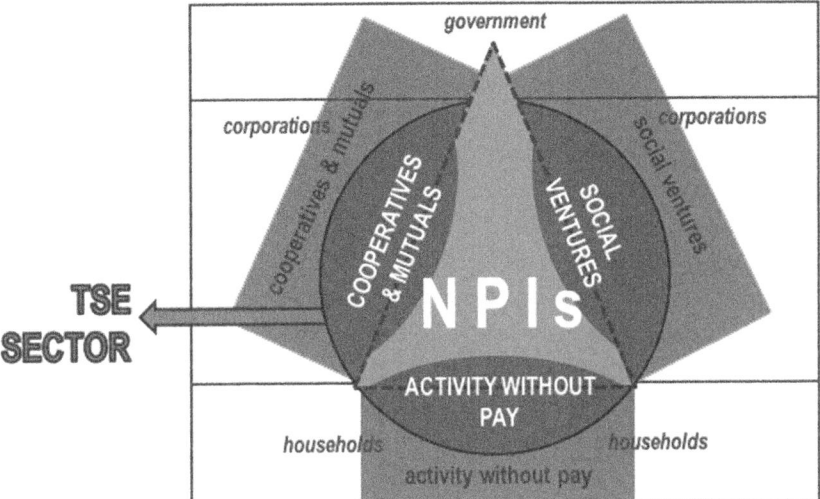

Fig. 2.1 Conceptualizing the third sector: a graphic representation

that is, government, for-profit businesses and household activities—from which the third sector must be distinguished in order to stay true to our basic philosophical conception of a set of institutions or activities that are *private*, primarily *public serving* in purpose, and engaging people *without compulsion*. This bottom-up review thus made it clear that formulating a consensus definition of the third sector required finding a way to differentiate those elements of these institutional and individual components that are "in-scope" of our proposed TSE sector from those that are "out-of-scope" by virtue of being much closer to for-profit businesses, government agencies or household activities.

Figure 2.1 provides a pictorial representation of the conceptualization task that the project thus faced. The circular line marks the hypothesized boundary of what we can term the TSE sector, and differentiates the institutional and individual-action components that are in-scope of this sector from those that are out-of-scope. Several features of our conceptualization task stand out starkly in this figure:

- First, the triangle in the middle represents the nonprofit institution set of entities that forms the core of the TSE sector. The centrality of this set of institutions to the TSE sector concept reflects the fact that the total prohibition on the distribution of profits under which these organizations operate in most European countries, coupled with their noncompulsory character, provides an exceptionally clear operational guide to the fact that these organizations embody the "public purpose" feature considered so central to the TSE sector concept. The central notion here is that a set of institutions in which individuals participate of their own free will without expectation of receipt of any distribution of profit must be perceived by them as serving an important public purpose. This roots the public purpose criterion in the actual behavior of a country's people rather than being imposed from outside. Except for a relative handful of NPIs created by governments and fundamentally controlled by them, almost the entire class of NPIs consequently falls within the scope of this TSE sector, and the defining features of in-scope NPIs could thus serve as the starting point for building our "consensus definition" of the TSE sector.

- Also notable in Figure 2.1 are the dotted lines separating NPIs from cooperatives, mutuals, social enterprises and activity without pay. These are intended to reflect the fact that some cooperatives, mutuals and social enterprises are also NPIs, and that some volunteer work takes place within NPIs.
- Thirdly, the conceptual map also makes clear that the TSE sector is quite broad, potentially embracing cooperatives, mutuals, social enterprises and volunteer work in addition to the many types of NPIs. It does so, however, in modular fashion, separately identifying the different types of entities rather them merging them into one undifferentiated mass, thereby making it possible for particular stakeholders to gain insight into their particular types of organizations and making clear some of the bases for variation in the size and structure of the TSE sector in different regions.
- Finally, and perhaps most importantly, the figure graphically illustrates the significant conceptual and definitional work that still remains, since not all cooperatives, mutuals, social enterprises or individual activity can be considered in-scope of the TSE sector. This is so, as noted earlier, because they do not all embody the philosophical notions that underlie the common understanding of what truly constitutes the TSE sector.

The task that remained, therefore, was to identify a set of operational features that could be used to differentiate the in-scope cooperatives, mutuals, and social enterprises from those that are out-of-scope. It is to our approach for completing this task that we therefore now turn.

4 Toward a Consensus Operational Conception of the TSE Sector

To carry out this task, we began with the existing consensus definitions of the NPI sector and volunteer work, respectively, and searched for ways to refine them to incorporate portions of these other potentially in-scope institutional and individual-action components while still adhering to the criteria of breadth, comparability, operationalizability and institutionalizability that we had set for ourselves at the outset. The resulting process was iterative, which means that it consisted of a series of rounds in which partners were asked to provide their input on a set of proposed operational characteristics, on the basis of which the defining features were modified or tweaked and submitted for additional review.

Two sets of hypothesized operational features emerged from this iterative review process: one for institutional units and one for individual human actions. The discussion below outlines these two sets of features separately and indicates how they came to be operationalized. Taken together, the result is a consensus operational definition of the TSE sector that rests on the firm ground of a bottom-up investigative process focusing on actually existing conceptualizations and manifestations of the third sector concept in many different European countries and regions, and that seems likely to work as well in other regions of the world.

4.1 Institutional Components

Following the strategy outlined above, we started our search for in-scope operational features of the institutional components of the TSE sector from the definition of the NPI sector already worked out and incorporated into the United Nations' *Handbook on Nonprofit Institutions in the*

System of National Accounts (2003) and subsequently integrated into the 2008 revision of the core System of National Accounts. This was possible, in part, because NPIs, at least those not controlled by government, have features that serve as useful embodiments of all three of the crucial philosophical notions central to the third sector concept—*privateness, public purpose* and *uncoerced participation*.

The first and third of these were reflected in the definitional requirement that in-scope NPIs be self-governing entities that individuals are free to join or not join voluntarily, and that are private, that is, institutionally separate from government, and not controlled by government, even though they may receive substantial financial support from government. The second was reflected in the fact that nonprofits are prohibited by law or custom from distributing any profits they may earn to their investors, directors or other stakeholders, and must operate under a "capital lock" that stipulates that any assets they accumulate must be dedicated to another nonprofit entity in the same or similar field in the event they cease operation or undergo a transformation into a for-profit entity. Along with the noncompulsory feature, this prohibition on the distribution of profit serves as a convenient and workable proxy for the notion of public purpose.[10]

With this as a starting point, it was an easy jump to realize, based on the input from our bottom-up investigation, that the other potential in-scope institutional components of the TSE sector could be identified by relaxing just one of the key operational features of in-scope NPIs: the feature requiring complete limitation on the distribution of organizational profits to directors or other stakeholders. This is the case because virtually all organizations primarily engaged in the production of public goods or public benefits of any kind, one of the defining features of true TSE sector entities, willingly accept some limitation on their pursuit of profit in order to stay true to their public-purpose mission. Many such organizations provide their goods or services at reduced cost or free of charge. Others engage individuals with disabilities or other barriers to employment, which can affect their productivity and increase costs. Still

---

[10] Employees of nonprofits are free to receive compensation for their work from the nonprofits, but such compensation must be reasonable and not excessive.

other organizations cross-subsidize certain members or participants based on their need rather than their ability to pay for goods or services because serving these individuals, rather than maximizing profits, is central to their missions. All such practices significantly limit the ability of these organizations to generate and distribute profits. *Relaxing the nonprofit distribution constraint to include organizations that can distribute some surpluses generated by their activities, but by law or custom are "significantly limited" in the extent of this distribution, can thus provide a suitable proxy for the concept of public purpose that is central to our philosophical concept of the third sector and hence offers the operational basis for differentiation between in-scope and out-of-scope cooperatives, mutuals, and social enterprises that we are seeking.*

Still needed, however, was a further clarification of what it means to be "significantly limited" in the distribution of profits. For this, it was necessary to examine existing practice in a wide range of countries, from which a number of more specific and concrete specifications were derived.

Out of this set of considerations emerged a consensus definition of the institutional components of the third sector that focuses on five defining features, each of which is translated into operational terms. An institutional unit—whether a NPO, an association, a cooperative, a mutual, a social enterprise or any other type of institutional entity in a country—must meet all five of these features to be considered "in-scope" of the third, or TSE, sector.

In particular, to be considered part of the TSE sector, entities must be:

- *Organizations*, whether formal or informal;
- *Private*
- *Self-governed*;
- *Noncompulsory*; and
- *Totally or significantly limited from distributing any surplus they earn* to investors, members or other stakeholders.

More specifically, each of these features was translated into operational terms as follows.

4.1.1 The Organization Feature

Organization means that the unit has some institutional reality. To be considered an *organization*, a unit need not be legally registered. What is important is that it possesses a meaningful degree of permanence, an internal organizational structure, and meaningful organizational boundaries. Informal organizations that lack explicit legal standing but involve groups of people who interact according to some understood procedures and pursue one or more common purposes for a meaningfully extended period (e.g. longer than several months) are included. Groupings that lack even these minimum features of permanence and understood operating procedures (e.g. ad hoc social movements or protest actions) can still be considered parts of the third sector under the individual-action component of the TSE sector discussed below.

4.1.2 The Private Feature

To be considered *private*, the organization must not be controlled by government. The emphasis here is not on whether the organization receives its income from government, even when this income is substantial; nor does it depend on whether the organization was originally established by a government unit or exercises government-like authority (e.g. issuing licenses to practice particular professions). The ultimate test of not being controlled by government is the ability of the organization's governing body to dissolve the organization on its own authority. This attribute distinguishes TSE organizations from businesses and nonmarket NPIs that are controlled by government units.[11]

---

[11] The *Satellite Account on Nonprofit and Related Institutions and Volunteer Work* developed under the auspices of the UN Statistical Division further specifies five factors to be considered in deciding whether an organization is controlled by government as follows:

1. If the government has the right to appoint the officers managing the TSE organization under its constitution, articles of association or other enabling instrument.
2. If the enabling instrument or a contractual agreement between a government and an organization contains provisions other than the appointment of officers that effectively allow the government to determine significant aspects of the general policy or program of the organization;

4.1.3 The Self-governing Feature

To be self-governing, the organization must bear full responsibility for the economic risks and rewards of its operations. The need for this defining feature arises from the interconnectedness of various institutional units through legal ownership. Following SNA procedures, we distinguish between legal and economic ownership and put the emphasis on the latter rather than the former. While a TSE organization may be created by a corporation, it is not considered to be controlled by that corporation so long as it retains full responsibility for the economic risks and rewards entailed in its operations. Entities that assume the economic risks and rewards for their operations are "self-governed" and thus institutionally separate from other units that may legally own them. Such self-governed units are allocated to economic sectors based on their own economic activities rather than those of the units that may legally own them. Thus, a for-profit business that is fully responsible for the economic risks and rewards of its operations is not in-scope of the TSE sector even though it is legally owned by a unit that is in-scope. Likewise, a TSE unit that is fully responsible for its economic and risks and rewards is still treated as in-scope of the TSE sector satellite account, even if it is legally "owned" by a for-profit corporation.

---

3. If receiving government funding determines significant aspects of the general policy or program of the organization; A TSE organization may be mainly financed by government and still not controlled by government if the organization is able to determine its policy or program to a significant extent;
4. If an organization must seek the approval of government before assuming risk or voting itself out of existence or if it is controlled by government or depends on government to shield it from risk.

A single indicator could be sufficient to establish control in some cases, but in other cases, a number of separate indicators may collectively indicate control. A decision based on the totality of all indicators will necessarily be judgmental in nature.

Borderline cases include organizations created by political processes but that operate quasi-independently of the agencies that established them (so-called GONGOs) as well as organizations that implement government-created responsibilities to oversee certain areas of economic or professional activity, such as regulating who can practice a profession, arbitrating labor-management relations, and so on. Such organizations may operate in close relationship with government authorities such that it may be difficult to decide whether they are institutional parts of government. The ultimate test is whether the leadership of such entities can dissolve the units on their own authority. If not, the entities are out of scope of the TSE sector as defined here.

4.1.4 The Noncompulsory Feature

To be considered *noncompulsory*, participation with the organization must be *free of compulsion* or coercion, that is, it must involve a meaningful degree of choice. Organizations in which participation is dictated by birth (e.g. tribes, families, castes), legally mandated or otherwise coerced, such as community service volunteering required to meet a court penalty or fulfill a military obligation, are excluded. Organizations in which membership is required in order to practice a trade or profession, or operate a business, can be in-scope so long as the choice of profession or business is itself a matter of choice.

This feature, combined with the limited profit-distribution requirement outlined below, serves as a proxy for a public-interest purpose, since organizations in which individuals freely choose to participate, but from which they can expect to secure only limited profit or none at all, must be organizations that serve some public purpose in the minds of those who are involved with them.

4.1.5 The Totally or Significantly Limited Profit-distribution Feature

To meet this condition, organizations must be prohibited, either by law, internal governing rules, or by socially recognized custom[12] from distributing either all or a significant share of the profits or surpluses generated by their productive activities to their directors, employees, members, investors or others. This attribute distinguishes TSE sector organizations from corporations, which permit the distribution of surpluses generated to their owners or shareholders. TSE organizations may accumulate surplus in a

---

[12] The reference to "socially recognized custom" refers to situations, common in a number of countries, where the formal body of laws governing nonprofits may be very limited for various reasons but where prohibitions on the distribution of profits to members or investors are firmly settled in social experience. This is consistent with 2008 SNA's (para 4.6) reference to a "legal or social entity" in its definition of an "institutional unit." Formal legal status typically stipulates what the organizations registered under it can legally do. If an organization is registered as a "non-profit" "non-stock" or "tax- exempt" entity, this not only establishes its legal status as an institutional unit, but also implies prohibition on profit distribution. By the same principle, "socially recognized custom" not only establishes the existence of an organization, but it also specifies what kind of organization it is, which may establish expectations about what happens with its surplus.

given year, but that surplus or its significant share must be saved or plowed back into the basic mission of the agency and not distributed to the organizations' directors, members, founders or governing board. In this sense, TSE organizations may be profitmaking but unlike other businesses they are nonprofit-distributing, either entirely or to a significant degree.

This condition embraces the full nondistribution-of-profit feature used to define "nonprofit institutions," but broadens it to embrace organizations that permit some distribution of profit (e.g. cooperatives, mutuals and social enterprises), but still restricts it to those of these entities that are required by law or custom to place some significant limit on such distribution. While the prohibition on distribution of any profit is self-explanatory, the determination that an organization has a significant limitation on profit distribution is based on the following four indicators, as shown in Fig. 2.2 and elaborated more fully below:

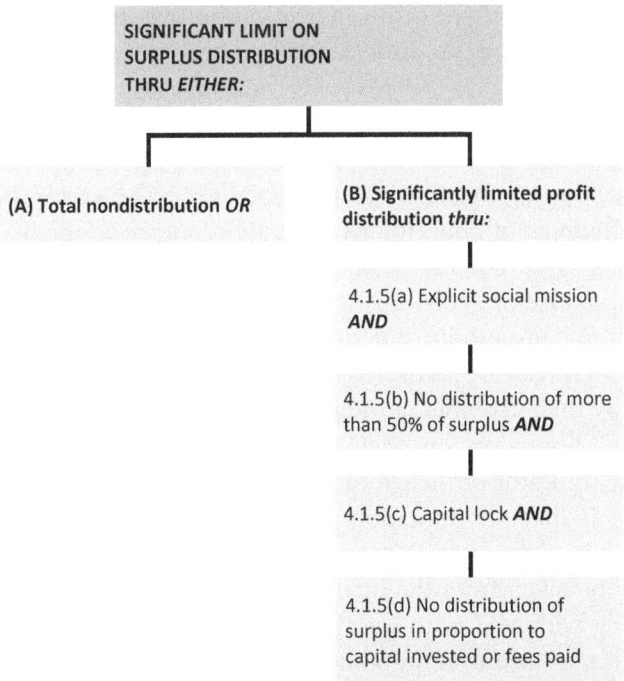

Fig. 2.2 Criteria for determining significant limit on surplus distribution for TSE in-scope institutional units

4.1.5(a) Public-purpose mission. *To be considered in-scope of the TSE sector, an organization must be bound by law, articles of incorporation, other governing documents or settled custom to the pursuit of a social purpose.* What constitutes a public or social purpose may vary widely among countries and over time, but the central concept is that the organization is legally committed to a mission that prioritizes the production of public goods or other social or environmental benefits of value to broadly defined communities over the maximization of profit. Various attempts have been made to characterize the concept of public purpose with special terms, such as "charitable" or "in the public interest," but these carry different meanings in different places and eras. Core concerns revolve around concepts of health, welfare, education, public safety, human and civil rights, overcoming inequalities, promoting employment, protecting human and civil rights and pursuing justice. The key, though, is to free organizations from the requirement to pursue profit maximization over the commitment to improving human or animal welfare, the environment or social solidarity.

4.1.5(b) Significant and binding limitation on distribution of profits. Important as a clear commitment to a public purpose is to the identification of organizations in-scope of the TSE sector, because of the diffuseness of conceptions of "public purpose," this is at best a "necessary" but "not a sufficient" determinant of public-purpose activity. In the case of NPIs, this is achieved through the prohibition on distributing any profits, but since cooperatives, mutual societies and social enterprises are permitted to distribute some of the surpluses generated by their activities, a suitable alternative is to require some "significant" limitation on their profit distribution as a comparable tangible indicator of their meaningful pursuit of public purpose. The key test is that the limitation must be sufficient to differentiate in-scope entities clearly from for-profit firms. What that standard should be may be taken from the international consensus that appears to be emerging with respect to social enterprises, institutions that are even more like for-profit corporations than are cooperatives and mutual. Several recent European laws thus stipulate that to be considered true "social enterprises," organizations must dedicate to the organization's social mission, and therefore not distribute, at least 50 percent of any profits they might earn. This standard might appropriately be applied to cooperatives and social enterprises as well.

In all these cases, however, some adjustment of this specific figure may be appropriate where the valid social mission of the units involves activities that have the effect of reducing the amount of profit earned. This could be the case, for example, where part of the social mission of the organizations is to subsidize the cost of products or services by selling them below market prices to members, or employ substantial numbers of persons suffering from some disability or chronic disadvantage, thus boosting the costs of training and social support. Such subsidies or extra costs could be considered part of the retained earnings in support of the organizations' social mission.

4.1.5(c) **Capital lock.** In addition to the requirement for a total or significant limitation on the distribution of profit, in-scope TSE units must also operate under laws, explicit governance provisions or, where such formal provisions were not in place when the organization was originally established, set social customs establishing a "lock" on any surplus retained. Such rules prohibit the distribution of the retained surplus and any other assets owned by the organization to its owners, directors or other stakeholders, in the event of the organization's dissolution, sale or conversion to "for-profit" status. Rather, any such retained surplus or assets must be transferred to another entity set up for a similar social purpose and subject to the same requirements as those in-scope of the TSE sector.

4.1.5(d) **Prohibition on any distribution of profits in proportion to capital invested or fees paid.** This prohibition is one of the defining features of cooperatives and mutual societies that differentiates them from other market producers (e.g. joint stock corporations) that typically distribute surpluses in proportion to invested capital or fees paid. This prohibition does not apply to payment of interest on invested capital so long as the interest does not exceed prevailing market rates or rates on government bonds. The purpose of this indicator is to differentiate cooperatives that primarily serve some social or other public purpose from those primarily seeking returns on invested capital. Prohibition of profit distribution in proprtion to capital invested applies only to coops; social enterprises by definition are not coops within the framework of the UN Handbook.

Each of these requirements is based on existing laws or customs in existence in some European countries, among at least some cooperatives, mutuals or social enterprises, though each may need further refinement once the range of practice is further analyzed. Thus, for example, to be designated as a "social cooperative" in Italy, organizations must maintain a labor force 30 percent of which must be people with certain specified special needs. The prohibition on the distribution of profit on the basis of investment or fees reflects one of the defining features of "social cooperatives" found in a prominent analysis of European cooperatives (Barea and Monzón 2006). And social enterprise laws in Belgium and France set the "no more than 50 percent" standard as the limitation on distribution of profit required for designation as a social enterprise in these countries.

All four of these indicators should be met to qualify as an entity subject to a "significant limitation on profit distribution." A decision based on the totality of these indicators will necessarily be judgmental in nature as, in some cases, some of these indicators may carry a different relevance and thus weigh differently on the final decision than others.

Summary. Taken together, therefore, this set of operational features meets the criteria we set for an acceptable conceptualization of the third sector that is at once broader than the nonprofit sector, consistent with the consensus philosophical precepts of the third sector concept that emerged from our bottom-up investigation and operationalizable enough to be integrated into existing statistical machinery. In the process, these features make it possible to foster the development of official "satellite accounts" on a TSE sector that is much broader than the one called for in the 2003 UN *NPI Handbook*, yet sufficiently differentiated from other institutional units to be integrated into national accounts statistical systems and win the support of national accounts officials. Reflecting this, the United Nations Statistics Division, working with one of the present authors, has approved for international review pending submission for final approval at a meeting of the United Nations' Statistical Commission at its next meeting, a proposed *Satellite Account on Nonprofit and Related Institutions and Volunteer Work* that embodies this conceptualization

In-scope under this core definition of the TSE sector are thus:

1. Virtually all *NPIs* as defined in the UN *Handbook on Nonprofit Institutions in the System of National Accounts*. This includes not only NPISH, but also "market NPIs" assigned to the corporations sectors in the System of National Accounts, so long as they embody the definitional features of NPIs. The only exceptions are those NPIs that are controlled by government (including official state churches) and units nominally registered as NPIs that de facto distribute profits (e.g. in the form of excessive compensation of directors or key stakeholders). Particular types of organizations— for example, hospitals, universities and cultural institutions—may be organized as "third sector" organizations in some countries and as governmental institutions or for-profit institutions in others. Indeed, all three forms of such institutions can exist in particular countries, but this definition makes it possible to determine which of these are truly NPIs and which not. Borderline cases can include political parties (in some countries, they may be controlled by government) and indigenous peoples' associations (in some countries their membership may be decided by birth or the organizations may exercise governmental authority).
2. Some, but very likely not all, *cooperatives and mutuals*. Cooperatives that are organized as nonprofits, or social cooperatives that operate under legal requirements stipulating a minimum of at least 30 percent of employees or beneficiaries that exhibit certain "special needs," would be clearly in-scope. So are other types of cooperatives and mutuals that meet the significantly limited profit-distribution feature. As a general rule, cooperatives and mutuals in northern European countries (such as Belgium, Germany or the Scandinavian countries) tend to lack such clear limitations on their distribution of profits and are therefore likely to be out-of-scope of the TSE sector. By contrast, southern European countries (Bulgaria, Greece, Hungary, Italy, Malta, Spain and Portugal) more often impose conditions on cooperatives and mutuals that have the effect of significantly limiting their distribution of profit. These cooperatives are more likely to be in-scope of the TSE sector so long as they meet the operational criteria for limited profit-distribution identified above. By contrast, market-oriented cooperatives that operate as profit-distributing businesses and are free to distribute all profits are out-of-scope. As a general rule, cooperatives and

mutuals in the financial services sector, such as banks and mutual insurance companies, would likely be out-of-scope since they have typically evolved into large-scale businesses that are hard to distinguish from regular, profit-seeking companies.
3. Social enterprises that are registered as NPIs, social or mutual activity cooperatives, community benefit corporations in the UK, special B-Corps in the USA or other countries, and entities operating as officially designated social cooperatives or social economy institutions in Belgium or France are likely in-scope of the third sector as identified here. So, too, are enterprises that belong to social enterprise networks that require the pursuit of significant social or environmental benefits. Social enterprises registered as regular corporations are either borderline cases or out-of-scope, as are companies that operate corporate social responsibility programs but otherwise have no significant limitation on their generation or distribution of profits.

Finally, all privately owned for-profit businesses, and all government agencies and units controlled by them, are out of the TSE scope.

4.2 Informal and Individual Components

In addition to organizations, the TSE sector embraces a variety of individual and informal activities. That portion of such activity undertaken to or through organizations is naturally recorded as part of the workforce of the in-scope organizations. Strictly speaking, the additional portion is the portion done directly for individuals or other families. In both cases, however, the task here is to differentiate the in-scope individual activities from normal leisure activities and recreation and from unpaid household activity, such as performing household chores, or helping members of one's close family.

Fortunately, much of the work of operationalizing this border has already been done and captured in the *Manual on the Measurement of Volunteer Work* issued by the International Labour Organization in 2011, and subsequently further ratified at the 19th International Conference of Labour Statisticians in 2013. The resulting conceptualization views the individual activity considered in-scope of the TSE sector as a form of unpaid *work*, thus differentiating it from activity one does for one's own or one's family's enjoyment, edification or quality of life. Under the resulting official, internationally sanctioned definition, volunteer work is thus defined as "unpaid, non-compulsory work; that is, time individuals give without pay to activities performed either through an organization or directly for others outside their own household or family."

We adopt this recommended definition here as suitable for identifying the individual activity considered in-scope of the TSE sector, with one difference: the TSE sector includes all direct volunteer work but only that organization-based volunteer work done through TSE organizations. Volunteer work carried out through government agencies or for-profit corporations are therefore not in-scope of the TSE sector.

More specifically, individual activities in-scope of the TSE sector as volunteer work under this definition must exhibit the following operational features:

They produce benefits for others and not just, or chiefly, for the person performing them. The test here is whether the activity could be replaced by that of a paid substitute. Thus, for example, time spent playing the piano for one's personal enjoyment would not be considered a TSE sector activity, whereas playing the piano for residents of a nursing home would qualify.

They are not casual or episodic. Rather, the activity must be carried on for a meaningful period of time, typically defined as an hour in a certain "reference period." Helping an elderly person across the street one time would thus not qualify as volunteer work, but serving as the unpaid crossing guard at a school would.

They are unpaid. That is, the person performing them is not entitled to any compensation in cash or kind. Although this feature is straightforward and self-explanatory, its application may be problematic in those circumstances where people performing these activities receive something of value that is not formally defined as compensation or wages. This may include token gifts of appreciation, accommodations, reimbursement of expenses or stipends. Under provisions embodied in a new regulation on the measurement of work issued by the ILO, receipt of pay that is less than one-third of the normal pay for a particular job does not disqualify such an activity from being in-scope of the TSE sector.

The activity is not aimed at benefiting members of one's household or their close family or families (e.g. next of kin—brothers, sisters, parents, grandparents and respective children).

The activity is noncompulsory, which means it involves a meaningful element of individual choice. To be considered noncompulsory:

- The person performing the activity must have the capacity to choose whether or not to undertake it.
- This excludes activities undertaken by minors or the mentally challenged.
- The person performing the activity must be able to cease performing it at any time if they so choose. If not, the activity is not noncompulsory.
- Performing the activity is not required by law, governmental decree or other legal obligation.
- If performing the activity is required to practice a trade, profession or similar economic activity or to complete educational requirements, then there must be a meaningful element of choice in the selection of that trade, profession, economic activity or educational program.
- Responding to a social norm or religiously inspired sense of personal obligation does not violate this noncompulsory feature.

Summary. The human action in-scope of the TSE sector under this definition is quite broad. It includes all uncompensated work performed either directly for people outside of one's close family or through an in-scope TSE organization to (i) improve a community; (ii) organize public, cultural, or religious events; (iii) promote public health, safety, or education; (iv) provide emergency relief or preparedness; (v) clean up the environment or rescue animals; (vi) help a person in need with food, assistance, or companionship; (vii) take part in, or organize, a demonstration or advocacy campaign; (viii) uncompensated pro-bono work undertaken in a professional capacity (e.g. legal or emotional counseling, review of scientific papers for publication, arbitration, etc.).

Forms of human action that are out of the scope of the TSE sector include all forms of legally mandated public service, such as volunteer work in lieu of compulsory military service, court-ordered community service, as well as public service requirements to fulfill mandatory educational requirements (e.g. volunteering required to graduate from high school); all forms of uncompensated training activities whose main purpose is the acquisition of occupational skills by the person performing them; and all activities linked to common crime (e.g. criminal gang involvement or acts of street violence).

All forms of employment-related activities and all forms of household activities (household work, socializing, leisure, etc.) are out-of-scope by definition, as is pro-bono technical assistance to the members of one's own household in any other way.

5 Conclusion and Next Steps

This chapter has offered a consensus conceptualization of a third/social economy/civil society or TSE sector—embracing institutional and individual-action components—that is rooted in an intensive review of different conceptions of third sector realities in the various regions of Europe as well as previous similar inquiries in other regions of the world. It is also one that can meet the standard of being institutionalizable in the major official statistical systems for measuring the size and scope of different sectors and forms of work globally. Indeed, this conceptualization has already been accepted by the United Nations Statistics Division for inclusion in a new version of the original 2003 United Nations *Handbook on the Measurement of Nonprofit Institutions in the System of National Accounts*, now renamed the *Satellite Account on Nonprofit and Related Institutions and Volunteer Work*.

Armed with this officially sanctioned conceptualization, statistical agencies in Europe (and elsewhere) will be equipped to generate systematic comparative data on a broad common core of institutions and forms of individual behavior that can reliably be considered to be within the scope of a broadened TSE sector that is clearly consistent with the fundamental philosophical conception of what a TSE sector consists of and with the central principles of the System of National Accounts. At the same time, the "modularity" of this framework allows the separate identification of the different components that are of interest to various stakeholders and more or less relevant to particular regions.

In the chapter that follows, we take up this challenge by offering a preliminary attempt to apply this conceptualization to the TSE sector in Europe in order to generate at least a tentative picture of the scope, scale and economic weight of the TSE sector that this conceptualization reveals.

References

Alcock, P., & Kendall, J. (2011). Constituting the third sector: Processes of decontestation and contention under the UK Labour governments in England. *Voluntas: International Journal of Voluntary and Non-profit Organisations, 22*(3), 450.

Amin, A., Cameron, A., & Hudson, R. (2002). *Placing the social economy*. London: Routledge.

Barea, J., & Monzón, J. L. (2006). *Manual for drawing up the satellite accounts of companies in the social economy: Co-operatives and mutual societies*. Liege: CIRIEC.

Bornstein, D. (2004). *How to change the world: Social entrepreneurs and the power of new ideas*. New York: Oxford University Press.

Chambers, S., & Kopstein, J. (2001). Bad civil society. *Political Theory, 29*(6), 837–865.

Chambers, S., & Kymlicka, W. (Eds.). (2002). *Alternative conceptions of civil society*. Princeton: Princeton University Press.

Chandhoke, N. (2001). The 'civil' and the 'political' in civil society. *Democratization, 8*(2), 1–24.

Cohen, J. L., & Arato, A. (1994). *Civil society and political theory*. Cambridge, MA: MIT Press.

Defourny, J. (2001). From third sector to social enterprise. In C. Borzaga & J. Defourny (Eds.), *The emergence of social enterprise* (pp. 1–28). London and New York: Routledge.

Defourny, J., Develtere, P., & Fonteneau, B. (Eds.). (1999). *L'économie sociale au Nord et au Sud*. Brussels and Paris: De Boeck.

Deutsch, K. (1962). *The nerves of government: Models of political communication and control*. New York: Free Press.

Edwards, M. (2009). *Civil society*. Cambridge: Polity Press.

Edwards, M. (2011). *The Oxford handbook of civil society*. New York: Oxford University Press.

Evers, A., & Laville, J.-L. (Eds.). (2004). *The third sector in Europe*. Cheltenham: Edward Elgar.

Fowler, A. (2002). Civil society research funding from a global perspective: A case for redressing bias, asymmetry and bifurcation. *Voluntas, 13*(3), 287–300.

Garton, J. (2009). *The regulation of organised civil society*. Oxford: Hart Publishing.

General Secretariat of the Council of the European Union. (2015, December). *The promotion of the social economy as a key driver of economic and social development in Europe* (Paras. 8,18, and 19. Doc No. 15071/15). Brussels.

Habermas, J. (1989). *The structural transformation of the public sphere: An inquiry into a category of bourgeois society*. Cambridge, MA: MIT Press.

Heinrich, V. F. (2005). Studying civil society across the world: Exploring the thorny issues of conceptualization and measurement. *Journal of Civil Society, 1*(3), 211–228.

Heins, V. (2002). *Das Andere der Zivilgesellschaft. Zur Archäologie eines Begriffs.* Bielefeld: Transcript.

Howell, J., & Pearce, J. (2001). *Civil society and development: A critical exploration.* Denver: Lynne Rienner.

International Labour Organization. (2011). *Manual on the measurement of volunteer work.* Geneva: International Labour Organization.

Kendall, J., & Thomas, G. (1996). The legal position of the voluntary sector in the UK. In J. Kendall & M. Knapp (Eds.), *The voluntary sector in the UK.* Manchester: Manchester University Press.

Lane, M. J. (2011). *Social enterprise: Empowering mission-driven entrepreneurs.* Chicago: American Bar Association.

Mogrovejo, R., Mora, A., & Vanhuynegem, P. (Eds.). (2012). *El cooperativismo en América Latina. Una diversidad de contribuciones al desarrollo sostenible.* La Paz: OIT, Oficina de la OIT para los Países Andinos.

Nicholls, A. (2006). *Social entrepreneurship: New models of sustainable social change.* Oxford: Oxford University Press.

Nickel, P. M., & Eikenberry, A. M. (2016). Knowing and governing: The mapping of the nonprofit and voluntary sector as statecraft. *Voluntas: International Journal of Voluntary and Non-profit Organisations, 27*(1), 392–408.

Pollack, D. (2004). Zivilgesellschaft und Staat in der Demokratie. In A. Klein, K. Kern, B. Geißel, & M. Berer (Eds.), *Zivilgesellschaft und Sozialkapital. Herausforderungen politischer und sozialer Integration* (p. 23). Wiesbaden: VS Verlag für Sozialwissenschaften.

Salamon, L. M. (1970). Comparative history and the theory of modernization. *World Politics, 23*(1), 83–103.

Salamon, L. M. (2010). Putting civil society on the economic map of the world. *Annals of Public and Cooperative Economics, 81*(2), 167–210.

Salamon, L. M., & Anheier, H. K. (Eds.). (1997a). *Defining the non-profit sector: A cross-national analysis.* Manchester: Manchester University Press.

Salamon, L. M., & Anheier, H. K. (1997b). In search of the nonprofit sector: The question of definition. In L. M. Salamon & H. K. Anheier (Eds.), *Defining the nonprofit sector: A crossnational analysis.* Manchester: Manchester University Press.

Salamon, L. M., Sokolowski, S. W., & Associates (Eds.). (2004). *Global civil society: Dimensions of the nonprofit sector* (Vol. II). Bloomfield, CT: Kumarian Press.

Salamon, L. M., Sokolowski, S. W., & Haddock, M. (2011). Measuring the economic value of volunteer work globally: Concepts, estimates, and a roadmap to the future. *Annals of Public and Cooperative Economics, 82*(3), 217–252.

Seligman, A. (1992). *The idea of civil society*. New York: Free Press.
Simsa, R. (2013). Gesellschaftliche Restgröße oder treibende Kraft? Soziologische Perspektiven auf NPOs. In R. Simsa, M. Meyer, & C. Badelt (Eds.), *Handbuch der Non-profit-Organisation: Strukturen und Management* (pp. 125–145). Stuttgart: Schäffer & Poeschel.
Six 6, P., & Leat, D. (1997). Inventing the British voluntary sector by committee: From Wolfenden to Deakin. *Non-profit Studies*, *1*(2), 33–46.
Teasdale, S. (2010). What's in a name? The construction of social enterprise. *TSRC Working Paper 46*, Birmingham and Southampton: Third Sector Research Centre.
Teune, S. (2008). Rechtsradikale Zivilgesellschaft—contradictio in adiecto? *Forschungsjournal Soziale Bewegungen*, *25*(4), 17–22.
U.K., Office for the Third Sector. (2006). *Partnership in public services: An action plan for third sector involvement*. London: Office for the Third Sector, Cabinet Office.
United Nations Statistics Division. (2003). *Handbook on non-profit institutions in the system of national accounts*. New York: United Nations.
Van Til, J. (1988). *Mapping the third sector: Voluntarism in a changing social economy*. New York: The Foundation Center.
Zimmer, A., & Priller, E. (2007). *Gemeinnützige Organisationen im gesellschaftlichen Wandel. Ergebnisse der Dritte-Sektor-Forschung*. Wiesbaden: VS Verlag für Sozialwissenschaften.

Open Access This chapter is distributed under the terms of the Creative Commons Attribution 4.0 International License (http://creativecommons.org/licenses/by/4.0/), which permits use, duplication, adaptation, distribution and reproduction in any medium or format, as long as you give appropriate credit to the original author(s) and the source, a link is provided to the Creative Commons license and any changes made are indicated.

The images or other third party material in this chapter are included in the work's Creative Commons license, unless indicated otherwise in the credit line; if such material is not included in the work's Creative Commons license and the respective action is not permitted by statutory regulation, users will need to obtain permission from the license holder to duplicate, adapt or reproduce the material.

3

The Size and Composition of the European Third Sector

Lester M. Salamon and Wojciech Sokolowski

Armed with this conceptualization of the third or social-economy (TSE) sector we are now in a position to estimate its dimensions and contours. But which dimensions can provide the most relevant description of this sector? Conventional economic measures, such as the monetary value of the sector's contribution to the national economy (the so-called Gross Value Added or GVA), may not be the best measure because a very substantial part of the TSE sector's contribution to economy and society is provided at below market prices or free of charge and relies on unpaid volunteer labor. Likewise, the number of organizations, another measure widely used in popular accounts, is also misleading due to vast differences in the size of organizations. A sector with a relatively small number of large or mid-sized organizations can carry more weight than one with many very small organizations, yet simple counts of organizations may disguise this. What is more, existing listings of organizations are notoriously unreliable because they tend not to be updated and fail to delete defunct organizations in a regular way.

L. M. Salamon (✉) • W. Sokolowski
John Hopkins University, Baltimore, MD, USA
e-mail: lsalamon@jhu.edu

Previous research (Salamon et al. 2004) has identified the following five dimensions as more revealing of important dimensions of the third sector and as providing the most useful basis in terms of which to compare a country's TSE sector to its counterparts in different countries and to other segments of its own society and economy:

1. *Workforce size*, both paid and volunteer. For reasons cited earlier, this variable provides a better measure of the level of activity that this sector accounts for than does the economic value of its output. Because such entities often engage part-time workers as well as full-time ones, simple headcounts can be misleading. Accordingly, this variable has to be measured in FTE terms, that is, a person working half time for a third sector organization (TSO) would be counted as one-half of an FTE worker. Similarly, a volunteer who works on average eight hours a week each week of the year would count as 1/5th of a full-time worker.[1]
2. *Workforce composition*. Unlike the business or government sectors, the TSE relies extensively on both volunteer and paid employment. Therefore, it is important to generate information on both forms of labor, and to be able to differentiate between the two. What is more, it is important to measure both volunteer work that is channeled through organizations and that provided directly to other individuals. This is so because in some countries organizations with paid staff are rare, but robust third sectors heavily reliant on volunteers may still be present and highly active.
3. *TSE sector activities*, which can be most conveniently measured by the shares of the TSE sector workforce in different activity fields. To facilitate comparison between TSE activities and those of the other sectors, we have used classification structures that have been developed to portray the composition of the other sectors as well.
4. *TSE Sector revenue sources*. TSE sector organizations receive their revenue from three kinds of major sources: government payments

---

[1] Since volunteers and some paid workers work part-time or episodically, we converted all employment data into FTE workers. This was done by dividing the total hours of paid or volunteer work in a given reference year by the number of hours considered to represent "full-time work," which we assume to be on average 1760 hours. This number varies from country to country and it is generally lower in high-income countries of Western Europe than in medium-income countries of Eastern Europe.

(including grants, contracts and reimbursements for services rendered to eligible parties); market sales of goods and services and membership dues paid by private parties; and philanthropic donations from private individuals, foundations and corporations. Unfortunately, existing international statistical systems, such as the System of National Accounts, obscure these different revenue streams by treating government grants along with philanthropy as transfers, and government contracts and vouchers as market sales.[2] Accordingly, great care must be taken to adjust the data to clearly reflect these three distinct sources;

5. *TSE sector institutional composition.* As noted in Chap. 2, the TSE sector as currently conceived includes at least four distinguishable components: in-scope NPIs, cooperatives and mutuals, social enterprises and direct volunteering, that is, volunteering not mediated by organizations.[3] As will become clear below, however, these are not wholly distinct categories, since some cooperatives, mutuals and social enterprises are also NPIs. This requires some careful adjustments to avoid double counting, since some data sources are not clear about this.

6. *The average annual growth of the TSE active workforce*, including both paid and volunteer workers, and its comparison to the growth of overall employment in the economy.

In developing the measures of these five dimensions of the TSE in the European Union and Norway, we utilize the following data sources:

1. A comprehensive study of nonprofit institutions in over 40 countries, including 20 European countries, carried out under the auspices of the Johns Hopkins University Comparative Non-Profit Sector Project (CNP)[4];

---

[2] Salamon, Lester M., S. Wojciech Sokolowski, and Associates. (2004). *Global Civil Society: Dimensions of the Nonprofit Sector*, Volume Two. Bloomfield: Kumarian Press.
[3] Volunteer work carried out through organizations is also included, but its full-time equivalent amount is included in the count of NPI workers and those cooperatives and mutuals that are also NPIs.
[4] For a description of this project and its methodology, see Salamon et al. 2004. For an analysis of its results in the light of prevailing theories, see Salamon et al. 2017.

2. A report on the social economy in the European Union prepared by the International Centre of Research and Information on the Public, Social and Cooperative Economy (CIRIEC)[5];
3. Nonprofit Institution Satellite Accounts and similar reports issued by the statistical agencies of Belgium, Czech Republic, Italy, Norway, Poland, Portugal and Sweden;
4. Time Use Surveys (TUSs) and other surveys in several European countries.[6]

It must be noted, however, that the estimates of the size and contours of the European TSE sector offered here are necessarily highly preliminary. This is so because the data available on the key components of this sector remain grossly incomplete and, even where available, seriously out

---

[5] José Luis Monzón Campos and Rafael Chaves Ávila, *The Social Economy In The European Union*, Brussels: European Economic and Social Committee, 2012. An update of this report was prepared in preliminary form and presented to the European Economic and Social Committee in June of 2017, but a final report with final estimates was not available as of the time this volume went into production. Based on the preliminary data, however, the basic estimates presented here would only be marginally affected by the updated estimates.

[6] Included here are the following sources: Miranda, V. (2011), "Cooking, Caring and Volunteering: Unpaid Work Around the World," OECD Social, Employment and Migration Working Papers, No. 116, OECD Publishing. doi: 10.1787/5kghrjm8s142en; Erstellt vom Institut für interdisziplinäre Nonprofit Forschung an der Wirtschaftsuniversität Wien (NPO-Institut), Freiwilliges engagement in österreich, Wien, 2009, http://www.bmask.gv.at; Główny Urząd Statystyczny, Wolontariat W Organizacjach I Inne Formy Pracy Niezarobkowej Poza Gospodarstwem Domowym—2011 (Volunteering Through Organizations And Other Types Of Unpaid Work Outside Own Household—2011, Warszawa, 2012; Pennerstorfer, A., Schneider, U. & Badelt, C. in: Simsa, R., Meyer, M. & Badelt, C.: (Hg.): Handbuch der Nonprofit-Organisation. Stuttgart 2013 (5. überarbeitete Auflage); oje, T. P., Fridberg, T., & Ibsen, B. (2006). Den frivillige sektor i Danmark. Omfang og betydning (Rapport 06:19). København: Socialforskningsinstituttet. Retrieved from: http://www.sfi.dk/Admin/Public/DWSDownload.aspx?File=%2fFiles%2fFiler%2fSFI%2fPdf%2fRapporter%2f2006%2f0619_Den_frivillige_sektor.pdf; Kaminski, P. (2005). Table1. The NPS in France, 2002 (version INSEE). Le compte des Institutions Sans But Lucratif (ISBL) en France (Année 2002). Paris: l'Institut National de la Statistique et des Études Économiques (INSEE); Nagy, R., & Sebestény, I. (2009). Table A 10 in Methodological Practice and Practical Methodology: Fifteen Years in Nonprofit Statistics (Hungarian Statistical Review Special Number 12). Budapest: Hungarian Central Statistical Office. Retrieved from: http://www.ksh.hu/statreview; ISTAT. (2014). Nonprofit institution profile based on 2011 census results. Rome: Istituto nazionale di statistica. Retrieved from: http://www.istat.it/en/files/2014/10/Nonprofit-Institution-Profile-based-on-2011-Census-results_EN_definitivo.pdf?title=Nonprofit+institutions+profile+-+9+Oct+2014+-+Full+text.pdf;

of date. Although a special *Handbook on Nonprofit Institutions in the System of National Accounts* was issued by the United Nations Statistical Division in 2003, only six EU countries plus Norway have seen fit to implement this *Handbook*. Similarly, while the Statistics Department of the International Labour Organization issued a *Manual on the Measurement of Volunteer Work* in 2011, only three countries in Europe have implemented it, leaving us dependent on TUS data that covers only 18 of the 27 EU countries. The Johns Hopkins Comparative Nonprofit Sector Project generated solid data on nonprofit institutions in 20 of the 27 EU countries, but these data were collected between the mid-1990s and the 2000s and have been updated for only a handful of the countries since then, making it necessary to rely on inevitably imperfect methods for "aging" the data. Systematic data on social enterprises are available on only a handful of countries, and even these use widely different definitions, and the data available on cooperatives make it difficult to determine what share meet the in-scope criteria for inclusion in the third sector and also what share are actually recorded as nonprofit institutions in various data sources.

Fortunately, a revised version of the UN *NPI* Handbook has been developed and is available for implementation. This *Satellite Account on Nonprofit and Related Institutions and Volunteer Work* adheres closely to the definition of the TSE sector offered in this report and therefore offers the hope of generating more reliable data on the European third sector than is currently available. But it remains to be seen whether European statistical and policy officials will support implementation of this important new piece of statistical machinery.

While preliminary, however, the data presented here offer a solid first approximation of the scale and contours of the European TSE sector carefully defined in operational terms consistent with official national accounts concepts and based on the best data and estimating techniques available. For a detailed description of the various data sources and estimating procedures used, see Annex B.

To present these estimates, the balance of this chapter falls into three sections. In the section that follows, we report our estimates of the aggregate dimensions of the TSE sector in 28 EU countries and Norway. In the second section, we examine regional variations in the scale and composition of the TSE sector to the extent permitted by the data. These latter findings, in turn, pose the puzzle that the final section of this chapter will seek to unravel.

1 The Contours of the European TSE Sector: The Aggregate View

1.1 An Enormous Economic Engine

Perhaps the major aggregate finding that has emerged from the data examined here is that, contrary to many popular assumptions, the European TSE sector is an enormous economic force, outdistancing most major industries in the scale of its workforce. Taken together, as of 2014, the latest date for which data are available, the European TSE sector engages an estimated 29.1 million FTE workers (paid and volunteer) in the 28 EU countries and Norway. The European TSE sector thus accounts for slightly more than 13 percent of the European workforce. This is significant because any industry that accounts for 5 percent of the employment of a country is considered to be a major industry. What is more, in the fields in which they operate, the TSE sector turns out to account for an even larger employment share.

Put somewhat differently, with over 29 million FTE workers, the European TSE sector has the third largest "workforce" of any industry in Europe, trailing only trade and manufacturing, but outdistancing the construction and transportation industries by 2:1, and the financial services industry by nearly 5:1 (see Fig. 3.1).

1.2 Volunteer Engagement

A second striking characteristic of the European TSE Sector is its engagement of volunteers in addition to paid employees. In fact, of the over 29 million FTE workers in the TSE sector in Europe, 55 percent—a total of

The Size and Composition of the European Third Sector 55

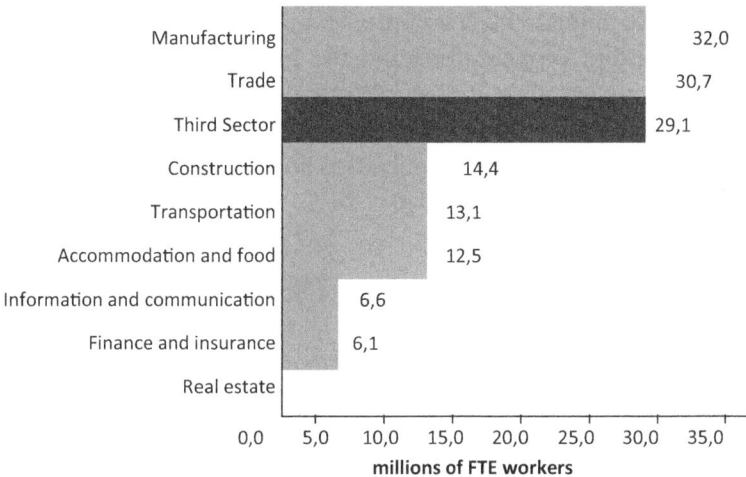

Fig. 3.1 Size of the European TSE workforce versus employment in major industries in 29 European countries, 2014

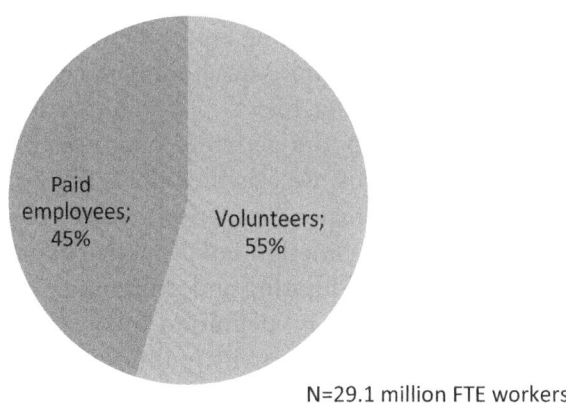

Fig. 3.2 Composition of European TSE workforce, FTE Paid versus Volunteer Workers in 29 European countries, 2014

16 million FTE workers—are volunteers (Fig. 3.2). This means that the European TSE sector employs more FTE volunteer workers than there are FTE workers of any sort employed in any major European industry but trade and manufacturing.

Of these 16 million FTE volunteer workers, nearly 7 million work through nonprofit organizations and the balance, roughly 9.0 million FTE volunteer workers, volunteer directly to help friends and neighbors outside of their own households or families. Clearly, this ability to mobilize a veritable army of volunteers is another potent measure of the reach and power of the TSE sector.

1.3   What does the European TSE Sector Do?

Not only are TSE sector organizations important in economic terms, but they are also important socially, politically and culturally. Indeed, third sector actors perform a multitude of social functions. For one thing, they are service providers, delivering significant shares of such services as health care, education, environmental protection, disaster relief and economic development promotion. Beyond this, however, they function as policy advocates, as promoters of a sense of community, as guardians of a crucial value emphasizing the importance of individual initiative for the common good and as vehicles for giving expression to a host of interests and values—whether religious, ethnic, social, cultural, racial, professional or gender-related (Salamon 2014a, b).

To gain some insight into the activities and functions that the European TSE sector performs, we classified the activities of the TSE sector workforce into three major categories: service, expressive and other functions.[7] The *service* function entails activities in education, social services, health care and housing and community development. Direct volunteer action, which by definition involves help to other households, is considered a service activity in this report. The *expressive* function comprises activities in culture and recreation, membership organizations—including labor unions—business and professional organizations, environmental organizations and religious congregations. Finally, the *other* function includes activities of charitable foundations, international organizations, as well as activities not elsewhere classified. Given the limitations of the existing data, more detailed

---

[7] See Appendix 1 for the methodology used in this estimation.

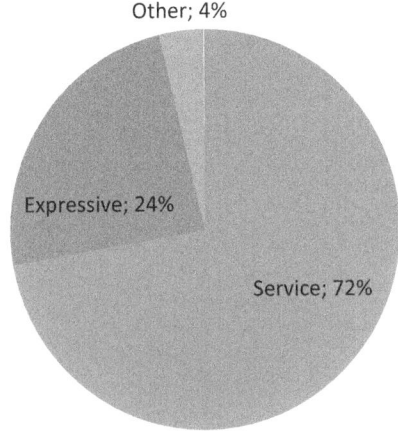

May not add to 100% due to rounding   N=29.1 million FTE workers

Fig. 3.3 European TSE sector workforce activity, by function in 29 countries, 2014

classification of TSE sector activity by industry is not possible at this time. As Fig. 3.3 shows, we estimate that the overwhelming majority (72 percent) of TSE sector workforce activity is devoted to the service functions of the sector. At the same time, a substantial 24 percent of the activity goes into expressive functions.

1.4   Revenue Structure

The revenue structure of the civil society sector differs markedly from what many observers tend to believe. While charitable giving attracts the most public and media attention, it turns out to account for a relatively small share of TSE sector revenue. Thus, as shown in Fig. 3.4, taken all together, charitable contributions—from individuals, foundations and corporations—account on average for only about 9 percent of overall TSE sector revenue in Europe. By contrast, private fee income, which includes private payments for goods and services, membership dues and investment income, accounts for a much larger 54 percent of income on average. Finally, *government support*, which includes grants, contracts and

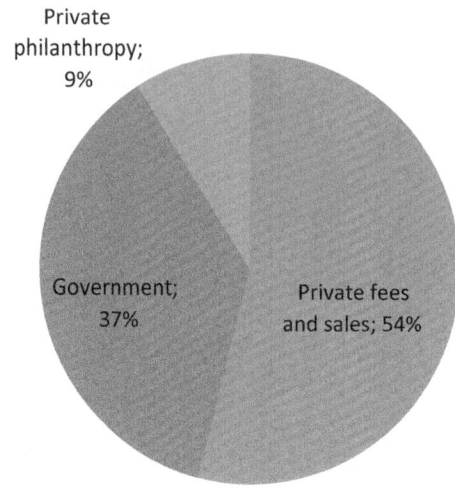

Excluding direct volunteer action

Fig. 3.4 European TSE sector revenue structure in 29 countries, 2014

reimbursements for services rendered to eligible private parties in such fields as health care or education, make up the balance of about 37 percent of TSE sector revenue.[8]

1.5 Institutional Structure

The final dimension of the European TSE sector that deserves attention is its institutional structure. As previously noted, this includes four elements: NPIs, cooperatives and mutual societies, social enterprises and all direct volunteer activities.[9]

---

[8] These estimates do not include any payments for direct volunteer action, which, if any, we assume to be insignificant. We furthermore assume that all income of cooperatives and mutual societies and social enterprises comes from market activities, and thus is considered to be fee income. Unfortunately, the data do not permit us to estimate the monetary values of these revenue streams at this time. For more information about this estimation methodology, see Annex 1.

[9] As previously noted, organization-based volunteering is treated here as an attribute of the organizations through which this work is mediated.

Several complications attend the separate depictions of these four components, however. For one thing, some cooperatives and mutuals are subject to a full nondistribution of profit constraint and thus are considered to be NPIs. Based on data available in at least one European country—France—we estimate that about 11 percent of the total recorded employment in cooperatives and mutuals is actually working in entities that are also NPIs. To avoid double counting, we have counted the workers in such cooperatives and mutuals as cooperative and mutual workers and adjusted our estimate of NPI employment accordingly. In addition, to ensure consistency with our definition of in-scope cooperatives and mutuals, a number of estimations had to be employed in countries where existing data for making the necessary distinctions was not available. Fortunately, solid statistical data were available in some countries that facilitated these estimates, as detailed more fully in Appendix 2.

Secondly, as already noted, reliable data on social enterprises, particularly those that meet our in-scope criteria, are unavailable on most countries. However, in a number of countries, special legal or technical categories have been adopted to identify such enterprises. Included here are entities that are legally registered or otherwise designated as "Work Integration Social Enterprises (WISE)," "sheltered employment establishments" or, in the case of the UK, "Community Interest Companies (CIC)." While it is not entirely clear how fully these designations line up with our definition of in-scope social enterprises, we were sufficiently encouraged that they provide a reasonable proxy to rely on them. Even so, data on employment in these forms of enterprises were available for only nine EU countries.[10] In the remaining countries, no such designations or other sources of data were available, though, as will become clear below, it was possible to make some rough imputations of the scope of such employment in the other countries.

Finally, in the case of volunteers, as previously noted, the portion of total FTE volunteer work that is carried out through other institutions is included in the data on the workforce of these other institutions and

---

[10] See section "Social Enterprises" of Appendix 2 for more details.

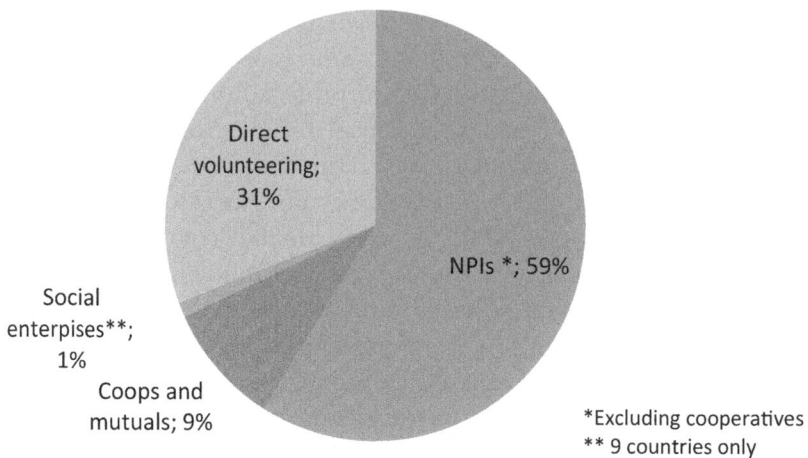

Fig. 3.5 Institutional structure of the European TSE Sector in 29 countries, 2014

broken out separately there. The direct volunteer work, that is, that volunteer work that is not mediated by other organizations but is carried out directly for persons outside the volunteer's family or household is reported separately.

Figure 3.5 shows the distribution of the TS workforce among the four components: direct volunteering, NPIs (excluding those that are cooperatives), cooperatives and mutuals (including those that are also NPIs), and social enterprises (including those that may be either cooperatives or NPIs), but only for the countries on which data are available.

It is clear that NPIs still engage the majority (59 percent) of the TSE sector workforce, and about 87 percent of the organizational component of the TSE sector. Of this NPI workforce, however, 40 percent is made up of FTE volunteers.

By contrast, cooperatives and mutual societies account for a much smaller 9 percent of the TSE sector workforce even with the cooperatives operating as NPIs included. In the case of social enterprises, their share of total TSE employment cannot be estimated precisely for reasons mentioned earlier, but it is likely to vary only between 1.0 and 2.1 percent, depending on whether we include only the nine countries in which we are able to find reasonable estimates or impute the scale of social enterprise employment in the other countries at the average rate for the countries for which data are available.

The final component of the TSE sector—direct volunteer action—accounts for a significant 31 percent of the FTE TSE sector workforce, and if the volunteers operating through nonprofit organizations are included, the overall volunteer share of total TSE sector's FTE employment would stand at 55 percent.

1.6 Longitudinal Changes

One final notable dimension of TSE activity has been its recent dynamism. Although we have longitudinal data on only one TSE institutional component, the nonprofit institutions (NPIs), and on only 12 EU countries, these limited data show that the TSE sector has recently been in the midst of significant growth in these countries—growing at a rate that exceeds the growth of overall employment in the economy.[11] Thus, paid employment in the NPI sector grew at an annual average rate of 3.4 percent in the 12 EU countries on which comparative time-series data are available (Fig. 3.6). By comparison, as also shown in Fig. 3.6, total employment in these 12 countries grew at an annual rate of only 0.6 percent.

Moreover, NPI employment growth outdistanced total employment growth in all but one country (Denmark). A particularly dramatic difference took place in Spain, where the NPI employment was growing at the annual rate of 6.6 percent between 2008 and 2013, while total employment shrank by 3.5 percent per year in the same time period.

2 A Diverse Sector: Regional Variations

Important though these aggregate features of the TSE sector are, however, they can be misleading. As one old joke puts it: even a statistician can easily drown in a creek that is on average 5 inches deep. Behind the

---

[11] We are indebted to Karl-Henrik Sivisend for assistance in assembling the data reported here. For a complete summary of sources, see Appendix 2.

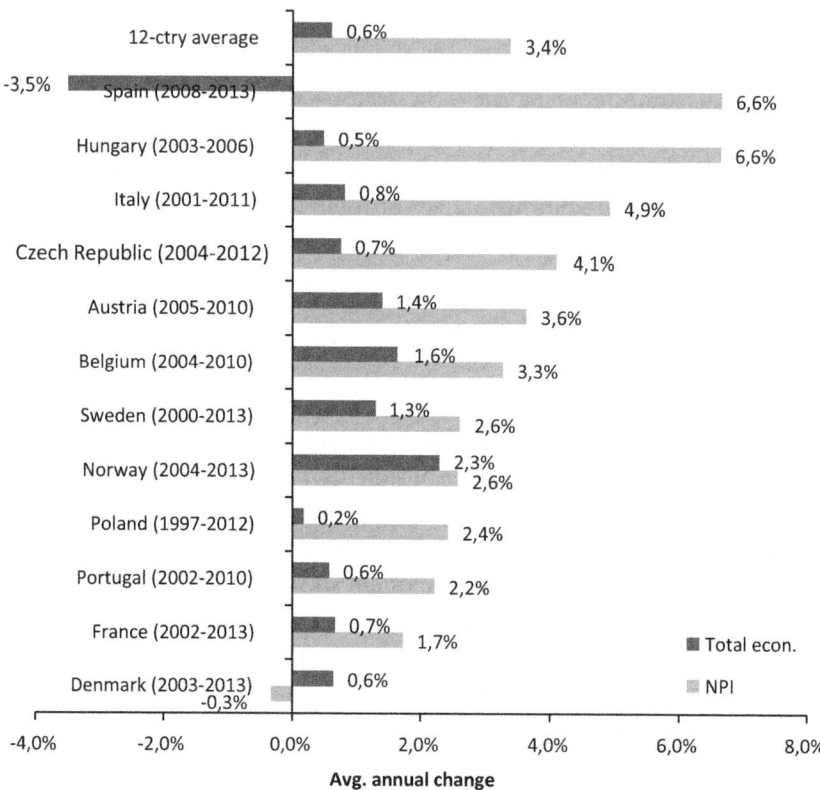

Fig. 3.6 Average annual change in employment in selected European countries, NPIs vs. Total economy

averages often lie some significant cross-national and regional variations. And that is certainly true of the European TSE sector, as our discussion in Chap. 2 above made clear.

To make sense of these variations, it is useful to examine them at the regional level. For this purpose, we have divided the EU countries into four regional groupings, which we term Northern Europe, Southern Europe, Scandinavia, and Central and Eastern Europe. Table 3.1 depicts the breakdown of European countries among these four regional clusters. To be sure, significant variations exist within these regional groupings as

The Size and Composition of the European Third Sector

Table 3.1 Regional grouping of EU countries plus Norway

Northern Europe	
Austria	Ireland
Belgium	Luxembourg
France	Netherlands
Germany	UK
Southern Europe	
Cyprus	Malta
Greece	Portugal
Italy	Spain
Scandinavia	
Denmark	Norway
Finland	Sweden
Central and Eastern Europe	
Bulgaria	Lithuania
Croatia	Poland
Czech Republic	Romania
Estonia	Slovakia
Hungary	Slovenia
Latvia	

well, and even within particular countries, but our data do not at this stage permit us to go below the regional level.

2.1 Regional Variations in Overall TSE Sector Scale

A useful starting point for this discussion of regional variations in the contours of the TSE sector is with the sector's basic scale. Countries differ, of course, in the size of their populations, so it is natural that larger countries will have larger TSE sector workforces than do smaller ones. To draw valid comparisons, therefore, we focus not on the absolute numbers, but on the share that the TSE sector workforce represents of the total number of people employed in each region. As Fig. 3.7 shows, that share varies from a high of 15 percent in the Northwestern European countries to a low of 9.5 percent in Central and Eastern Europe.[12]

---

[12] See Appendix 2 for the values for individual countries.

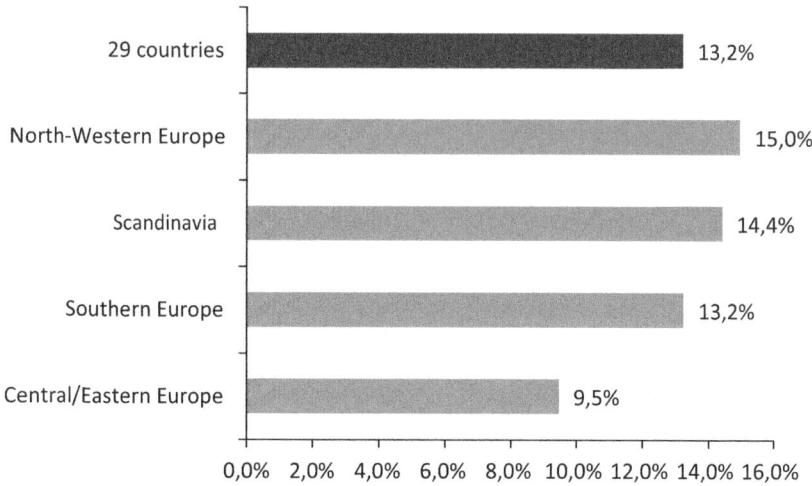

Fig. 3.7 European TSE sector workforce as a percent of total employment, by region, 2014

2.2 Regional Variations in the Institutional Composition of the TSE Sector Workforce

These overall disparities in the relative size of the TSE sector among regions are overshadowed, moreover, by the much larger disparities in the composition of the third sector in the different European regions. This is fully consistent with our discussion of regional variations in Chap. 2 above, but still deserves emphasis here. Thus, as shown in Fig. 3.8, in Central and Eastern Europe, 70 percent of third sector employment takes the form of direct volunteering. By contrast, employment in NPIs—both paid and volunteer—accounts for a much smaller 22 percent. This contrasts sharply with Northwestern Europe, where 60 percent of the TSE sector employment is in NPIs, much of it in paid positions, while employment in coops accounts for about 12 percent, social enterprises for less than 1 percent, and direct volunteering a relatively small 27 percent. This testifies to the still-embryonic nature of the more formal third sector institutions in the formerly Soviet-dominated territories and their much more robust development in the continent's advanced northwestern tier.

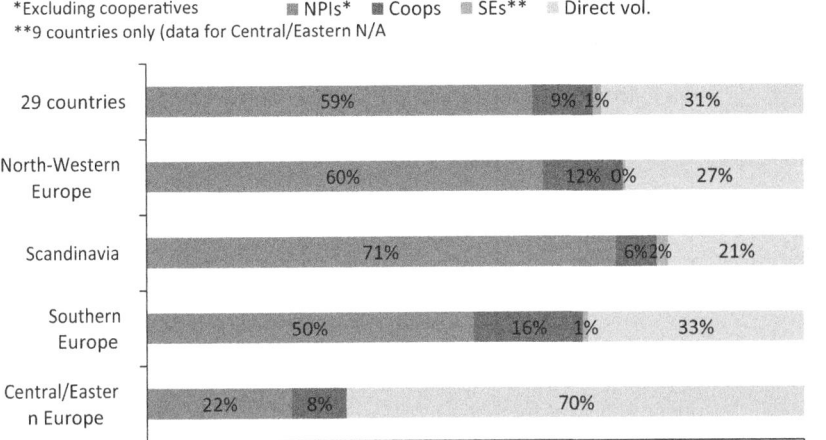

Fig. 3.8 Institutional composition of EU TSE sector workforce, by region, 2014

Southern Europe is different again, with an exceptionally high 16 percent of TSE sector employment in cooperatives, 1 percent in social enterprises, a similarly quite high 33 percent in direct volunteering, and a relatively low 50 percent of employment in NPIs.

2.3 Regional Variations in European TSE Sector Functions and Revenue Patterns

Other dimensions of the European third sector—the scope of activity by field and the revenue structure—also vary considerably by region. Due to data availability limitations, however, we can only examine these variations on a much smaller set of European countries and on a smaller set of institutions—that is, only for the NPI components of the TSE sector and only for the 20 countries covered by the Johns Hopkins Comparative Nonprofit Sector Project. As Fig. 3.9 shows, the distribution of service and expressive activities of NPIs is very different in the Scandinavian countries than it is in Northern and Southern Europe. Thus, in the Scandinavian region, 57 percent of nonprofit FTE employment is

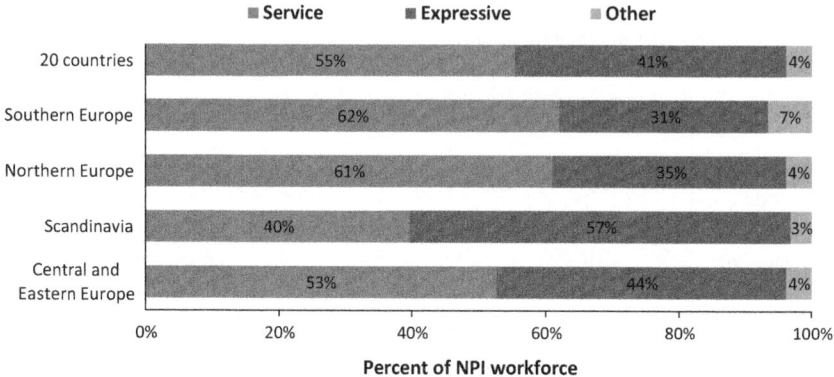

Fig. 3.9 European NPI workforce, by function, by region, 20 EU countries

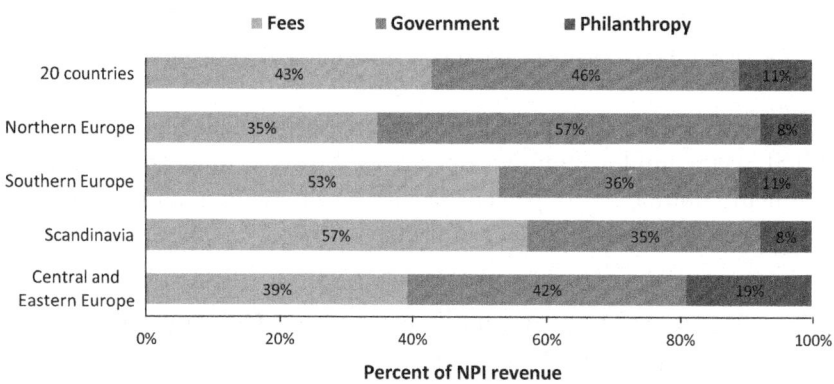

Fig. 3.10 NPI revenue structure, by region, in 20 EU countries

devoted to expressive functions and only 40 percent to service ones. By contrast, in Northern and Southern Europe, these proportions are reversed, with over 60 percent of TSE sector effort devoted to service provision and a much smaller 31–35 percent devoted to expressive functions. This reflects the much greater reliance on government for service provision in the Scandinavian lands and the long-standing tradition of nonprofit involvement in advocacy and sport activities there.

Similar disparities characterize the revenue structure of NPIs across Europe, as shown in Fig. 3.10. Thus, "fee income" (comprising market sales, membership dues and interest earned) is the dominant revenue source for NPI entities in the Scandinavian countries, accounting for 57 percent of NPI revenue, whereas government is the dominant source in Northwestern Europe outside of Scandinavia, with a similar 57 percent of revenue coming from governmental sources in this region. Lacking both substantial government and fee income, NPIs in Central and Eastern Europe rely disproportionately on philanthropy, which accounts for 19 percent of NPI income, twice the share that it provides to the much larger NPI sectors in Scandinavia and Northern Europe.

2.4 Summary

As this section has shown, behind the aggregate picture of the European third sector lie some enormous cross-regional variations. What is more, these variations apply to each of the dimensions of the TSE sector that we have been able to examine, and often in apparently confusing ways. What has caused these variations? Is it possible that these variations hold the key to explaining what it is that determines the size, shape, functions and financing of the TS sector across Europe? It is to this intriguing set of questions that we turn in the next section.

3 Explaining Cross-national Variations in TSE Sector Dimensions[13]

Cross-national dimensions in different manifestations of TS activities have not, of course, totally escaped public scrutiny. Public officials, journalists, foundation officers, civil society activists and volunteers have long had hunches about different levels and manifestations of third sector activities among countries and regions, even though they have

---

[13] This section draws heavily on Lester M. Salamon, S. Wojciech Sokolowski, and Megan Haddock, *Explaining Civil Society Development: A Social Origins Approach*. Baltimore, MD: Johns Hopkins University Press, 2017.

lacked solid empirical verification. Yet, the popular explanations of these differences are at best unconvincing and often misleading.

Perhaps the most popular explanation links these cross-country differences in the manifestations of TS activities to different cultural values and sentiments. The key element of this line of argument is that social institutions such as civil society organizations result from the development of certain values, attitudes and norms of behavior, many of which are supposedly rooted in religious convictions and teachings. Societies that espouse norms and values favorable for charity, self-governance or altruism will have stronger nonprofit and philanthropic sectors than societies in which such impulses are weaker.

Variants of this argument can be found in the academic literature as well. For example, Banfield attributed the backwardness of southern Italy to a prevalent, but dysfunctional, moral code that he termed "amoral familism" that impeded cooperation among families or clans and thus the growth of associational ties. Fukuyama proposed a similar cultural explanation of the sources of civil society growth, emphasizing the cultural value of "trust." Societies exhibiting high levels of trust create self-governing associations in both business and social life, whereas low-trusting societies rely on familial ties while the management of public affairs is carried out by a centralized authority (the state). "A thriving civil society," Fukuyama therefore explains, "depends on a people's habits, customs, and ethics—attributes that can be shaped only indirectly through conscious political action and must otherwise be nourished through an increased awareness and respect for culture."[14]

Another line of argument, developed by American economists and popularized by the spread of the neoliberal ideology during the past 30 years, attributes these differences to the degree of heterogeneity of demand for public goods. According to this theory, the inability of the market to supply the level of collective goods that citizens demand necessitates that such goods are paid for by public funding rather than through ordinary market transactions. However, when the demand for public

---

[14] Edward Banfield. (1958). *The Moral Basis of a Backward Society.* New York: Free Press.; Francis Fukuyama. (1995). *Trust: The Social Virtues and the Creation of Prosperity.* New York: The Free Press.;

goods is diversified due to different preferences of different socio-demographic groups, it is difficult to obtain the level of political consensus needed to secure sufficient public funding for such goods. According to this theory, this set of circumstances leads to the growth of the nonprofit sector to supply the collective goods that neither the market nor the state can provide. This theory thus predicts that the lower the level of heterogeneity in a population, the higher the level of government provision of public welfare services, and therefore the lower the level of TS development needed to provide the "collective goods" that citizens demand. In other words, the third sector should be less prominent where government spending is highest, and vice versa.[15]

Neither of these theories is very consistent with the findings reported here, however. So far as the cultural theories, and their religious grounding, are concerned, Europe, and especially the European Union countries, show a remarkable degree of cultural and religious similarity by global standards. All these countries share virtually identical religious roots—the Greco-Roman civilization and Christianity. Virtually every European country's religious tradition emphasizes the importance of social solidarity, altruism, helping others, civic virtues and engagement in public affairs. Clearly, a factor that is so ubiquitous can hardly be counted on to explain the enormous variations that exist in the manifestations of the TSE sector in Europe. Indeed, countries with very similar religious traditions, such as Italy, Ireland and Poland, all predominantly Catholic nations, have very different levels of TSE sector activities, especially with regard to their organizational component. Portugal and Spain share not only the same religion, but also the same cultural tradition, yet they differ markedly in their TSE sector manifestations.

This, of course, does not mean that cultural norms, values and ideologies play no role in TSE sector development, but that the relationship between the ideological influences and TSE is far more complex than the cultural sentiments theories claim. On the one hand, the norms and values can constrain even powerful social interests. At the same time,

---

[15] Burton Weisbrod. (1977). *The Voluntary Independent Sector*. Lexington: Lexington Books; Henry Hansmann. (1987). "Economic Theories of Nonprofit Organizations." In Walter W. Powell (ed.), *The Nonprofit Sector: A Research Handbook*, pp. 27–42. New Haven: Yale University Press.

whether particular values or norms gain support or legitimacy can be influenced by their consistency with group interests. Max Weber recognized this latter point in his concept of "elective affinity," the tendency of social actors to lean toward cultural norms and values that align with their predispositions and group interests ([1904–05] 1958, see also Howe, 1978). Thus, according to Weber, Protestant religious doctrines emerging in fifteenth- and sixteenth-century Europe gained ground in important part because they were more aligned with the economic interests of wealthy merchants than the traditional Catholic teaching renouncing worldly possessions.

This suggests that rather than being treated as general influences without observable causal links to particular social groupings or specific institutional outcomes, the cultural and ideological influences must be linked to the power and actions of specific social actors. For example, the long-standing Catholic doctrine of subsidiarity, holding that social issues ought to be addressed by the social unit closest to the family, including, of course, the parish, provided a convenient template for conservative elements to use in resisting worker pressures for expanded state-provided social welfare protections in nineteenth century Germany by channeling such protections through politically "safe," religiously affiliated, nonprofit organizations. Hence, as will be explained more fully later in this chapter, this created a pattern of TSE development that we term "welfare partnership."

With regard to the economic theories linking the rise of the third sector to a combination of market failure and government failure that constrains government social welfare spending and leads to increased reliance on nonprofit groups, the evidence presented here roundly refutes them. Indeed, far from being more limited, the European third sector is much larger and more robust in precisely those regions—Northwestern Europe and Scandinavia—where government social welfare spending is higher. This refutes both these market failure/government-failure theories and the common perception that Western European countries have built "welfare states." In fact, what they have built are "welfare partnerships" in which governments have turned massively to nonprofit organizations to deliver state-funded social welfare services. This has been possible because, unlike the USA, most European countries have developed what Lijphart terms "consensus democracy," which differs from the winner-take-all image embodied in the government-failure theory by making provision for proportional representation of minority interests.[16] This makes it possible to build consensuses among various interest groups and thereby generate support for a much broader array of public goods than the hypothesized "median voter" might want and eliminates the binary "either-or" choice between government or third sector provision by designing cooperative arrangements that engage both. This may explain why the inverse relation between government social welfare spending and the size of the civil society sector predicted by the economic theory turns out to be powerfully refuted by much of the cross-national data we have assembled.

How, then, are we to account for the significant differences in TSE sector size and contours among the different European regions? Drawing in part on Robert Putnam's influential study of the significant variations in the scope and scale of the nonprofit sector in Southern and Northern Italy, which Putnam links to different social class power relations in these different regions,[17] the two authors of this chapter have developed a broader "social origins" theory of third sector development that links the development of the third sector to different configurations of power relations among social groupings and institutions in various countries during the period of industrialization and modernization (Salamon et al. 2017). Thus, for example, in countries where industrial and commercial elements were able to diffuse the influence of conservative landed elites and consolidate their own political and economic power during the period of industrialization, they were able to impose national policies favorable to their economic interests in limited government involvement in economic and social affairs, and reliance on markets and private initiative in addressing the social problems resulting from industrialization. The consequence was the emergence of a "Liberal pattern" of civil society development, characterized by fairly substantial TSE sector institutions, but mostly

---

[16] Lijphart, Arendt. (1999). *Patterns of Democracy: Government Forms and Performance in Thirty Six Countries.* New Haven: Yale University Press.

[17] Robert Putnam. (1993). *Making Democracy Work: Civic Traditions in Modern Italy.* Princeton: Princeton University Press.

dependent on private sources (fees and charity) for their support. In Europe, this pattern is most visible in the UK and Switzerland.

In countries where industrialization and the partial liberalization of social relations led to the substantial growth of a working class and of organizations representing its interests, but not to the point of displacing the dominant position of landed and/or industrial or commercial elites, a decidedly different pattern emerged characterized by greater state-sponsored social welfare protections—but channeled through "safe," religiously affiliated, private voluntary organizations. This produced a "Welfare Partnership pattern" of civil society sector development, mostly focused on service activities instead of protest and advocacy, heavily subsidized by the state, but safely held in check by conservative religious or other institutions. This pattern was most pronounced in the Northwestern European countries, especially in Germany and the Netherlands, but subsequently adopted by other countries now making up the EU.

Yet another pattern emerged where the power of both industrial and rural elites had been weakened by a rising working class along with small-farmer agrarian elements and urban professionals, creating a favorable environment for implementing generous governmental social welfare provisions. The upshot here was a social-democratic pattern where social welfare services are treated as a "right" of all citizens—not a gift bestowed by charitable institutions—and are delivered directly by governmental institutions subject to popular control by citizens.[18] In Europe, this pattern emerged in the Scandinavian countries and Austria.

Still another pattern of civil society development could emerge where pre-modern landed elements retain power into the modern era and prolong economic stagnation that threatens a country's sovereignty. To counteract this threat, particularly in the face of foreign pressures, military leaders, senior civil servants, urban professionals or modernizing elites stage a revolutionary takeover of state institutions in order to push

---

[18] K. H. Sivesind, and P. Selle (2010) "Civil society in the Nordic countries: Between displacement and vitality." In R. Alapuro and H. Stenius (Eds.), *Nordic Associations in a European Perspective* (pp. 89–120). Baden-Baden: Nomos Verlagsgesellschaft.

through programs of rapid industrialization and modernization. To keep popular forces at bay and make it possible to channel whatever surplus is produced into modernization rather than consumption, such modernizing elites often find it necessary to limit personal freedoms and, particularly, restrict the growth of civil society organizations that could challenge governmental dominance and disrupt the rapid modernization agenda through demands for greater political voice and better living standards. This results in a "Statist pattern" of third sector development characterized by a highly constrained civil society sector operating in a narrow range of fields deemed critical for national development. One consequence of this constraint on third sector organizational development is a shifting of social welfare protections from the organizational to the informal social sphere. In Europe, this pattern first emerged in Russia, Turkey, Spain and Portugal, but after World War II, was forcibly exported to Central and Eastern Europe countries on the bayonets of the Red Army.

This social origins theory thus does a better job of explaining the regional variations in TSE sector dimensions in Europe than do the alternative theories. First, it explains why the size of the organizational component of the TSE sector in Eastern European countries is markedly smaller than that elsewhere in Europe, while the size of direct voluntary action is markedly larger (Fig. 3.7). Until the 1990s, the Central and Eastern European countries remained tied to the statist pattern under which the organizational component of the TSE sector remained firmly in strict state control. As the legitimacy of the political regime waned, so did the legitimacy of these state-controlled civic organizations. As a consequence, virtually all spontaneous civic activities were conducted in the informal sphere of neighborly self-help activities and unorganized social movements. Although the economic and political reforms of the 1990s and the subsequent EU accession dramatically changed the environment in which civic organizations operate, the norms of social behavior that favor direct volunteer action over participation in organized civic action still linger.

A similar process took place in the Mediterranean countries, many of which fell under the statist regime during modernization. However, unlike in Central and Eastern Europe, the statist regimes in the Mediterranean countries were democratized much earlier, in 1945 in Italy and in the early 1970s in Spain and Portugal. Also, these countries joined the EU much earlier than their Eastern European counterparts. Consequently, they enjoyed the benefits of a supportive environment for civic organizational development for a considerably longer period than the CEE countries. They also had partially Church-inspired cooperative institutions operating in financial and related spheres that muted the dominance of capitalist institutions and fostered broader cooperative and mutual ties. Cooperative institutions also emerged in Central and Eastern Europe, but with much greater state involvement and control.

The social origins theory also helps us understand the otherwise puzzling dominance of expressive over service activities in the third sector of the Scandinavian countries, as contrasted with the countries in northwestern Europe (Fig. 3.8). The social origins theory accounts for this difference by noting that conservative landed and industrial elements retained substantial power well into the late-nineteenth century and channeled social welfare provisions for workers through safe, religiously affiliated nonprofit organizations, producing a characteristic welfare partnership pattern with the religious organizations serving as junior partners of governments in delivering publicly funded welfare services. In the Scandinavian countries, by contrast, landed elites were weakened and a robust small-farmer agrarian class took its place and made common cause with the emerging working class to push for a social-democratic regime in which public welfare services were expanded and delivered predominantly by the state. Because the welfare state took care of many tasks such as child care and elderly care, the families got more time to participate and volunteer in the culture, sports and recreation areas, which grew rapidly from the 1960s as the welfare state matured and a leisure society emerged

The social origins theory also explains why the government share of nonprofit revenue is considerably higher in Northern Europe than elsewhere in Europe (Fig. 3.9). Northwestern Europe, especially Germany and the Netherlands, pioneered the policies of harnessing civic organizations into the provision of publicly funded services.

Although the original impulses behind these policies were to counteract the radicalization of the working class, they proved to be a very effective mechanism of public service delivery that combines the security of public funding with the responsiveness of relatively small and nonbureaucratic civic organizations. As a result, the welfare partnership pattern continued to develop even after the original motivation behind it lost its relevance.

To summarize, the social origins theory of third sector development thus carries us considerably far down the road toward explaining the diverse size, shape, functions and support structure of the TSE sector in Europe, and does so considerably better than the alternative explanations that have been deployed up to now. What the analysis here shows is that while the TSE sector may be a conduit for altruistic sentiments and personal preferences, the size of the sector and the shape that it takes depend heavily on the broader structures of power relationships in society. Restoring considerations of power to the center of analysis of the third sector thus emerges as a central imperative if we are to understand the path that civil society development takes.

This analysis also suggests a significant connection between the growth of the TS and the strength of labor movements and their political extensions. This connection is often missed in public perception, as "civil society" and "organized labor" are often seen as two separate social institutions pursuing wholly disparate, if not mutually antagonistic, goals. But the contribution of the labor movement to the development of the civil society sector is significant and takes two different forms. In the first place, organized labor has created a wide array of self-help groups and clubs serving the needs of the working class. And second, organized labor's demands have often leveraged government policies that create favorable conditions for general civil society sector growth.

The social origins theory can not only explain existing developments, but also help forecast the future. This can offer valuable insights into possible outcomes in rapidly changing parts of the world, and it can offer useful insights for the design of public policies facilitative of robust third sector development. But for these topics, it is necessary to turn to subsequent chapters of this book.

Appendix 1: Estimates of TSE Sector FTE workforce in EU and Norway, by Component, 2014

Region Country	NPIs (FTE)[a]			Coops & mutuals (FTE)[b]			Social enterprises Paid (FTE)	Direct volunteers (FTE)	Total TSE (FTE)	NPIs* as % of total national employment			Coops & mutuals as % of national employment			% of total national employment		Total TSE sector (%)
	Paid	Volunteers	Total	Paid	Volunteers	Total				Paid (%)	Volunteers (%)	Total (%)	Paid (%)	Volunteers (%)	Total (%)	Social enterprises (%)	Direct volunteers (%)	
Northern Europe	**7,218,017**	**4,652,448**	**11,870,465**	**970,006**	**68,588**	**1,038,593**	**291,630**	**3,435,587**	**16,636,275**	**6.3**	**4.0**	**10.3**	**0.8**	**0.1**	**0.9**	**0.3**	**3.0**	**14.4**
Austria	156,825	228,541	385,366	33,629	5420	39,050	8000	200,141	632,557	3.8	5.6	9.4	0.8	0.1	0.9	0.2	4.9	15.4
Belgium	450,454	129,210	579,664	13,534	429	13,963	75,000	185,867	854,494	9.9	2.8	12.8	0.3	0.0	0.3	1.7	4.1	18.8
France	1,562,866	1,059,883	2,622,749	161,546	12,117	173,663	40,052	139,572	2,976,036	6.1	4.1	10.2	0.6	0.0	0.7	0.2	0.5	11.5
Germany	2,343,848	1,278,256	3,622,104	486,161	29,324	515,485	–	1,479,321	5,616,911	5.9	3.2	9.1	1.2	0.1	1.3	–	3.7	14.1
Ireland	179,306	48,102	227,407	23,322	692	24,014	–	76,636	328,058	9.4	2.5	11.9	1.2	0.0	1.3	–	4.0	17.1
Luxembourg	22,544	17,979	40,523	1025	90	1116	–	9664	51,303	9.2	7.3	16.5	0.4	0.0	0.5	–	3.9	20.9
Netherlands	847,082	482,389	1,329,471	99,121	6243	105,364	–	281,756	1,716,591	10.3	5.9	16.1	1.2	0.1	1.3	–	3.4	20.8
United Kingdom	1,655,091	1,408,089	3,063,181	151,668	14,271	165,939	168,578	1,062,630	4,460,326	5.4	4.6	10.0	0.5	0.0	0.5	0.6	3.5	14.6
Southern Europe	**2,019,483**	**1,161,168**	**3,180,651**	**985,787**	**62,633**	**1,048,421**	**50,035**	**2,096,122**	**6,375,228**	**4.2**	**2.4**	**6.6**	**2.0**	**0.1**	**2.2**	**0.1**	**4.3**	**13.2**
Cyprus	23,044	18,378	41,422	2687	237	2924	–	15,238	59,583	6.4	5.1	11.4	0.7	0.1	0.8	–	4.2	16.4
Greece	243,424	194,137	437,561	8550	754	9304	–	180,156	627,022	6.9	5.5	12.4	0.2	0.0	0.3	–	5.1	17.7
Italy	871,952	555,246	1,427,199	598,387	42,144	640,531	17,635	812,383	2,897,748	3.9	2.5	6.4	2.7	0.2	2.9	1.1	3.6	13.0
Malta	10,512	8384	18,896	133	12	144	–	7327	26,368	5.8	4.6	10.4	0.1	0.0	0.1	–	4.0	14.5
Portugal	186,750	54,752	241,501	28,629	928	29,557	–	166,405	437,463	4.2	1.2	5.4	0.6	0.0	0.7	–	3.7	9.7
Spain	683,800	330,272	1,014,071	347,402	18,558	365,960	32,400	914,613	2,327,044	3.9	1.9	5.8	2.0	0.1	2.1	1.2	5.3	13.4
Scandinavia	**466,852**	**667,357**	**1,134,210**	**196,250**	**31,373**	**227,623**	**6492**	**510,273**	**1,878,597**	**3.7**	**5.3**	**9.0**	**1.6**	**0.2**	**1.8**	**0.1**	**4.1**	**15.0**
Denmark	132,969	110,538	243,508	39,682	3649	43,331	3483	123,637	413,958	4.9	4.1	9.0	1.5	0.1	1.6	0.1	4.6	15.3
Finland	67,000	78,146	145,146	54,409	7019	61,428	459	145,159	352,192	2.7	3.2	5.9	2.2	0.3	2.5	1.1	5.9	14.4
Norway	84,054	143,637	227,691	–	–	–	–	85,647	313,339	3.2	5.5	8.7	0.0	0.0	0.0	–	3.3	11.9
Sweden	182,829	335,036	517,865	102,159	20,705	122,864	2550	155,830	799,109	3.8	7.0	10.9	2.1	0.4	2.6	1.2	3.3	16.7
Central and Eastern Europe	**612,859**	**319,805**	**932,664**	**310,054**	**21,718**	**331,771**	–	**2,920,538**	**4,201,535**	**1.4**	**0.7**	**2.1**	**0.7**	**0.0**	**0.7**	–	**6.6**	**9.5**

(continued)

Region	NPIs (FTE)[a]			Coops & mutuals (FTE)[b]				Social enterprises Paid (FTE)	Direct volunteers (FTE)	Total TSE (FTE)	NPIs[a] as % of total national employment			Coops & mutuals as % of national employment			Social enterprises (%)	Direct volunteers (%)	Total TSE sector (%)
											Paid (%)	Volunteers (%)	Total (%)	Paid (%)	Volunteers (%)	Total (%)			
Country	Paid	Volunteers	Total	Paid	Volunteers[c]	Total													
Bulgaria	16,538	6898	23,436	21,902	1010	22,912		–	183,595	229,944	0.6	0.2	0.8	0.7	0.0	0.8	–	6.2	7.7
Croatia	70,512	29,412	99,924	–	–	–		–	107,770	207,694	4.5	1.9	6.4	0.0	0.0	0.0	–	6.9	13.3
Czech Republic	98,156	25,442	123,597	33,864	971	34,835		–	269,964	428,396	2.0	0.5	2.5	0.7	0.0	0.7	–	5.4	8.6
Estonia	20,074	8373	28,448	5224	241	5464		–	38,931	72,843	3.2	1.3	4.6	0.8	0.0	0.9	–	6.2	11.7
Hungary	84,203	15,965	100,168	48,978	1027	50,005		–	255,532	405,705	2.1	0.4	2.4	1.2	0.0	1.2	–	6.2	9.9
Latvia	34,144	14,242	48,386	233	11	244		–	50,334	98,964	3.9	1.6	5.5	0.0	0.0	0.0	–	5.7	11.2
Lithuania	6889	2874	9763	4757	219	4977		–	74,919	89,659	0.5	0.2	0.7	0.4	0.0	0.4	–	5.7	6.8
Poland	196,338	159,266	355,604	149,742	13,434	163,176		–	1,243,900	1,779,242	1.2	1.0	2.2	0.9	0.1	1.0	–	7.8	11.1
Romania	24,976	32,502	57,479	28,303	4074	32,377		–	515,288	605,144	0.3	0.4	0.7	0.3	0.0	0.4	–	6.0	7.0
Slovakia	18,286	7002	25,289	14,980	634	15,615		–	146,491	187,394	0.8	0.3	1.1	0.6	0.0	0.7	–	6.2	7.9
Slovenia	42,743	17,829	60,572	2070	96	2166		–	33,813	96,551	4.7	1.9	6.6	0.2	0.0	0.2	–	3.7	10.5
Total	**10,317,211**	**6,800,779**	**17,117,990**	**2,462,097**	**184,311**	**2,646,408**		**348,156**	**8,962,520**	**29,091,636**	**4.7**	**3.1**	**7.8**	**1.1**	**0.1**	**1.2**	**0.2**	**4.1**	**13.2**
EU+Norway																			

Bold print indicates regional totals; regions are composed of countries listed below each bold print line

[a] Excluding coops and mutuals that are NPIs
[b] Includes coops and mutuals that are NPIs
[c] Includes only volunteering in coops and mutuals that are NPIs
– Data not available

Appendix 2: Methodology for Estimating the Size of the Third Sector in Europe

Following the conceptual framework developed by the TSI project, the TSE sector consists of the following components: nonprofit institutions, cooperatives and mutuals, social enterprises and individual human activities outside organizations. According to this conceptual framework, all nonprofit institutions not controlled by government are in in-scope of the TSE sector. However only some cooperatives, mutual associations and social enterprises meet the TSE sector's definitional features, that is, those that are not controlled by government and are significantly limited by law or widely acknowledged custom from distributing any profits they earn to members, investors or other stakeholders. This framework also limits the individual activities in scope, as those that constitute work without pay performed for public benefit rather than for the benefit of the volunteers' households or families. Data sources therefore had to be found that would provide a way to draw these operational distinctions. The methodology used in this project to estimate the size and related characteristics of the TSE sector's paid and volunteer workforce therefore had to estimate each of these components separately and then add these estimates together to arrive at the estimate of the size and related characteristics of FTE employment in the entire TSE sector while avoiding potential double counting. The discussion below covers the methodology and data sources utilized in estimating these various parameters for each of these components in turn.

Nonprofit Institutions (NPIs)

The existing data sources on employment in NPIs include the Johns Hopkins Comparative Nonprofit Sector Project (JHU/CNP)(Lester M. Salamon, S. Wojciech Sokolowski and Megan Haddock (2017), *Explaining Civil Society Development: A Social Origins Approach*, Baltimore: Johns Hopkins University Press), NPI Satellite Accounts compiled by national statistical agencies, and other semi-official data sources. The JHU/CNP data cover both paid and volunteer employment in the in-scope NPIs, as defined in chapter two of this book. These data sources cover 18 EU countries (Austria, Belgium, Czech Republic, Denmark, Finland, France, Germany, Hungary, Ireland, Italy, Netherlands, Poland, Portugal, Romania, Slovakia, Spain, Sweden and the UK) and Norway. For most of these countries, the data reported in these sources were "updated" to 2014 by calculating the ratios of NPI employment to total employment for the year for which the data were originally reported, and then applying these ratios to the 2014 total employment in the respective countries (as reported by Eurostat). This approach thus assumes, conservatively, that the NPI share of the total employment remained more or less constant over time even though the limited time-series data reported above suggests that nonprofit employment is growing more rapidly than overall employment in all the countries for which such data are available.

For two of these countries, France and Portugal, however, newer, reliable data were published in time to be incorporated into this analysis. For France, the data come from the *Atlas Commente de l'economie Sociale et Solidarie 2014, Observatorie National de L'ESS—CNRES*. For Portugal, the data come from the satellite account for social economy released by Statistics Portugal.[19]

For the remaining 10 EU countries on which no NPI data are available, a regression-based estimation methodology was used. This methodology used a multivariate linear regression model to estimate the NPI share of total employment in the EU and non-EU countries on which NPI data are already available, and then applying the regression equation to countries for which no NPI data exists. Several predictor variables were tested, and the following were selected based on the amount of explained variance they accounted for in the base countries: (a) per Capita GDP in USD; the services share of GVA; and the revenue of NPISH units as a share of GDP.[20] This model explains 71.5 percent of variance (66 percent

---

[19] These data were downloaded from: https://www.ine.pt/xportal/xmain?xpid=INE&xpgid=ine_destaques&DESTAQUESdest_boui=278817467&DESTAQUESmodo=2&xlang=en

[20] NPISH stands for Nonprofit Institutions Serving Households. Prior to revisions of the System of National Accounts in 2008, NPISH was the only portion of the entire nonprofit sector visible in official economic statistics guided by the System of National Accounts. Formally, NPISH covers organizations that receive all or most of their income from philanthropy, though some countries apply it more broadly.

adjusted). For the 12 EU and non-EU countries on which NPISH data were not available, the missing data were replaced by averages for Eastern and Western Europe, respectively.

The regression equation was used to predict the NPI share of total employment in 10 countries for which CNP or NPI satellite account statistical data on NPIs were not available. In several of these countries, adjustments had to be made to the estimated NPI share values to restrict its variability to the actually observed ranges in the countries for which solid data were available:

For the five countries where the estimated value of the NPI share was lower than the lowest observed value in the 18-country data set, the lowest observed value (for Romania) was used;

For the two countries where the predicted value was higher than the highest observed value in the 18-country data set, the highest observed value was applied.

This estimation methodology results in a reasonably accurate estimate of NPI employment in the 10 countries as a group, but predictions for individual countries may be less reliable and should therefore be viewed with caution. These 10 countries as a group account for only about 5 percent of the NPI workforce (paid and volunteers) covered by this study.

Data for predictor variables come from the national accounts aggregates available at the UN Statistics Division website http://data.un.org/Explorer.aspx?d=SNAAMA

Cooperatives and Mutual Societies

The data on employment in cooperatives and mutual societies were drawn mostly from a report prepared by José Luis Monzón Campos and Rafael Chaves Ávila entitled *The Social Economy in the European Union*, Report drawn up for the European Economic and Social Committee by the International Centre of Research and Information on the Public, Social and Cooperative Economy (CIRIEC, 2012), covering the year 2010. The report provides paid employment data on all EU member countries covering the following separately identified types of organizations: cooperatives, mutuals and associations. The CIRIEC team updated these data through 2014 and reported the tentative results in a June 2017 briefing for the European Economic and Social Committee. However, no published version of these estimates was available as of the date the present publication went to press, and too little documentation of the sources of the tentatively released data were available to judge their validity. The 2010 data published in 2012 were therefore used as the basis for the estimates used here for most countries. Based on a comparison of these two data sets, we have confidence that the overall picture presented in this report would not have been affected significantly were we to have used the tentatively released newer data.

For a variety of reasons, while the CIRIEC data provided a starting point for our estimates of the employment and other features of in-scope cooperatives and mutuals for most countries, these data had to be adjusted to meet the operational criteria for such in-scope entities identified above. There were three reasons for this:

- First, because the CIRIEC data took as given the varying legal definitions of cooperatives, mutuals and associations found in the separate countries, rather than the operational criteria specified here. As a result, it appears to have included substantial numbers of cooperatives and mutual, particularly in the financial services field, that operate very much like regular for-profit banks and insurance companies and are therefore out-of-scope of the TSE sector as defined in Chap. 2 of this book;
- Second, little account seems to have been taken of the fact that a significant, but still unknown, number of cooperatives are actually NPIs, creating significant potential double counting in the estimates
- Finally, the data available to Monzón and Chaves tended to rely on practitioner assessments and unverified administrative registration records, both of which tend to overestimate the scope of actual employment in this field.

Fortunately, to deal with these potential problems, we had available four more reliable and rigorous sources of data on cooperative and mutual employment: data generated by official statistical agencies or high-level research institutions in Portugal, France, Poland and Norway. All four of these sources reported cooperative and mutual employment levels that fell well below those reported in the CIRIEC data. Not only did this provide better estimates of the actual cooperative and mutual employment in these countries, but also they provided a statistically persuasive basis for estimating the "correction factors" needed to bring the CIRIEC estimates into better alignment with the criteria we adopted to identify the in-scope cooperatives and mutuals. In particular, to eliminate possible out-of-scope units, we followed a procedure recommended by statisticians at Statistics Portugal, which identified cooperatives and mutual societies operating in the financial sector as most likely to be out-of-scope of the TSE sector as we defined it.[21] Using the resulting Portugal data and a more detailed breakdown of cooperatives and mutuals available in a 2014 French *Atlas Commente de l'economie Sociale et Solidarie* (Tableau 16), we were able to generate an empirically verified estimate of the average share of the total cooperative and mutual employment reported in the CIRIEC report that was likely to fit our definition of in-scope cooperative and mutual employment in Europe. Similar adjustments became possible in Poland, where statistical sources put the estimate of in-scope cooperative and mutual employment far lower than the adjustments found to be necessary In Portugal and France.[22] To be conservative, we applied the average adjustment factor of the CIRIEC estimates found to be appropriate in France and Portugal (53.1 percent) to the CIRIEC estimates in all other countries except Poland and Norway. In the case of Poland, we used the Polish statistical office figures for Poland's estimate. Since Norway is not an EU member country, the data for this country were not included in the CIRIEC publication. However, an NPI Satellite Account (NPISA) produced by Statistics Norway in accord with the United Nations *Handbook on Nonprofit Institutions in the System of National Accounts* yielded solid data on NPIs in Norway and the Norwegian TSI project research team determined that all cooperatives and mutuals that are in-scope of the TSE sector in Norway were included

---

[21] Email communication from Ms. Cristina Ramos, National Accounts Statistician, Statistics Portugal, January 20, 2017 and February 6, 2017.
[22] Personal communication, Slawomir Nalecz, national account statistician, Government Statistical Office, Poland.

in the NPI Satellite Account (NPISA) released by Statistics Norway, and those not covered by the Norwegian NPISA were likely to be out-of-scope of our consensus definition.

To avoid double counting of cooperatives that may be treated as NPIs in various countries' statistics, we developed an estimate of this possible overlap using data available in the French *Atlas Commente de l'economie Sociale et Solidarie 2014*, Tableau 16. In particular, in consultation with French experts, we took as given that cooperatives and mutuals operating in the field of social action were likely to be NPIs. Employment in "social action" cooperatives and mutuals in France accounts for about 11 percent of total in-scope employment in those two types of institutions (after excluding employment in the financial cooperatives and mutuals). We applied this rate to the estimated in-scope employment in cooperatives and mutuals in the remaining countries covered by this book to determine the approximate shares of cooperative and mutual employment that also qualify as NPI employment. In our discussion of the institutional breakdown of the TSE sector workforce in Chap. 3, we included this employment in cooperatives and mutuals that are also NPIs with the cooperative and mutual employment and subtracted it from the estimate of NPI employment.

Social Enterprises

Very limited reliable data on social enterprises are available at this time. The TSI project country assessments suggested that since most of the in-scope social enterprises are already included in the NPI or cooperative data, it was not generally possible to separate them out for most countries. The only clearly identifiable social enterprises are those that have been registered as such under the special legal categories that some countries have recently established for such entities. These categories are variously identified as "Work Integration Social Enterprises" (WISE), "sheltered employment establishments" and, in the case of the UK, "Community Interest Companies (CIC)." Only nine European countries have established such categories, however. In eight of these countries (Austria, Belgium, Denmark, Finland, France, Italy, Spain and Sweden), employment in WISEs and sheltered employment establishments could be estimated using information provided in country reports of the European Commission's publication *A map of social enterprises and their eco-systems in Europe* (European Union, 2014).[23] Estimates of employment in CICs in the UK were derived by combining data on the number of active social enterprise establishments provided in an official business register available at http://download.companieshouse.gov.uk/en_output.html, with data on average employment per establishment available in the UK country report included in the European Commission's *Map of social enterprises and their eco-systems in Europe*. In the remaining countries, social enterprises operate mostly as NPIs or cooperatives, making it highly likely that they are already included in our data, though it was not possible to report on them separately. Using the data on these nine countries, we estimated that social enterprises accounted for roughly 1 percent of TSE sector employment in Europe. To get some sense of the potential scale of such enterprises in the other countries, we developed two additional estimates—one assuming that the share that social enterprise employment would represent of total TSE employment in these other countries would be on a par with the average in the nine countries on which solid data were available, and the other assuming that the social enterprise share of TSE sector employment in these other countries would likely be on a par with that in the country with the lowest such share among countries for which data are available. It turned out that using the lower estimate would boost the overall share of social enterprise employment from 1 percent to 1.3 percent, and that the higher share would boost it from 1 percent to 2.3 percent—still well within the range of our initial 1 percent estimate.

Direct Volunteering

The data on direct volunteering come from estimates based on national TUSs as reported by OECD. Methodological documentation on national TUS used for these estimates is in Miranda V. (2011) "Cooking, Caring and Volunteering: Unpaid Work Around the World," OECD Social,

---

[23] This publication is accessible at: http://ec.europa.eu/social/keyDocuments.jsp?pager.offset=0&&langId=en&mode=advancedSubmit&year=0&country=0&type=0&advSearchKey=socentcntryrepts&orderBy=docOrder.

Employment and Migration Working Papers, No. 116, OECD Publishing. doi: 10.1787/5kghrjm8s142-en.

TUS assigns the time respondents spend on various activities during a 24-hour period and extrapolates those values to the entire population. This allows estimation of the total time spent on these activities by the entire adult population of a country during the period of one year, and converting that time to FTE employment, assuming 1760 hours per FT job, though this latter number may actually vary from country to country. Time spent on "care for non-household members" reported in TUS tabulations was used as a proxy for direct volunteering. This probably underestimates direct volunteering that does not involve helping other households, such as unorganized community work or protest actions.

Eighteen European countries are covered by the TUS data in the OECD report. The countries are: Austria, Belgium, Canada, Denmark, Estonia, Finland, France, Germany, Hungary, Ireland, Italy, Netherlands, Norway, Poland, Portugal, Slovenia, Spain, Sweden and the UK. However, for Poland, an alternative data source (GUS, *Volunteering Through Organizations And Other Types Of Unpaid Work Outside Own Household*—2011, Warsaw, 2012) offers a more accurate estimate based on the methodology outlined in the ILO *Manual on the Measurement of Volunteer Work*. The value reported in the latter source is about 5 percent lower than that estimated from the TUS data for Poland. For the remaining 11 countries covered by this report, the averages calculated separately for Western and Eastern Europe, respectively, were used.

The estimation methodology used the average number of minutes per adult spent on caring for nonhousehold members reported in the TUS, and multiplied that number by 365 days and by the size of the adult population (15-65 years of age) in a respective country to estimate the total number of hours spent on these activities during one year. That number was then converted to FTE workers by dividing it by 1760 hours.

Estimation of the TSE Sector Size

Employment in each of the institutional components described above (1 through 4) was summed up for each of the 29 countries covered by this chapter to arrive at the total size of the workforce (paid and volunteers) in the TSE sector. The values presented here are conservative estimates of that size due to a limited ability to estimate social enterprises and the accurate value of employment in cooperatives.

Estimation of Service and Expressive Shares of the Workforce

The core data for estimating the relative shares of service and expressive activities of the TSE sector workforce were collected through the Johns Hopkins Comparative Nonprofit Sector Project for 20 European countries. Unweighted country averages of these shares were calculated to estimate the respective shares of the NPI component of the workforce engaged in these respective activities in the remaining EU countries. In the case of the cooperative, mutual, social enterprise and direct volunteering components of the TSE workforce, it was assumed that these workers were entirely involved in service activities. Although it is possible that some direct volunteering involved expressive activities, this kind of direct volunteering was not captured by the TUS data that asked only about help for other households. Our estimate therefore unavoidably likely underestimates the expressive share of the TSE sector workforce.

Estimation of TSE Sector Revenue Shares

The core data for estimating the shares of TSE sector revenue coming from government payments (grants, contracts and reimbursements), fees (market sales, membership dues and investments), and private philanthropy in NPI revenues were collected through the Johns Hopkins Comparative Nonprofit Sector Project for 20 European countries. Unweighted country averages of these shares were calculated to estimate the respective shares of NPI revenue for the remaining countries. Since, in the European context, government reimbursements for individual services account for most of government support to NPIs, and such reimbursements are reported in conventional economic statistics as market sales to individuals, our estimate of government support of TSE sector organizations will diverge from estimates provided in conventional economic statistics.

This NPI estimate of revenue shares from these three main sources was then supplemented by data for cooperatives, mutuals and social enterprises, which assumed that this revenue comes chiefly from fees and market sales. The value of direct volunteering, estimated at the replacement cost, was counted as private philanthropy and factored in proportionally to the direct volunteering share of the TS workforce.

Summary of Sources of Data on TSE Sector Average Annual Employment Changes by Country

Compiled by Karl Henrik Sivesind, Institute for Social Research, Norway

Austria
Number of employed persons 2005 and 2010: Pennerstorfer, A., Schneider, U. & Badelt, C. in: Simsa, R., Meyer, M. & Badelt, C.: (Hg.): *Handbuch der Nonprofit-Organisation. Stuttgart 2013* (5. überarbeitete Auflage).
Volunteering FTE 1997: Heitzmann, Karin (2001): *Dimensionen, Strukturen und Bedeutung des Nonprofit Sektors. Eine theoretisch-konzeptionelle und empirische Analyse für Österreich.* Wien: Facultas Copy Store.
Volunteering FTE 2000: Badelt, Christoph and Hollerweger, Eva (2007): Ehrenamtliche Arbeit im Nonprofit Sektor, in: Badelt, C./Meyer, M./Simsa, R. (eds.), *Handbuch der Nonprofit Organisationen. Strukturen und Management* (4., überarbeitete Auflage ed., pp. 503-531). Stuttgart: Schäffer-Poeschel.
Volunteering FTE 2006: Statistik Austria (2008): *Struktur und Volumen der Freiwilligenarbeit in Österreich. Bericht im Auftrag des BMSK.* Wien: Bundesministerium für Soziales und Konsumentenschutz.

Belgium
FTE employment, and sources of funding 1995 from: Salamon, L. M., Anheier, H. K., List, R., Toepler, S., Sokolowski, S. W., & Associates. (1999). *Global civil society. Dimensions of the nonprofit sector, Volume I.* Baltimore, MD: The Johns Hopkins Center for Civil Society Studies.
Number of employed persons, and sources of funding 2004 from:
Institut des comptes nationaux. (2007). *Comptes nationaux. Le compte satellite des institutions sans but lucratif 2000-2004.* Bruxelles: Banque nationale de Belgique. Retrieved from: https://www.nbb.be/doc/dq/f/dq3/histo/nfds0004.pdf Number of employed persons 2010, and sources of funding from:
Institut des comptes nationaux. (2007). *Comptes nationaux. Le compte satellite des institutions sans but lucratif 2009-2010.* Bruxelles: Banque nationale de Belgique. Retrieved from: https://www.nbb.be/doc/dq/f/dq3/nfds.pdf

Sources of funding 2008:
Salamon, L. M., Sokolowski, S. W., Haddock, M., & Tice, H. S. (2013). *The state of global civil society and volunteering comparative nonprofit sector* (Working Paper no. 49). Baltimore, MD: Johns Hopkins University, Center for Civil Society Studies. Figure 12: NPI revenue, by source, by country.

Czech Republic
Number of employed persons 2004 and 2012 from: http://apl.czso.cz/pll/rocenka/rocenka.indexnu_en_sat
Sources of funding 2009: Salamon, L. M., Sokolowski, S. W., Haddock, M., & Tice, H. S. (2013). *The state of global civil society and volunteering comparative nonprofit sector* (Working Paper no. 49). Baltimore, MD: Johns Hopkins University, Center for Civil Society Studies. Figure 12: NPI revenue, by source, by country.

Denmark
FTE paid employment and volunteering, and sources of funding 2003 from: Boje, T. P., Fridberg, T., & Ibsen, B. (2006). *Den frivillige sektor i Danmark. Omfang og betydning* (Rapport 06:19). København: Socialforskningsinstituttet. Retrieved from: http://www.sfi.dk/Admin/Public/DWSDownload.aspx?File=%2ffiles%2fFiler%2fSFI%2fPdf%2fRapporter%2f2006%2f0619_Den_frivillige_sektor.pdf
FTE paid employment and volunteering, and funding from donations 2013 from: Boje, T. P. (2016). *Danmark NPO sektoren inøgletal—foreløbige tal for det nationale sample*. Roskilde: Roskilde Universitet.

France
FTE employment 2002: Kaminski, P. (2005). Table1. The NPS in France, 2002 (version INSEE). *Le compte des Institutions Sans But Lucratif (ISBL) en France (Année 2002)*. Paris: l'Institut National de la Statistique et des Études Économiques (INSEE).
FTE employment 2013:Connaissance locale de l'appareil productif (CLAP) Caractéristiques des établissements au 31 décembre 2013. Paris: l'Institut National de la Statistique et des Études Économiques (INSEE).
Sources of funding 2005 and 2011: Tchernonog, V. (2013). Les associations entre crise et mutations: les grandes évolutions. Paris: Association pour le Développement des Données sur l'Economie Sociale(ADDES). Retrieved from: https://hal- paris1.archives-ouvertes.fr/halshs-00962135/fr/

Germany
Data on full-time equivalent employment in the third sector in 2007 are from the business register 2011. Thanks to Holger Krimmer, Head of civil society research at Stiftverband für die Deutsche Wissenschaft.

Hungary

The number of the employees of nonprofit organizations, 1993–2006 from: Nagy, R., & Sebestény, I. (2009). Table A 10 in *Methodological Practice and Practical Methodology: Fifteen Years in Nonprofit Statistics* (Hungarian Statistical Review Special Number 12). Budapest: Hungarian Central Statistical Office. Retrieved from: http://www.ksh.hu/statreview

Volunteering 1995 for the whole third sector p. 308: Salamon, L. M., Anheier, H. K., List, R., Toepler, S., Sokolowski, S. W., & Associates. (1999). *Global civil society. Dimensions of the nonprofit sector, Volume I*. Baltimore, MD: The Johns Hopkins Center for Civil Society Studies.

Italy

Number of employees and outworkers of active non-profit institutions and sources of funding 2001 and 2011 retrieved from: ISTAT. (2014). *Nonprofit institution profile based on 2011 census results*. Rome: Istituto nazionale di statistica. Retrieved from http://www.istat.it/en/files/2014/10/Nonprofit-Institution-Profile-based-on-2011-Census-results_EN_definitivo.pdf?title=Non profit+institutions+profile+-+9+Oct+2014+-+Full+text.pdf; http://dati-censimentoindustriaeservizi.istat.it

Netherlands

FTE paid employment and volunteering, and sources of funding 2002 from: Dekker, P., & Kuhry, B. (2007). CNP Data Master for the Netherlands 2002. Personal communication.

Norway

FTE employment 2006 and 2013 from: Statistisk sentralbyrå. (2015).
Table 08520: Full-time equivalent persons, by activity (ICNPO). *Satellite account for non-profit institutions*. Retrieved from https://ssb.no/orgsat

Poland

FTE paid employment 2012: Wilk, R., Knapp, A., & Borysiak, K. (2014). Ekonomiczny wymiar działalności badanych organizacji (The economic dimension of the activities of the organizations). In K. Goś-Wójcicka (Ed.), Trzeci Sektor w Polsce: Stowarzyszenia, fundacje, społeczne podmioty wyznaniowe, organizacje samorządu zawodowego, gospodarczego i pracodawców w 2012 r (The third sector in Poland: associations, foundations, faith-based charities, professional and business associations, employers' organizations in 2012). Warsaw: Central Statistical Office of Poland, pp. 104 & 106.
http://stat.gov.pl/obszary-tematyczne/gospodarka-spoleczna-wolontariat/gospodarka-spoleczna-trzeci-sektor/trzeci-sektor-w-polsce-stowarzyszenia-fundacje-spoleczne-podmioty-wyznaniowe-samorzad-zawodowy-i-gospodarczy-oraz-organizacje-pracodawcow-w-2012-r-,1,3.html?BHT-9530df09-411f-4044-a26e-8e451762e454.0

FTE volunteering: Volunteering 1995 for the whole third sector p. 328: Salamon, L. M., Anheier, H. K., List, R., Toepler, S., Sokolowski, S. W., & Associates. (1999). *Global civil society. Dimensions of the nonprofit sector, Volume I*. Baltimore, MD: The Johns Hopkins Center for Civil Society Studies. table 5.5.9. p. 209, in Nałęcz, S. & Goś-Wójcicka, K. (Eds). (2012). Wolontariat w organizacjach i inne formy pracy niezarobkowej poza gospodarstwem domowym—2011 (Volunteering thorough organizations and other types of unpaid work outside own household—2011). Warsaw: Central Statistical Office of Poland.

Sources of funding 2012: table 4(5) Annex tables in Goś-Wójcicka, K. (Ed.) (2014). Trzeci sektor w Polsce: Stowarzyszenia, fundacje, społeczne podmioty wyznaniowe, organizacje samorządu zawodowego, gospodarczego i pracodawców w 2012 r (The third sector in Poland: Associations, foundations, faith-based charities, professional and business associations, employers' organizations in 2012)

Thanks to Sławomir Nałęcz for help with sources and calculations.

Portugal
Number of employees 2002: Salamon, L. M., Sokolowski, S. W., & Associates (Eds.). (2004). *Portugal: Workforce, expenditures, and revenue data (2002)*. Baltimore: Johns Hopkins Center for Civil Society Studies. Retrieved from: http://ccss.jhu.edu/wp-content/plugins/download-monitor/download. php?id=Portugal_Data_2002.pdf

Number of employees and sources of funding 2006: Salamon, L. M., Sokolowski, S. W., Haddock, M., & Tice, H. S. (2012). *Portugal: Portugal's nonprofit sector in comparative context, 2006*. Baltimore: Johns Hopkins Center for Civil Society Studies in collaboration with Instituto Nacional de Estatistica—INE. Retrieved from: http://ccss.jhu.edu/wp-content/plugins/download-monitor/download.php?id=Portugal_Comparative-Report_FINAL_4.2012.pdf

FTE paid employment 2010: Misericórdias, Fundações, Associações e outras OES Quadro 1.1—Principais indicadores por grupos de entidades da Economia Social (2010)

Welfare share of employment: (Ensino e Investigação, Saúde e Bem-Estar, Ação Social) Gráfico 1.2—Emprego remunerado na ES (ETC)

Instituto Nacional de Estatística. (2013). *Conta Satélite da Economia Social 2010*. Estatísticas oficiais. Lisboa: Instituto Nacional de Estatística, I.P. Retrieved from: https://www.ine.pt/ngt_server/attachfileu.jsp?look_parentBoui=157544893&att_display=n&att_download=y

Total FTE employment and welfare employment 2010 is missing in the ILOSTAT database. Source: Table A.4.17—Full-time equivalent employment by industry (N.°; annual), Portuguese National Accounts—ESA2010, base 2011.

Spain

Number of employees 2008: Monzón, J. L. *Las grandes cifras de la economía social en España. Ámbito, entidades y cifras clave. Año 2008*. Valencia: CIRIEC. Cuadro 2.38. Entidades singulares de la economía social. Año 2008; Cuadro 2.41. Asociaciones activas: empleados, voluntarios y gastos por actividad; Cuadro 2.46. Fundaciones privadas al servicio de los hogares activas por actividad principal. Año 2008

Systeme Innovación y Consultoría. (2015). *The third sector of social action in 2015: Impact of the crisis* (Executive summary) Madrid: Plataforma de ONG de Acción Social/Plataforma Tercer Sector. Retrieved from: http://www.plataformaong.org/ciudadaniaactiva/tercersector/executive_summary_TSSA_in_2015_impact_of_t he_crisis.pdf

There is no data on total nonprofit employment in 2013. It is estimated by adding the number of non-welfare employees in 2008 to the welfare employees from 2013. The assumption is that non-welfare employment has been on the same level in real numbers, while the data shows that the welfare employment has increased. This means that Spain has had a decrease in non-welfare employment from 1995 to 2013 of −0.53 percentage points per year, while total NPO employment has increased by 0.11 percentage points per year due to documented welfare growth. If growth had been estimated by using 2008 data, the decrease in non-welfare employment would have been −0.81 and total NPO employment would have decreased by −1.17 percentage points per year. This would seem to be a too strong decline given the recent growth in welfare employment. In addition, total employment has declined in real numbers from 2008 to 2013, which further increases the share of the NPO sector. On the welfare field, the NPO employment has increased fast while the total employment has grown slightly in health and social services from 2008 to 2013.

Volunteering data for 2008 seem to be not comparable (number of volunteers, not FTE?).

Volunteering 1995 for the whole third sector p. 166: Salamon, L. M., Anheier, H. K., List, R., Toepler, S., Sokolowski, S. W., & Associates. (1999). *Global civil society. Dimensions of the nonprofit sector, Volume I*. Baltimore, MD: The Johns Hopkins Center for Civil Society Studies.

Sweden

Number of employees 1992: Lundström, T., & Wijkström, F. (1997). *The nonprofit sector in Sweden*. Manchester: Manchester University Press.

Number of employees 2000 for NPO welfare: Sveriges officiella statistik. (2009). Table 15. Sysselsatta fördelat på verksamheter och kön år 2007, in *Finansiärer och utförare inom vård, skola och omsorg 2007* (Sveriges Oficiella Statistik, Serie Offentlig ekonomi OE 29 SM 0901): Statistiska centralbyrån. Retrieved from: http://www.scb.se/Statistik/OE/OE0112/2007A01/OE0112_2007A01_SM_OE29SM0901.pdf

Number of employees 2002 for the nonprofit sector: Wijkström, F., & Einarsson, T. (2006). *Från nationalstat til näringsliv. Det civila samhällets organisasjonsliv i förändring* (Rapport. Stockholm: Ekonomiska Forskningsinstitutet, Handelshögskolan i Stockholm).
FTE volunteering 2005: Olsson, Lars-Erik, Lars Svedberg & Eva Jeppson Grassman (2006), Medborgarnas insatser och engagemang i civilsamhället— några grundläggande uppgifter från en ny befolkningsstudie. Arbetsrapportserie nr 39. Sköndal: Sköndalsinstitutet.
Number of employees 2013 for the nonprofit sector: Statistics Sweden. (2015). Tabell 13. Sektorindelad statistik över det civila samhället, 2013. *The Civil Society 2013—Satellite accounts and surveys*. Örebro: Statistics Sweden. Retrieved from: http://www.scb.se/Statistik/_Publikationer/NV0117_2013A01_BR_X105BR1501.pdf
Number of employees 2013 for the nonprofit welfare services: Sveriges officiella statistik. (2015). Table 13: Employment within education, health care and social services 2000, 2008–2013. Finansiärer och utförare inom vård, skola och omsorg 2013: Statistiska centralbyrån. Retrieved from: http://www.scb.se/Statistik/OE/OE0112/2013A01/OE0112_2013A01_SM_OE29SM1501.pdf
Sources of funding for the nonprofit sector 2007: Sveriges officiella statistik. (2009). Table 1-3 in *Finansiärer och utförare inom vård, skola och omsorg 2007: Statistiska centralbyrån*. Retrieved from: http://www.scb.se/sv_/Hitta-statistik/Publiceringskalender/Visa-detaljerad-information/?W=serie&publobjid=11229There is only information about income for market producing nonprofit units.
Sources of funding for the nonprofit sector 2013: Statistics Sweden. (2015). Tabell 10. Transfereringsinkomster per verksamhet enligt ICNPO, 2013 in *The Civil Society 2013—Satellite accounts and surveys*. Örebro: Statistics Sweden. Retrieved from: http://www.scb.se/Statistik/_Publikationer/NV0117_2013A01_BR_X105BR1501.pdf

Switzerland
FTE employment and sources of funding for 2005: Helmig, B., Gmür, M., Bärlocher, C., von Schnurbein, G., Degen, B., Nollert, M., Salamon, L. M. (2011). *The Swiss Civil Society sector in a comparative perspective* (VMI Research Series Volume 6). Fribourg: Institute for Research on Management of Associations, Foundations and Cooperatives (VMI), University of Fribourg. Retrieved from: http://www.vmi.ch/de/165-vmi_forschungsreihe.html

References

Banfield, E. (1958). *The moral basis of a backward society*. New York: Free Press.
Fukuyama, F. (1995). *Trust: The social virtues and the creation of prosperity*. New York: Free Press.

Hansmann, H. (1987). Economic theories of nonprofit organizations. In W. W. Powell (Ed.), *The nonprofit sector: A research handbook* (pp. 27–42). New Haven: Yale University Press.

ISTAT. (2014). *Nonprofit institution profile based on 2011 census results*. Rome: Istituto nazionale di statistica. Retrieved from http://www.istat.it/en/files/2014/10/Nonprofit-Institution-Profile-based-on-2011-Census-results_EN_definitivo.pdf?title=Nonprofit+institutions+profile+-+9+Oct+2014+-+Full+text.pdf

Kaminski, P. (2005). Table1. The NPS in France, 2002 (version INSEE). Le compte des Institutions Sans But Lucratif (ISBL) en France (Année 2002). Paris: l'Institut National de la Statistique et des Études Économiques (INSEE).

Lijphart, A. (1999). *Patterns of democracy: Government forms and performance in thirty six countries*. New Haven: Yale University Press.

Monzón Campos, J. L., & Ávila, R. C. (2012). *The social economy in the European Union*. Brussels: European Economic and Social Committee.

Nagy, R., & Sebestény, I. (2009). Table A 10 in methodological practice and practical methodology: Fifteen years in nonprofit statistics (Hungarian Statistical Review Special Number 12). Budapest: Hungarian Central Statistical Office. Retrieved from http://www.ksh.hu/statreview

Putnam, R. D. (1993). *Making democracy work: Civic traditions in modern Italy*. Princeton, NJ: Princeton University Press.

Salamon, L. M. (2014a). *Leverage for good: An introduction to the new frontiers of philanthropy and social investment*. New York: Oxford University Press.

Salamon, L. M. (2014b). *The new frontiers of philanthropy: A guide to the new actos and tools reshaping global philanthropy and social investment*. Oxford: Oxford University Press.

Salamon, L. M., Sokolowski, S. W., & Associates (Eds.). (2004). *Global civil society: Dimensions of the nonprofit sector* (Vol. II). Bloomfield, CT: Kumarian Press.

Salamon, L. M., Sokolowski, S. W., & Haddock, M. A. (2017). *Explaining civil society development: A social origins approach*. Baltimore: Johns Hopkins University Press.

Sivesind, K.-H., & Selle, P. (2010). Civil society in the Nordic countries: Between displacement and vitality. In R. Alapuro & H. Stenius (Eds.), *Nordic associations in a European perspective* (pp. 89–120). Baden-Baden: Nomos.

United Nations Statistics Division. (2003). *Handbook on non-profit institutions in the system of national accounts*. New York: United Nations.

Weisbrod, B. A. (1977). *The voluntary nonprofit sector*. Lexington, MA: D.C. Heath.

Open Access This chapter is distributed under the terms of the Creative Commons Attribution 4.0 International License (http://creativecommons.org/licenses/by/4.0/), which permits use, duplication, adaptation, distribution and reproduction in any medium or format, as long as you give appropriate credit to the original author(s) and the source, a link is provided to the Creative Commons license and any changes made are indicated.

The images or other third party material in this chapter are included in the work's Creative Commons license, unless indicated otherwise in the credit line; if such material is not included in the work's Creative Commons license and the respective action is not permitted by statutory regulation, users will need to obtain permission from the license holder to duplicate, adapt or reproduce the material.

4

The Roles and Impacts of the Third Sector in Europe

Bernard Enjolras and Karl Henrik Sivesind

The development of social enterprises, social investment, social finance and new philanthropy (Salamon 2014a, b; Nicholls et al. 2010) has triggered an increasing focus on the measurement of the social value and social impact of the programs, operations and organizations of the third sector. Funders and policymakers want to know whether their funds and policies make a difference, and TSOs have been increasingly eager to be in a position to respond to these demands. More than that, as a distinctive set of organizations and behaviors, the third sector is regularly called upon to demonstrate that it generates social value that is distinctive, both in kind and quantity, from the other social sectors. In addition, since, in contrast to the corporation sector whose value is measured by market prices, the third sector lacks an automatic mechanism to document the benefits it generates, an array of valuation tools and measuring devices has had to be developed to accomplish this task.

B. Enjolras (✉) • K. H. Sivesind
Institute for Social Research (ISF), Oslo, Norway
e-mail: bernard.enjolras@socialresearch.no;
karl.henrik.sivesind@socialresearch.no

Most of the scholarly literature relative to the roles and functions of TSOs is related to the evaluation of impact at the organizational level, and is primarily concerned with the service function of TSOs. By contrast, systematic evidences of the impact of the third sector at the macro level and in relation to the sector's supposedly distinctive functions are lacking.

In this chapter, we seek to fill this gap, to shift the focus of impact assessment from the organizational level to the macro-sectoral level, to the third sector as a whole, asking, "What difference does the third sector make for society?" In doing so, moreover, we focus our attention not on the service functions of the sector but on certain distinctive *functions* of TSOs and volunteering compared to government, corporations and households. Included here are: the third sector's *expressive role*, allowing individuals and groups to freely express their values, interests and concerns in artistic, religious, cultural, ethnic, social, recreational and occupational areas; *value guardian role*, promoting freedom of speech, civil liberties or debates about norms and values as society changes; and *advocacy role*, providing links to the policymaking process for individuals, neighborhoods and different kinds of private interests. This civil society role is an essential part of a democratic society ruled by law because the legitimacy of political power relies on public discussions, hearings and consultations with affected groups. The TSE sector includes, among other things, voluntary associations and civic and advocacy organizations that have the potential for bridging multiple levels of governance. Given an open political culture, it represents an essential democratic infrastructure.

Measuring such impact is challenging, however. To find out if there is an impact of the third sector on society, we must answer the question, "What would have happened without the activity of third sector entities?" Many social scientific approaches can be used for this kind of counter-factual analysis, such as comparing changes over time before or after the third sector activity, comparing groups or countries that have experienced a certain third sector activity with those that have not, or using statistical methods that make it possible to control for the most important factors other than the third sector activity. It is particularly important to control for the effect of self-selection. People who volunteer for TSOs may already have characteristics that are assumed to be the result of their third sector involvement, such as a high level of civic engagement and sense of well-being. What is more, it is often difficult to differentiate between cause and effect. Countries that allow free expres-

> *Third sector impact* means, within the context of this chapter, direct or indirect, medium- to long-term consequences of the distinctive features of volunteering or of the third sector organizations on individuals or on the community, ranging from neighborhoods to society in general.

sion may be more conducive to the presence of TSOs. If that is so, it would be a mistake to attribute the openness to free expression to the third sector's presence.

Untangling these relationships and assessing the available information in light of them is the objective of this chapter. To do so, the chapter proceeds as follows. The first section starts by defining what different roles the third sector may play in society, and what indicators can potentially be used to tell if this activity results in impacts on other parts of society. In the second section, we look at some existing efforts to measure certain types of TSIs and assess what they can tell us about the actual impact that the third sector has. A third section then examines under what circumstances such impacts may be produced and what prevents them from emerging. Finally, we try to sum up what can be concluded from these various studies and assessments about the socioeconomic impact of the European third sector.

1   Impact Areas

The TSE sector has some characteristics that make it different from other parts of society consisting of corporations, the government and households. Based on these characteristics and the way TSOs are supposed to behave, we can state some hypotheses about the expected impact of these organizations and of the sector as a whole.

TSOs may be seen as fulfilling four *functions* or *roles*: economic, social, political and communicative. For each of these functions, it is also possible to differentiate the "mainstream" contribution of these organizations—that is, what TSO have in common with governmental and for-profit organizations—from their specific contribution—that is, the functional features that are especially characteristic or even exclusive to these organizations.

From an *economic* viewpoint, TSOs provide both goods and services, but also organize expressive activities in the domains of sport, culture, arts and so on. They mobilize voluntary resources—voluntary work and donations—that are more difficult to mobilize, if not impossible, for other organizational forms. Additionally, they are most often oriented toward other ends than economic ends, even if in the pursuit of these ends they develop economic activities. From the *political and communicative*[1] perspectives, TSOs have the potential to constitute a counter-power to the state and economic powers, to act as schools of democracy and also constitute a communicative space where value contention is made possible. Being a space of associational life, TSOs have the capacity to promote and sustain norms and values of public interests and practices of civic engagement. They also have the potential to organize different types of identities and interests and to play a mediating and representative role in interacting with other societal spheres such as the state, the market or the family, influencing policies and attitudes. Being a communicative space, they have the capacity to enable debates, confrontations and contentions among individuals and organized actors animated by different values, interests and identities. By the play of these political and communicative functions, they contribute to the democratic infrastructure and might instigate social, axiological (value-based) and political transformations impacting other societal spheres. From the *social* point of view, TSOs constitute a space of value pluralism and freedom and contribute to the maintenance of norms and values. From this viewpoint, the third sector is fundamental for enhancing and protecting the diversity of particular values, cultural practices and citizens' initiatives in all domains of social life. TSOs are also instrumental to the maintenance of norms and value that are more universal, such as those of solidarity, inclusion, trust and public interest. For this reason, they potentially have the capacity to contribute to the social integration of individuals and groups and to foster solidarity across differences.

---

[1] Insofar as third sector organizations are both constitutive and actors of the public sphere. The public sphere can be defined as comprising the institutional communicative spaces that facilitate public discussion and the formation of public opinion (see: Habermas 1989).

For each of the roles played by TSOs, it is possible to infer a set of expected impacts at the individual, organizational, community and societal levels. Some of these impacts are likely to be distinctive (idiosyncratic) to TSOs, whereas other impacts can be common to those of other types of social actors. For example, if there were no TSE organizations with paid employment in social services funded by the government—such as institutions for elderly care—there probably would be public and for-profit providers performing those services. This is not to say that the social impacts of for-profit or government organizations providing the same services would be identical to those resulting from third sector provision, as TSOs, because of their distinctive features, innovate services in numerous fields, serve a more needy clientele, deliver services at a more human scale, stay in the game when government funding declines and so on. Hence, it is possible to differentiate the "mainstream" contributions of these organizations—that is, what TSOs have in common with governmental and for-profit organizations—from their distinctive contributions—that is, the functional features that are more characteristic, if not exclusive, to these organizations.

Based on reviews of previous research, these functions and roles can be translated into five domains of impact (Simsa et al. 2014; Enjolras 2015a, b):

- Well-being and quality of life
- Innovation
- Civic engagement, empowerment, advocacy and community building
- Economic impacts
- Human resources impacts

In the following section we will present some evidence of TSI based on analyses and reviews of research conducted by this project (on the basis of available data) related to the impact domains outlined above: civic engagement and advocacy; wellbeing and quality of life; human resources; and social innovation. However, as already stated, there are methodological problems related to previous research on impacts, and we address as far as possible these issues in our subsequent analysis.

2 Selected Evidence of TSIs

2.1 Some Methodological Challenges

A review of the literature on TSIs on human resources and community by Kamerāde (2015) reveals the complexity of assessing the impact of the third sector at different levels. Indeed, impacts can be, first, assessed in terms of the consequences of voluntary participation for individuals involved in TSOs. The same literature review (Kamerāde 2015) concludes that evidence from a range of studies in different disciplinary fields suggests that the third sector makes an important impact; however, this impact is not equally accessible or widespread. The presence of TSOs is not an easy or straightforward solution for inequalities in participation and representation, or social integration problems, as their effects again vary between different social groups and types of organizations. This literature review highlights the unequal distribution of positive effects on individuals of participation in TSOs. More specifically, individuals who already have better wellbeing and health, and higher social trust, are more likely to be involved in the third sector, which, in turn, contributes to better health and wellbeing. In addition, individuals and groups who have fewer resources or who are already less advantaged in society are less likely to become involved in voluntary associations to promote their interests, satisfy their needs or make changes in policy favorable to them. Moreover, the effects of voluntary participation are gendered and can vary by age, employment status, income, type of association and type of involvement. In some cases, for particular groups, involvement in voluntary associations can have negative consequences.

This review points toward a major methodological issue plaguing TSI studies: many studies rely almost exclusively on analyses of cross-sectional data where volunteering and its hypothesized impact have been measured simultaneously. Although these studies provide valuable empirical evidence that is an important link in a chain of causal reasoning, in many of these studies, the causal relationships often have been assumed rather than demonstrated—in important part, because of the absence of data enabling the use of adequate methods for demonstrating the causal relationships.

Furthermore, most of the studies on TSI have been conducted in a selected number of European countries, mainly in the UK, Netherlands, Germany, Norway, Belgium and the Czech Republic. Taking into account that the functions and extent of third sector involvement vary by social and institutional context, this raises the question of how far the impact findings from these institutional settings can be generalized across Europe and to other cultural and institutional contexts.

In spite of those methodological shortcomings, several studies of impact at both the individual and societal levels undertaken within the TSI project (based on available existing data) and outside it display mixed evidence about the impact of the third sector.

2.2 Impact on Civic Engagement, Empowerment, Advocacy and Community Building

Third sector organizations have long been viewed as arenas for civic and political participation and as schools for democracy (Almond and Verba 1963; Tocqueville 2000 [1835]). Closely related to this line of thinking is the emphasis recently placed on the third sector as a major contributor to social capital, to those bonds of trust and reciprocity without which neither democracy nor markets can operate (Putnam 1993, 2000). Howard and Gilbert (2008), for example, find empirical support for the Tocquevillian argument, according to which those persons with greater levels of involvement in voluntary organizations also engage in more political acts, have higher life satisfaction and are more trusting of others than those who do not. TSOs also are thought to play a central political role by channeling, articulating and advocating individuals' and groups' interests and values (Habermas 1998) and by participating in policy networks (Rhodes 1997) or advocacy coalitions (Sabatier 1998).

Political engagement and trust. As shown by Figs. 4.1 and 4.2, at the national macro-level, cross- national comparisons consistently display a correlation between indicators of social capital and of political engagement, on the one hand, and the size of the third sector, on the other hand. The Nordic countries and Northern European countries are characterized by high levels of social trust and political engagement, while

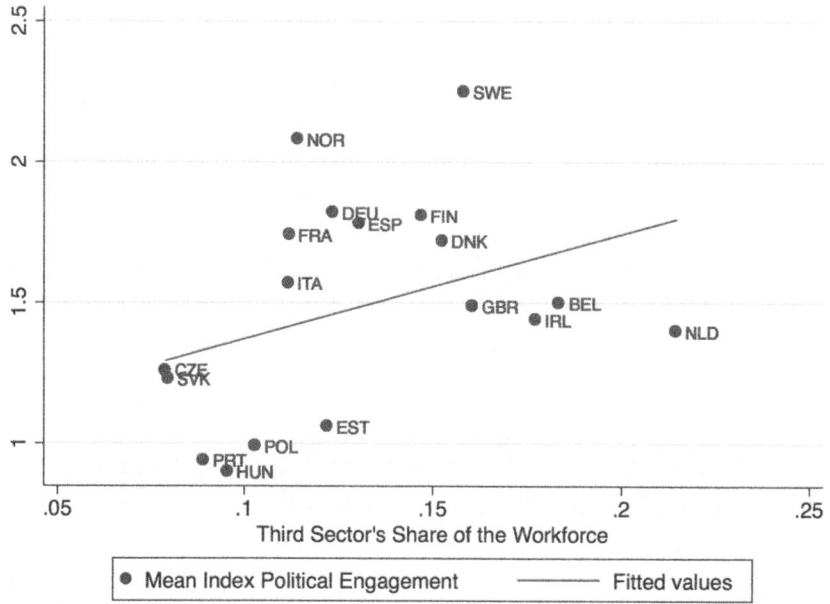

Fig. 4.1 Political engagement by relative size of third sector workforce (20 EU countries)

Eastern European countries display the lowest levels of trust and political engagement and the Southern European countries falling in between these two. High scores on these indicators coincide with vibrant civil societies, absence of corruption, strong trust in institutions, high scores on all indices of economic and gender equality and a culture of adherence to laws and regulations alongside a critical attitude toward politicians and excessive state power.

Robert Putnam's empirical work on Italy suggests that a vibrant civil society sector causes elevated levels of trust in a society (Putnam 1993). But to what extent is the result replicated in other countries?

Interestingly, research at the individual level investigating whether individuals who participate as volunteers in TSOs have higher levels of social trust and political engagement than those who do not volunteer has shown that, when corrected for potential self-selection effects, there is little evidence of such an effect, at least so far as the level of social trust

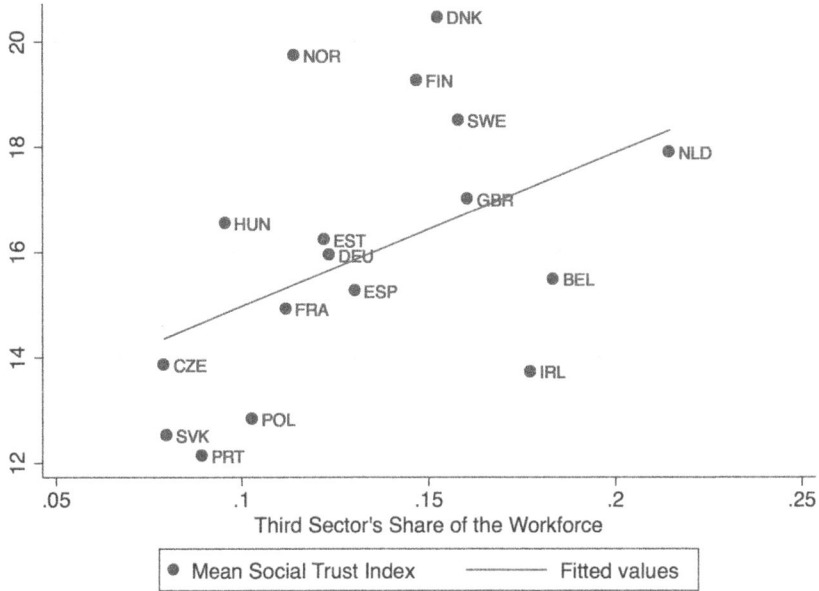

Fig. 4.2 Social trust by the relative size of the third sector workforce (20 EU countries)

is concerned (Claibourn and Martin 2000; Freitag 2003; Enjolras 2015a, b). At the very least, there is little uniformity in this relationship among nations.

Instead of the third sector, other studies attribute high levels of trust to the role played by the welfare state and redistribution. While some authors emphasize lack of social inequality (Bjørnskov 2006; Delhey and Newton 2005; Uslaner 2003), others view institutions of the (welfare) state or the rule of law as the crucial force fostering generalized trust in society (Rothstein 2001). Rothstein and Stolle (2008) have, for example, argued that the welfare state has a particular role in generating trust by sustaining values such as impartiality, equality before the law, respect for human rights, equality of opportunity and efficiency. According to these authors, it is the quality of policy implementation and service delivery by the welfare state that has the strongest bearing on generating trust among citizens. On this account, the role of the third sector in enhancing trust is secondary in comparison to the role of the state.

A third explanation of the results portrayed in Figs. 4.1 and 4.2, and one favored here, emphasizes the societal externalities created by dense networks of TSOs, producing impacts that extend beyond the members and volunteers of the individual TSOs, through the production of non-excludable benefits and resources to broader groups of people. In other words, at the societal (macro) level, participation in TSOs is associated with a set of "emergent" properties (Kawashi and Berkman 2014) that are inherent in the social structure and networks generated by the existence of dense networks of TSOs. In other words, this means that, at the societal level, a high density of TSOs enhances a structure of social interactions that is qualitatively different from the one enhanced by a low density of TSOs. Three macro-level mechanisms may help to explain such effects: (1) social contagion, (2) informal social control and (3) collective efficacy.

Social contagion refers to the fact that behaviors spread more quickly through a tightly knit social network. Behaviors can spread in a network through the diffusion of information or through the transmission of behavioral norms. The social networks constituted by a dense third sector are expected to enhance norms and behaviors that are central to TSOs and volunteering, such as trust and civic and political engagement.

Informal social control refers to the ability of individuals in a community to maintain social order, that is, to step in and intervene when they witness deviant behavior by others. The likelihood of informal policing increases with the degree of cohesion of the community, that is, the degree to which its members are socially connected to each other. A high density of TSOs is expected to entail more cohesive social networks and, consequently, a higher likelihood for informal social control, impacting on trust, health-related behavior and civic behaviors.

Collective efficacy is the group-level analog of the concept of self-efficacy, that is, it refers to the ability of a collective to mobilize to undertake collective action. When individuals are connected to each other through TSOs, mobilizing is made easier and free riding more difficult inasmuch as it risks damage to one's reputation as well as provokes social sanctions (i.e. ostracism). Additionally, individuals who are not members of a TSO but are connected through social networks to its members will be able to draw upon the organizational infrastructure and capacity

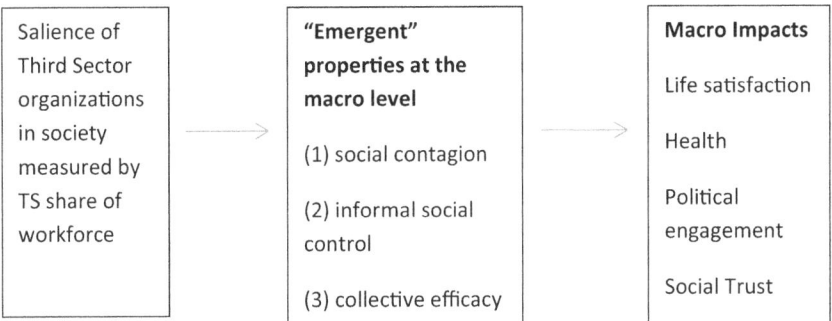

Fig. 4.3 Macro impact explanatory model

already established by the organization. Collective efficacy may be a significant factor influencing political engagement (Bandura 2000).

The density of the third sector at the societal level, measured by the third sector workforce (both volunteers and paid workers) is seen as generating macro-level socioeconomic impacts, by the play of emergent properties, according to the explanatory model displayed in Fig. 4.3.

A way to identify a potential socioeconomic impact, mediated by emergent properties, of the third sector at the macro level consists in assessing whether the size of the third sector, measured in terms of its workforce's share in the total workforce of the country, is positively associated with the aggregated indicators of social trust and political engagement, when controlling for other aggregated measures that can influence these indicators, such as the GDP per capita, the level of inequalities measured by the GINI index, the level of social expenditures in the country and the employment rate in the country. The results of the linear regressions of the indicators of trust and political engagement in relation to the size of the voluntary sector (share of the third sector' workforce in the total workforce) and the other control variables are presented in Table 4.1.

The empirical analysis investigates whether the size of the third sector approximated by the share of the third sector workforce (including paid and volunteer work) in the total workforce of the country is associated with social trust, self-reported health, happiness and political engagement. The analyses are based on data for 20 countries (European Union countries : Belgium, Czech Republic, Denmark, Estonia, Finland, France, Germany, Hungary,

Table 4.1 Linear regression of social trust index, political engagement index, self-reported well-being and self-reported health by country

	Social trust		Political Engagement	
	Model 1	Model 2	Model 1	Model 2
Employment rate	.127***	.125***	.008***	.009***
GDP per Capita	.000***	.000***	.000***	.000***
Gini Index	−3.766***	−3.941***	1.564***	1.570***
Social Expenditures	.116***	.105***	.032***	.035***
TS share of Workforce	–	7.590***	–	−2.046***
Constant	2.727***	2.681***	−1.203***	−1.187***
R-squared	.480	.489	.721	.747
Change in R-squared	–	.009	–	.026

*$p>0.10$, **$p>=0.05$, ***$p>0.001$

Ireland, Italy, Lithuania, the Netherlands, Poland, Portugal, Slovakia, Spain, Sweden, the UK and non-European Union country: Norway).

For each country, the *dependent variables* are the means of self-reported indices of health, subjective well-being political engagement and social trust. The means are calculated using the European Social Survey data (European Social Survey, 2012) consisting of a representative sample of the population including all persons aged 15 and over resident within private households, regardless of their nationality, citizenship, language or legal status. The data relative to the *independent variables* have two origins. The data concerning the third sector's share of the total workforce are provided by Salamon and Sokolowski (2016), whereas the other macro indicators were extracted from the OECD (2012) database.

For each dependent variable (social trust and political engagement), two models are displayed: model 1 shows the association of the dependent variable with a set of independent variables (employment rate, GDP per capita, Gini index as indicator for inequalities, and social expenditures) excluding the third sector share of the workforce, whereas model 2 includes this last variable. Introducing the third sector share of the workforce improves the goodness of fit of the model (R-squared) and shows the contribution of the third sector to social trust and political engagement.

The size of the third sector is heavily positively associated with the level of social trust. Social trust is also negatively associated with the degree of inequalities (GINI index). Even if a simple linear regression is not sufficient for inferring a causal relation between third sector size and social trust, and if the possibility of reverse causation cannot not be excluded, the data supports our explanatory model when it comes to social trust, in spite of a contribution to R-squared being weak. At the same time, the added explanatory power attributable to the third sector is quite small, suggesting that the other factors in the model carry most of the explanatory power.

The size of the voluntary sector is negatively associated with the level of political engagement, and political engagement seems to increase when the level of inequality is higher. This reflects the fact that, with the exception of Sweden, the countries with the highest levels of political engagement are not the ones having the biggest third sector.

The potential macro socioeconomic impact of the degree of development of the third sector in different European countries has been conceptualized as the result of emergent macro-level properties linked to the social structure (social networks) generated by TSOs and their activities. From this viewpoint, the more developed the third sector, the greater are its emergent properties at the macro level and the higher its impact. While at the individual level (Enjolras 2015a, b), when correcting for potential selection effects, there is no evidence that active volunteering in TSOs has a positive impact on individual social trust, a simple test of this impact model at the aggregated level—looking at the associations between the size of the third sector in 20 European countries and social trust and political engagement—shows some support for the existence of an impact of the size of the third sector on social trust.

2.3   Impact on Well-being and Quality of Life

A second range of potential impacts of the third sector relate to citizen well-being and quality of life. TSOs have long been associated with the provision of human services that contribute to wellbeing and the quality of life. In fact, this role of the sector is a principal focus of what has long been the dominant economic theory of the third sector, which views the existence of this sector as resulting from a demand for services that neither the market nor government can provide due to inherent failures of these alternative institutions—that is, the "free rider" problem in the case of markets and the need for majority support in the case of governments (Hansmann 1980; Weisbrod 1977). The Stiglitz report emphasized the

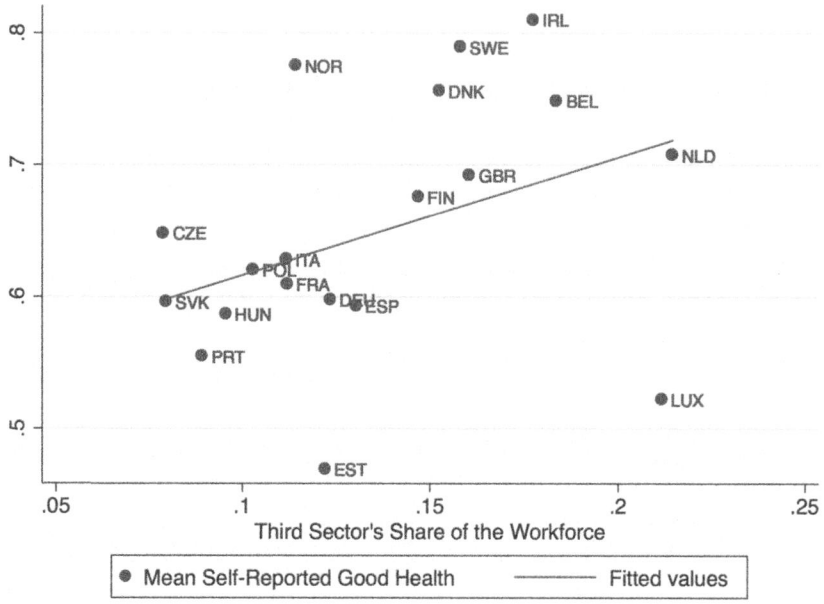

Fig. 4.4 Self-reported health by relative size of third sector workforce (20 EU countries)

need to "shift emphasis from measuring economic production to measuring people's wellbeing," (Stiglitz et al. 2009). But well-being involves more than concrete services. It also includes subjective factors, such as feelings of security, sense of well-being, confidence and a sense of belonging (Cummins 2000), all of which have also been associated with TSOs.

As shown in Figs. 4.4 and 4.5, at the societal level, cross-national comparisons consistently display a correlation between indicators of health and wellbeing, on the one hand, and the size of the third sector, on the other hand.[2]

As we did with the socioeconomic indicators of trust and political engagement, we can identify the socioeconomic impact of the third sec-

---

[2] The analyses are based on European Social Survey (2012) data for 20 countries. The *self-reported health* indicator is based on the questions: "How is your health in general?"— "very good, good, fair, not very good, poor." The *subjective well-being* indicator used in the analyses is a measure of people's evaluations of their lives as a whole, elicited by a widely used generalized single-item question: "All things considered, how satisfied are you with your life as a whole these days?" on a scale from 1 being completely dissatisfied to 10 being completely satisfied.

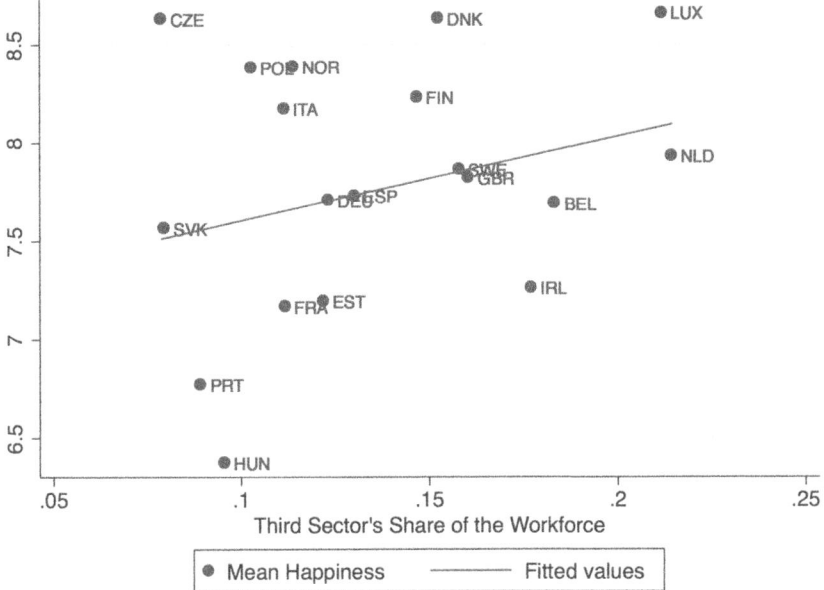

Fig. 4.5 Self-reported wellbeing by third sector workforce (20 EU countries)

Table 4.2 Linear regression of self-reported well-being and self-reported health by country

	Well-being		Health	
	Model 1	Model 2	Model 1	Model 2
Employment rate	.043***	.0442***	.000***	.000***
GDP per Capita	.000***	.000***	.000***	−1.56e−06***
Gini Index	−2.315***	−2.367***	−1.669***	−1.654***
Social Expenditures	−.000***	.004***	.004***	.003***
TS share of Workforce	–	−2.812***	–	.841***
Constant	5.028***	5.064***	.995***	.984***
R-squared	.464	.481	.450	.516
Change in R-squared	–	.017	–	.066

tor at the macro level by assessing whether the size of the third sector (measured in terms of its workforce's share in the total workforce of the country) is positively associated with the aggregated indicators of health and wellbeing. The results of this analysis are presented in Table 4.2.

The size of the voluntary sector is negatively associated with the level of self-reported well-being after controlling for the other variables that might affect well-being. In addition, levels of well-being decrease with inequalities. At the aggregated level, the size of the third sector is positively associated with self-reported health, though the added explanatory power of this variable is highly limited compared to the other factors identified. In both models, however, the contribution of the third sector share of the workforce (measured by the change in R-squared) is relatively weak, meaning that the explanatory power is being carried mostly by the other variables. Here, too, the macro socioeconomic impact of the third sector on population health in different European countries can be understood as the result of emergent macro-level properties linked to the social structure (social networks) generated by TSOs and their activities.

2.4 Impact on Human Resources

Another important perspective on the impacts of the third sector relate to the impacts these organizations have not on the society at large but on those who work in TSOs. This set of impacts has been emphasized most explicitly by students of volunteering, but it also applies to paid personnel. Thus, for example, Rochester *et al.* (2010) emphasize the benefits accruing to volunteers in terms of increased satisfaction, personal achievement, social networks and relations, skills, personal development, enhanced employability, improved mental and physical health and wellbeing. Similarly, Wilson (2000) identifies four areas where research has pointed to the positive consequences of volunteer work for the volunteer: citizenship (volunteers are more politically active and trusting than nonvolunteers), antisocial behavior (being a volunteer keeps young people out of trouble), health and well-being (volunteers enjoy better health in old age, have better self-esteem and self-confidence and higher levels of life satisfaction) and socioeconomic achievement. Additionally, TSOs offer a space for work integration for individuals excluded from the labor market and provide job experience to young people, to individuals with disability and to the long-term unemployed. Different works have also emphasized the positive impacts accruing to paid staff in TSOs, including higher job satisfaction because of the higher "pro-social" motivations (Benz 2005; Borzaga and Tortia 2006; Rose-Ackerman 1996) or greater fairness (Leete 2000; Tortia 2008). The literature suggests that people who volunteer enjoy good health (Moen et al. 1993; Musick et al. 1999; Oman et al. 1999; Post, 2005; Brooks 2006). They are also more likely to report being happy and are less likely to suffer from depression (Musick and Wilson 2003; Thoits and Hewitt 2001; Wheeler et al. 1998; Whiteley 2004; Borgonovi 2008). There is also evidence that volunteering positively influences political participation and engagement (Armingeon, 2007).

However, most of the evidence of the positive contribution of volunteering for the volunteers is based on established correlations between volunteering and measures of individual health, well-being or civic engagement. While these correlations are well established, they may be a result of selection bias.

Individuals who already have a greater sense of well-being and better health, higher social trust or levels of political engagement are more likely to be involved in the third sector and are more likely to answer questions about their health and well-being. The positive correlation between volunteering and self-reported health, subjective wellbeing and political participation may therefore be spurious

To address this issue, a study from the *Third Sector Impact Project* (Enjolras 2015a, b) uses different matching estimation methods (Caliendo and Kopeinig 2008; Guo and Fraser 2015) in order to eliminate the effect of self-selection by constructing a control group that is as similar as possible to the treatment group of interest with respect to observable characteristics. This is done by creating matching estimators by modeling the probability of participating in the treatment given the observed characteristics of the participants in the "treatment group." Volunteers are then matched on the basis of this probability to nonvolunteers in order to compare a "treatment group" (the participants) to a "control group" (the nonparticipants), ensuring that the members of both groups have the same socioeconomic characteristics (based on the variables used to estimate the probability of participation in those groups). The average treatment effect is then the mean difference in outcomes across these two groups. The results, based on the European Social Survey data for 23 European countries, show that volunteering has a minimal impact on self-reported health, no impact on self-reported wellbeing, but a significant impact on political engagement (Enjolras 2015a, b).

Another study from the *Third Sector Impact Project* (Kamerāde and Bennett 2015) focuses on voluntary work during unemployment. It investigates whether volunteering can compensate for the loss in manifest and latent benefits associated with paid work and thus improve unemployed individuals' well-being and mental health. Drawing on data from 29 European countries, and using matching estimators, this study concludes that the impact of volunteering on unemployed individuals' well-being and mental health depends on generous welfare benefits. The positive effects of volunteering during unemployment are not unconditional. Theuy obtain when some environmental conditions relative to the level income of unemployed volunnteers are met. In other words, volunteering may improve well-being and health if basic needs are met, but does not compensate for the lack of satisfaction of these basic needs.

The two surveyed analyses show that neither for people in general, nor for more marginalized groups like unemployed individuals, volunteering by itself does not significantly improve health and well-being when measured at the individual level. However, we do not presently know enough about the potential benefits of volunteering for different groups in the population, and the effect may vary with the type of organization, the tasks performed, the number of hours volunteered and the frequency of volunteering. Only a few community studies make it possible to analyze some of these variables.

2.5 Impact on Social Innovation

While the economic theories assign a primary role to the state and the market and view the third sector as merely a supplement to these other two sectors, filling in services that the other two sectors fail to supply, a second body of literature views the third sector as a source of pioneering social innovations that government and the market subsequently copy or support. This view has been conceptually articulated most fully in the notion of "interdependence" between the government and the third sector. Because of the transaction costs involved in mobilizing governments to act and the free rider problems that keep market actors from responding to many social and economic problems, it is TSOs that frequently come forward to identify unattended problems and devise innovative solutions to them (Salamon 1987, 1996). Social economy literature has also stressed this role of third sector entities, in their case, mutuals, cooperatives and social enterprises, as significant sources of social innovation and social change, contributing to labor market integration, fighting social exclusion and poverty, creating social capital and developing new services and ways to address unmet social need (Chaves and Monzón 2012; J. Defourny and Develtere 1999; Julià and Chaves 2012; Nicholls 2004). TSOs are spaces of freedom and unforced activities where volunteers and professionals in partnership with other stakeholders are in position to respond creatively to new challenges, to develop new forms of organization and interactions and to respond to social demands that are traditionally not addressed by the market or existing institutions. Indeed, TSOs are in a position to generate both types of social innovations that Greffe (2003) identifies—*macro-social innovations* such as new forms of social organization or networked approaches to addressing public problems, as well as *micro-social innovations* such as new services that the market does not supply, as well as attention to economic or social values that market production fails to advantage (such as social integration, wellbeing, sustainable development).

The potential contribution of third sector and volunteering to *social innovations* can be seen on different levels. At the micro level, they can be an important element affecting the socioeconomic development of societies by helping individuals in need, enhancing their capabilities and promoting well-being. Changing the form of governance, as well as the development of local communities, can be distinctive impacts of third sector social innovations on the meso-level. Social innovations at the macro level can involve transforming the ways in which society thinks and acts. Building new social relations can also be a main component of the macro-level impact of third sector social innovations. However, evidence demonstrating the TSI on social innovation remains quite limited (Bežovan 2016). Fortunately, some further research supported by the FP7 project is actively exploring this topic.[3]

---

[3] Such as EFESEIIS (http://www.fp7-efeseiis.eu) and ITSSOIN (http://itssoin.eu).

3 Can the TSE Sector Expand Civil Liberties and the Public Sphere?

The socioeconomic impacts of TSOs are contingent on the political and institutional context in which the third sector is embedded. Path dependency and social origins theories address both the nature of the *civil society regime* in which these organizations operate and the *institutional space of freedom* that the state grants to these organizations. Both the type of civil society regime and the space of freedom are determined by the state of identifiable power relationships among key social groupings during turning points in the historical evolution of societies (Salamon et al. 2017). These appear as crucial factors influencing the type and degree of impact that the TSE sector can make on society.

This chapter started by defining some areas where potential impacts of the TSE sector may be observed. Some of the most important impacts are related to the civil society role of TSOs in linking citizens and the policymaking processes; this role is among the most distinctive roles of the TSE sector that cannot be substituted by the other sectors of society—corporations, government or households. However, it is also very difficult to measure this kind of impact. The best option is to observe changes in the civil society role over time and what effects this may have on democracy and civil liberties over time, or, even better, to compare the development in countries with some important common historical characteristics to see what policies and structures may inhibit or promote the civil society role of the TSE sector.

A third sector impact project's study of civil liberties and volunteering in six former Soviet bloc countries examines whether volunteering is an outcome of democratization rather than a driver of it. It analyzes how divergent democratization pathways in six countries of the former Soviet Union have led to varied levels of volunteering, using data from the European Values Study.

The results show that Latvia, Lithuania, and Estonia—which followed a path toward EU accession—have high and increasing levels of civil liberties and volunteering. In Russia and Belarus, following another path, civil liberties have remained low and volunteering has declined. Surprisingly, despite the Orange Revolution and increased civil liberties, volunteering rates in Ukraine have also declined. The case of Ukraine indicates that the freedom to participate is not always taken up by citizens. The findings suggest it is not volunteering that brings civil liberties, but rather that increased civil liberties lead to higher levels of volunteering (Kamerāde et al. 2016), a finding that is consistent with the social origins theory contention that patterns of power shape the space for civil society development and hence the scope and scale of civil society organization development (Salamon et al. 2017).

Another historical and comparative study examines the role and impact of the third sector in the transformative processes of post-socialist countries by comparing Slovenia, the Czech Republic and Croatia, showing different paths for the third sector depending on the role played by the state (Bežovan 2016).

From the very beginning, civil society initiatives played an important role in the changes that occurred in post-socialist countries like the Czech Republic, Slovenia and Croatia. They were, in different ways, initiators of changes in the late 1980s and an active part of the new overall agenda on development in the 1990s and onwards.

It is interesting to compare these countries because there are important similarities in their historic background. Before World War I, they were all part of the Austro-Hungarian Empire, which was relatively liberal regarding the expression of the major nationalities and languages. This also meant that there was a high level of popular participation in the cultural sphere in these countries. During the communist era, civil liberties were repressed and there were confrontations between civil society in different forms and the authoritarian regime. Dissidents, often with support from the west, focused on promoting human rights and political pluralism. A multi-party system and parliamentarian democracy were almost synonymous with the concept of civil society. During the 1990s, there were frequent confrontations with the authoritarian regime in Croatia, while in Slovenia, there was more dialogue, as independent intellectuals and civic movements with younger participants played the role of setting up political parties (Bežovan 2004). However, there were different political understandings of the role of civil society. In Czechoslovakia, President Vaclav Havel saw civil society and public debate as essential for the creation of good citizens, and promoted decentralization of state responsibilities.

After the split into the two sovereign states in 1993, Vaclav Klaus, president of the Czech Republic, had different views. He supported the introduction of a competitive party system, but saw the market as the central instrument to promote human freedom and creativity. He was very suspicious of the term civil society and preferred the indirect participation of citizens rather than giving nonprofit organizations a privileged role as mediators between citizens and the government. These different views became paradigmatic for the development of civil society in the advanced Central Eastern European countries.

In political debates, civil society was often recognized as a revolutionary force and as part of the opposition. NGOs were under political attack from the ruling parties and governmental organizations, and there was no support for tax incentives or increased organizational participation in policymaking. They have even been accused of being agents of foreign powers or officially characterized as a "self-proclaimed civil society" (Bežovan 2004). On the other hand, there was a "parochial" structure of organizations often divided on the same issues as political parties, and often seen as mostly interested in securing government and other grants. The concept of civil society was associated with a struggle against the ruling regime and the dominant political culture, in which the old Soviet era mass organizations (related to the Communist party) were an integral part.

However, the process toward EU accession was important for strengthening the legitimacy of the civil society organizations and giving them a role as stakeholders in policymaking and policy implementation (Frič 2009). Crucial influences in the recent development of the sector came from the EU in the form of membership, financial support and technical help.

In the last 25 years, it is evident that civil society has become a respected stakeholder in all three countries, with certain differences that can be attributed to path dependency, the role of international donors, and the speed of accession to the EU. Thus, for example, in the 1990s, the countries were in different positions in relation to the dissolution of the former states of Yugoslavia and Czechoslovakia. Croatian and to a lesser extent Slovenian development was marked by the Balkan war, which made a long-lasting impact on society. The legacy of dissident culture and the financial aid of foreign donors increased the gap between citizens and civil society organizations in the Czech Republic and Croatia. Civil society is weak in engaging citizens in the Czech Republic and Croatia, while civil society appears to enjoy more space and legitimacy in corporatist Slovenia.

This comparison shows that the impact of TSOs depends on the policy environment for the third sector, political openness of the government for cooperation, and on the capacity developed by the TSOs. The institutional infrastructure for sector's development (resource centers, funding programs, pilot projects) is important for sustainable development and for innovative third sector practices (Bežovan 2016).

4 Does the European Third Sector make a Socioeconomic Impact?

The previous chapter shows that the TSE organizations and volunteers are a significant economic sector of activity in Europe. In this chapter, we have assessed the available evidence about the contribution of this TSE sector to the socioeconomic development and democratic governance of European societies through systematic reviews of research and new analyses of data. This indicates that the impact of the TSE sector is significant albeit difficult to assess empirically. This is because the activities of organizations and volunteers can have impacts in different social domains and on different levels, from individuals to local communities and society in general, and the research front is less advanced in some of these areas than others are. However, there is no support for unconditional and general claims about the third sector's contribution to improvement of health, well-being, innovation, social capital, empowerment or economic development.

There is a potential for individual benefits of membership or volunteering in TSOs. However, these positive impacts are not equally accessible or do not spread among the population. Individuals who already have better wellbeing, health and social trust are more likely to be active as members or volunteers in the third sector. Groups and individuals with fewer resources or who are already less advantaged are less likely to become members or volunteers in voluntary organizations to promote their interests, satisfy their needs or make changes in policy favorable to them. This seriously complicates the task of sorting out cause and effect. Moreover, the effects of voluntary participation are gendered and can also vary by age, employment status, income, type of association and type of involvement (Kamerāde 2015). In short, third sector activity is not a simple solution to individual or social problems. Those that have the largest potential benefits from TSIs are less likely to be involved, which represents a challenge for how to design third sector activities and support programs (Kamerāde 2015).

Our research shows that better health and well-being may be a result of who decides to volunteer, rather than an effect of volunteering for the general population. However, political engagement may increase as a result of volunteering. Among the unemployed, volunteering may improve mental health and well-being, but only when there are generous welfare benefits. These findings indicate that the impacts of the third sector depend not only on the activities that take place, but also on the kind of support and conditions the governments provide.

At the macro level, assessing the socioeconomic impact of the third sector confronts much of the same difficulties encountered at the micro level. In the absence of a unified data collection apparatus on the third sector at the European level, reliable longitudinal data on the third sector are difficult to obtain. Methodologically, the same difficulties related to identifying a causal link between a given feature of the third sector and expected impacts apply, given the potential existence of confounding factors not accounted for in the statistical models. Additionally, when aggregating individual behaviors at the macro-level, potential emergent properties—such as social contagion, informal social control and collective efficacy—that may lead to divergent results at the micro and macro levels, have to be taken into account. Our results show that participating in volunteering activities does not have an impact on individual well-being, health and level of social trust when correcting for potential self-selection. However, that does not mean that the same pattern applies at the macro level. Indeed, the size of the third sector seems to be positively correlated with social trust and health. This is in line with the assumption that the third sector is important as an infrastructure, even in areas where individual experience with volunteering does not have an effect. A vital civil society can contribute to breaking the vicious circle of distrust, corruption and bad government because people see that there are organizational structures they can work through to promote change.

When we compare the role of the third sector in the transformation of the post-communist countries during the last 25 years in Slovenia, the Czech Republic and Croatia, we also see the importance of the relations with the government. In all three countries, the TSOs have tried to play a civil society role, expand the public sphere, and promote civic liberties. However, there are significant differences in how they succeeded depending on what the social origins theory would suggest are the prevailing structures of power and the resulting institutional infrastructure enabling citizens to work for changes in policies. This, in turn, depends on previous history, but also on the present political circumstances.

Knowledge about the impacts of the third sector on other parts of society is scattered and inconclusive. Measurement of the third sector's size, structure and composition can take advantage of standardized procedures, definitions and typologies, such as the ILO *Manual on the Measurement of Volunteer Work*[4], and the UN *Handbook on Nonprofit Organizations in the System of National Accounts*[5], soon to be issued in a revised, expanded version that covers the third sector as conceptualized in this report. Most important for this present chapter, the resulting newly revised UN handbook, entitled *Satellite Account on Nonprofit and Related Institutions and Volunteer Work*, contains a new chapter that lays out a comprehensive strategy keyed to the new UN Sustainable Development Goals for measuring systematically and comparatively the impact of the TSE sector on the achievement of these goals. Unfortunately, these procedures are not fully implemented across Europe, a consequence being the poor quality of available data about the third sector and volunteering. Whereas a theoretical understanding of the functions, roles and specific features of TSOs points in the direction of a wide array of potential socio-

---

[4] Manual on the Measurement of Volunteer Work, International Labour Organization 2011 (ILO Manual).
[5] UN Handbook on Nonprofit Institutions in the System of National Accounts, 2003 (UN Handbook).

economic impacts at different levels of analysis, the scarcity and limited quality of the available data means that the empirical validation of these theoretical insights is only possible to a limited extent. Research on the impact of the third sector is in an early phase, and we need to further develop impact indicators and methods that can reliably identify causal links between third sector activities and micro and macro impacts. Hopefully, as the new UN TSE Satellite Account document comes online, countries, with the encouragement of the European Commission and Eurostat, will take measures to implement it across Europe.

References

Almond, G. A., & Verba, S. (1963). *The civic culture: Political attitudes and democracy in five nations*. Boston: Little, Brown and Company.

Armingeon, K. (2007). Political participation and associational involvement. In J. W. van Depth, J. R. Montero, & A. Westhilm (Eds.), *Citizenship and involvement in European democracies*. London: Routledge.

Bandura, A. (2000). Exercise of human agency through collective efficacy. *Current Directions in Psychological Science, 9*(3), 75–78.

Benz, M. (2005). Not for the profit, but for the satisfaction? Evidence on worker well-being in non-profit firms. *Kyklos, 58*(2), 155–176.

Bežovan, G. (2004). *Civilno društvo*. Zagreb: Nakladni zavod Globus.

Bežovan, G. (2016). The role and impact of the Third Sector in transformative process: A comparison of post-socialist countries Slovenia, Czech Republic and Croatia. *TSI Working Paper Series No. 13*, Seventh Framework Programme (grant agreement 613034), European Union. Brussels: Third Sector Impact.

Bjørnskov, C. (2006). Determinants of generalized trust: A cross-country comparison. *Public Choice, 130*, 1–21.

Borgonovi, F. (2008). Doing well by doing good. The relationship between formal volunteering and self-reported health and happiness. *Social Science & Medicine, 66*, 2321–2334.

Borzaga, C., & Tortia, E. (2006). Worker motivations, job satisfaction, and loyalty in public and nonprofit social services. *Nonprofit and Voluntary Sector Quarterly, 35*(2), 225–248.

Brooks, A. C. (2006). *Who really cares? The surprising truth about compassionate conservatism*. New York: Basic Books.

Caliendo, M., & Kopeinig, S. (2008). Some practical guidance for the implementation of propensity score matching. *Journal of Economic Surveys, 22*(1), 31–72.

Chaves, R., & Monzón, J. L. (2012). Beyond the crisis: The social economy, prop of a new model of sustainable economic development. *Service Business: An international Journal, 6*(1), 5–26.

Claibourn, M., & Martin, P. (2000). Trusting and joining? An empirical test of the reciprocal nature of social capital. *Political Behavior, 22*(4), 269–291.

Cummins, R. A. (2000). Objective and subjective quality of life: An interactive model. *Social Indicators Research, 52*, 55–72.

Defourny, J., & Develtere, P. (1999). Social economy: North and South. In J. Defourny, P. Develtere, & B. Fonteneau (Eds.), *Social economy: The worldwide making of a third sector* (pp. 25–56). Brussels: De Boeck.

Delhey, J., & Newton, K. (2005). Predicting cross-national levels of social trust: Global pattern or Nordic exceptionalism? *European Sociological Review, 21*(4), 311–328.

Enjolras, B. (2015a). Measuring the impact of the third sector: From concept to metrics. *TSI Working Paper No. 5*, Seventh Framework Programme (grant agreement 613034), European Union. Brussels: Third Sector Impact.

Enjolras, B. (2015b). The impact of volunteering on volunteers in 23 European countries. *Third Sector Working Paper No. 4*, Seventh Framework Programme (grant agreement 613034), European Union. Brussels: Third Sector Impact.

European Social Survey. (2012). Retrieved from http://www.europeansocialsurvey.org/data/download.html?r=6

Freitag, M. (2003). Social capital in (dis)similar democracies: The development of generalised trust in Japan and Switzerland. *Comparative Political Studies, 36*(8), 936–966.

Frič, P. (2009). The third sector and the policy process in the Czech Republic: Self-limited dynamics. In J. Kendal (Ed.), *Handbook on third sector policy in Europe-multi-level processes and organized civil society* (pp. 184–206). Cheltenham: Edward Elgar.

Greffe, X. (2003). Innovation, value added and evaluation in the third system: A European perspective. In *The Non-profit Sector in a Changing Economy* (pp. 189–220). Paris: OECD.

Guo, S., & Fraser, M. W. (2015). *Propensity score analysis*. London: Sage.

Habermas, J. (1989). *The structural transformation of the public sphere: An inquiry into a category of bourgeois society*. Cambridge, MA: MIT Press.

Habermas, J. (1998). *Between facts and norms*. Cambridge: The MIT Press.

Hansmann, H. (1980). The role of non profit enterprise. *Yale Law Journal, 89*(2), 835–898.
Howard, M., & Gilbert, L. (2008). A cross-national comparison of the internal effect of participation in voluntary organizations. *Political Studies, 56,* 12–32.
International Labour Organization. (2011). *Manual on the measurement of volunteer work.* Geneva: International Labour Organization.
Julià, J. F., & Chaves, R. (2012). Introduction: Social economy, a third sector in a plural people- oriented economy. *Service Business: An International Journal, 6*(1), 1–4.
Kamerāde, D. (2015). Third sector impacts on human resources and community: A critical review. *Third Sector Impact Working Paper No. 3*, Seventh Framework Programme (grant agreement 613034), European Union. Brussels: Third Sector Impact.
Kamerāde, D., & Bennett, M. (2015). Unemployment, volunteering, subjective well-being and mental health. *TSI Working Paper Series No. 7*, Seventh Framework Programme (grant agreement 613034), European Union. Brussels: Third Sector Impact.
Kamerāde, D., Crotty, J., & Ljubownikow, S. (2016). Civil liberties and volunteering in six former Soviet Union countries. *Nonprofit and Voluntary Sector Quarterly, 45*(6), 1150–1168. https://doi.org/10.1177/0899764016649689.
Kawashi, I., & Berkman, L. F. (2014). Social capital, social cohesion, and health. In L. F. Berkman, I. Kawachi, & M. M. Glymour (Eds.), *Social epidemiology* (pp. 290–319). Oxford: Oxford University Press.
Leete, L. (2000). Wage equity and employee motivation in nonprofit and for-profit organizations. *Journal of Economic Behavior & Organization, 43,* 423–446.
Moen, P., Dempster-McCain, D., & Williams, R. M. (1993). Successful aging. *American Journal of Sociology, 97,* 1612–1632.
Musick, M. A., Herzog, A. R., & House, J. S. (1999). Volunteering and mortality among older adults: Findings from a national sample. *Journals of Gerontology Series B, 54*(3), 173–180.
Musick, M. A., & Wilson, J. (2003). Volunteering and depression: The role of psychological and social resources in different age groups. *Social Science & Medicine, 56,* 259–269.
Nicholls, A. (2004). Social entrepreneurship: The emerging landscape. In S. Crainer & D. Dearlove (Eds.), *Financial times handbook of management* (3rd ed., pp. 636–643). Prentice Hall/Financial Times.
Nicholls, A., Paton, R., & Emerson, J. (Eds.). (2010). *Social finance.* Oxford: Oxford University Press.

Oman, D., Thoresen, C. E., & McMahon, K. (1999). Volunteerism and mortality among the community-dwelling elderly. *Journal of Health Psychology, 4*, 301–316.

Post, S. G. (2005). Altruism, happiness, and health: It's good to be good. *International Journal of Behavioral Medicine, 12*(2), 66–77.

Putnam, R. D. (1993). *Making democracy work: Civic traditions in modern Italy*. Princeton, NJ: Princeton University Press.

Putnam, R. D. (2000). *Bowling alone*. New York: Touchstone.

Rhodes, R. A. W. (1997). *Understanding governance: Policy networks, governance, reflexivity, and accountability*. Buckingham: Open University Press.

Rochester, C., Ellis Paine, A., Howlett, S., & Zimmeck, M. (2010). *Volunteering and society in the 21st century*. Basingstoke: Palgrave Macmillan.

Rose-Ackerman. (1996). Altruism, nonprofits, and economic theory. *Journal of Economic Literature, XXXIV*, 701–728.

Rothstein, B. (2001). Social capital in the social democratic welfare state. *Politics & Society, 29*(2), 207–241.

Rothstein, B., & Stolle, D. (2008). The state and social capital—An institutional theory of generalized trust. *Comparative Politics, 40*(4), 441.

Sabatier, P. A. (1998). The advocacy coalition framework: Revisions and relevance for Europe. *Journal of European Public Policy, 5*(1), 98–130.

Salamon, L. M. (1987). Of market failure, voluntary failure, and third party government: Toward a theory of government -nonprofit relations in the modern welfare state. *Journal of Volontary Reasernch, 16*, 1.

Salamon, L. M. (1996). *Partners in public service: Government-nonprofit relations in the modern welfare state*. Baltimore: Johns Hopkins University Press.

Salamon, L. M. (2014a). *Leverage for good: An introduction to the new frontiers of philanthropy and social investment*. New York: Oxford University Press.

Salamon, L. M. (2014b). *The new frontiers of philanthropy: A guide to the new actos and tools reshaping global philanthropy and social investment*. Oxford: Oxford University Press.

Salamon, L. M., & Sokolowski, S. W. (2016). Beyond nonprofits: Reconceptualizing the third sector. *Voluntas, 27*, 1515–1545.

Salamon, L. M., Sokolowski, S. W., & Haddock, M. A. (2017). *Explaining civil society development: A social origins approach*. Baltimore: Johns Hopkins University Press.

Simsa, R., Rausher, O., Schober, C., & Moder, C. (2014). Methodological guidelines for impact assessment. Third Sector Impact *Working Paper No. 1*,

Seventh Framework Programme (grant agreement 613034), European Union. Brussels: Third Sector Impact.

Stiglitz, J. E., Sen, A., & Fitoussi, J.-P. (2009). *Report by the commission on the measurement of economic performance and social progress*. Retrieved from www.stiglitz-sen-fitoussi.fr

Thoits, P. A., & Hewitt, L. N. (2001). Volunteer work and well-being. *Journal of Health and Social Behavior, 42*(2), 115–131.

Tocqueville, A. (1955/2000). *Democracy in America*. New York: Vintage Books.

Tortia, E. (2008). Worker well-being and perceived fairness: Survey-based findings from Italy. *The Journal of Socio-Economics, 37*, 2020–2094.

Uslaner, E. M. (2003). *Trust, democracy and governance: Can government politics influence generalised trust?* New York: Palgrave Macmillan.

Weisbrod, B. A. (1977). *The voluntary nonprofit sector*. Lexington, MA: D.C. Heath.

Wheeler, J. A., Gorey, K. M., & Greenblatt, B. (1998). The beneficial effects of volunteering for older volunteers and the people they serve: A meta-analysis. *International Journal of Aging and Human Development, 47*, 69–79.

Whiteley, P. (2004). *The art of happiness: Is volunteering the blueprint for bliss?* London: Economic and Social Research Council.

Wilson, J. (2000). Volunteering. *Annual Review of Sociology, 26*, 215–240.

Open Access This chapter is distributed under the terms of the Creative Commons Attribution 4.0 International License (http://creativecommons.org/licenses/by/4.0/), which permits use, duplication, adaptation, distribution and reproduction in any medium or format, as long as you give appropriate credit to the original author(s) and the source, a link is provided to the Creative Commons license and any changes made are indicated.

The images or other third party material in this chapter are included in the work's Creative Commons license, unless indicated otherwise in the credit line; if such material is not included in the work's Creative Commons license and the respective action is not permitted by statutory regulation, users will need to obtain permission from the license holder to duplicate, adapt or reproduce the material.

5

Barriers to Third Sector Development

Annette Zimmer and Benedikt Pahl

1 Introduction: A Success Story and a Clouded Horizon

There are many reasons why the third sector throughout Europe looks back upon a remarkable success story in terms of economic growth, cooperation with governments and civic engagement. Firstly, the unique position of third sector organizations (TSOs) in between "the market" and "the state" allows TSOs to combine the best of these two worlds: the entrepreneurial spirit and energy of the market with the common weal and public good orientation that is generally associated with the state. When governments started to modernize the public sector and looked for partners in the

---

A. Zimmer (✉) • B. Pahl
Institut für Politikwissenschaft, Westfälische Wilhelms-Universität,
Münster, Germany
e-mail: zimmean@uni-muenster.de

provision of public and social services, statist countries, in particular, opted in favor of welfare partnerships with TSOs (Freise and Zimmer 2004; Osborne and Gaebler 1992). Secondly, very often, TSOs are offspring of the social movements of the 1970s and 1980s, such as the ecological and the women's self-help movements. When these movements were successively institutionalized, they gave way to the establishment of numerous TSOs in many Western European countries (Staggenborg 2013; Johnston and Noakes 2005; Roth and Rucht 2008). Thirdly, in many countries of the Western world, the shift from an industrial to a service economy was accompanied by increased societal affluence. Blue- and white-collar workers had increasingly more leisure time at their disposal that was at least partly invested in activities affiliated with TSOs. As a result, the popularity of expressive TSOs, such as sport or hobby clubs, increased significantly and translated into a remarkable growth of the sector in terms of the number of organizations. In this vein, foundations became more and more popular in many countries, since private wealth had been growing due to Europe's peaceful development after World War II.

Moreover, TSOs in Europe were part of the "third wave of democratization" (Huntington 1991). In Spain and Portugal, repressive authoritarian regimes, which had lasted more than 40 years, finally came to an end in the mid-1970s, giving way to a reintegration of the Mediterranean countries into a democratic Europe. Both countries joined the European Union in 1986 (Dedman 2010). Furthermore, the end of the Soviet Union and the ensuing breakdown of socialist rule in Eastern Europe constituted a further milestone and a remarkable window of opportunity for civic engagement and third sector development. The new and unexpected freedom to organize and to form social groups was heavily used and put to work by social activists and former dissidents all over Eastern Europe. As documented by the work of John Keane (1998) and others (e.g. Mansfeldova et al. 2004; Havel and Keane 1985), the impact of the historic change was reflected in the remarkable growth rate of associations throughout the region. In other words, the third sector can look back upon a remarkable development all over Europe that brought the region full-force into what one scholar termed "a global associational revolution" (Salamon 1994), a significant upsurge of organized voluntary activity not only in Europe, but throughout the world.

Compared to the 1990s and 2000s, the general picture facing the third sector in Europe is currently less encouraging. Two decades ago, the future looked bright for the European Union. Central and Eastern European countries, cut off from the dynamic social and economic developments in the West since World War II, were integrated into the European Union, enlarging it to 28 member states. Covering a territory of more 1,600,000 square miles and with a population of over 510 million, the European Union developed into a major political entity. Today, Europe no longer serves as a role model for a harmonic reconciliation of democracy and economic growth. In many European countries, political stability and the reputation of the Union have been put into question. Unemployment rates are stuck at unacceptable levels in many European countries, particularly in the Mediterranean and in Eastern Europe. The Euro hardly managed to survive the economic crisis of 2008. Among the affluent countries in central and northern Europe, tendencies to leave the so-called Euro-Zone are increasingly gaining popularity. Indeed, as opinion polls show, the European Union as a concept has suffered a significant loss of support. Also, civil society, the third sector and its organizations are no longer perceived as key problem solvers by the European Commission. Jacques Delors had a mission and vision regarding the role and function of TSOs in Europe (Delors 2004; Kendall et al. 2009: 347). The Commission under Romano Prodi focused on the "voice function" of TSOs, which was particularly highlighted in the Commission's White Paper on European Governance of 2001 (European Commission 2001). Today, the sector does not enjoy a top priority on the Commission's agenda. If at all, TSOs play a certain role as social enterprises providing public social services (European Commission 2014; Defourny 2014).

Despite these caveats, Europe's third sector is remarkable in terms of size and scope, as clearly shown in Chap. 3. However, several developments have accrued to dim the prospects of Europe's third sector. Before going into detail by focusing on the barriers and hurdles TSOs in Europe are currently confronted with, we will first draw the attention to the enormous variety of the third sector in Europe. In a second step, we will allude to general societal and political trends that might impact on the sector. Among those also is the European Commission as a key actor providing funds for TSO activities and, at the same time, supporting fierce competition between for-profit and TSOs in the welfare domain. Against this background, common barriers and problems, almost every country in Europe is confronted with, will be highlighted. The chapter will be concluded by a more facetted picture of how the third sector tries and manages to cope with the identified hurdles in the different European countries.

2 Third Sector Impact Country Clusters

There is no question the third sector stands out for its variety in terms of fields of activity, traditions, relationships with government and organizational/legal forms. As Chap. 2 of this report noted, there is no single European law on any of the manifestations of the third sector in Europe. Some countries have no law, others have one or two references embracing the totality of the sector's operations, and others have multiple legal structures pertaining to each of a dozen or more types of third sector entities. As Chap. 3 has shown, the European countries are highly different with respect to the size and scope of the sector.

Under the umbrella of the Third Sector Impact (TSI) project, we undertook a substantial body of research analyzing key barriers for third sector development in the countries under study: Austria, Croatia, France, Germany, the Netherlands, Poland and Spain. The countries were grouped regionally and in accordance to their proximity to a specific pattern of civil society development. Thus, as outlined in Chap. 3 and summarized in Table 5.1, a number of countries in Northern or North Central Europe exhibit a pattern that has been identified as a "welfare

Table 5.1 Grouping of TSI Countries by Pattern of Third Sector Development

Model	Countries
Liberal	UK
Welfare partnership	Netherlands, Germany, France, Austria (rural areas)
Social democratic	Norway, Austria (urban areas)
Statist	Poland, Croatia, Spain*

Source: Salamon et al. (2017)

partnership." Included here among our TSI project countries are the Netherlands, Germany, France and the rural areas of Austria. These countries or regions look back upon a tradition of close cooperation in human service delivery between the third sector and the welfare state. In all, religious politics and strong conservative as well as social-democratic elites kept social welfare provision in the hands of party or religiously affiliated TSOs. In these countries, TSOs have traditionally served a partnership role vis-à-vis the state, particularly in the welfare domain. TSOs in welfare partnership countries used to be protected from commercial competitors, and hence enjoyed privileged access to funding through government protection or, more specifically, through legal regulations. Their TSO sectors have consequently had unusually high levels of government support and a dominance of paid staff in their workforces.

A considerably different pattern emerged in the UK. Here, state support for the third sector, and indeed for social welfare services, has long been far less pronounced than in the welfare partnership countries, a residue of the power of commercial and industrial elites and the historic weakness of labor elements. The mobilization of labor in World War II opened the country to elements of the welfare partnership model, but only partly, leaving behind a third sector more reliant on private than on public resources.

Two of our project countries exhibit a social-democratic model of civil society development, though in one of them (Austria) this reflects a bifurcation of the country's social welfare system between urban—in particular Vienna—and rural areas, with the urban areas displaying a social-democratic model characterized by direct delivery of social welfare services and a third sector much more strongly focused on sports, recreation and expressive activities, while the rural areas exhibit a welfare partnership pattern with the heavy involvement of Church-sponsored organizations.

Finally, three of our countries—Poland, Croatia and Spain—retain distinctive elements of a statist pattern fastened on the countries by modernizing elites in the military or authoritarian parties that restrained third sector development. One of these countries, Spain, is clearly in transition from a statist past to a welfare partnership future, and the other two are on a similar path, but a decade behind.

As Chap. 3 also notes, and as Salamon and colleagues have pointed out (Salamon et al. 1999; Salamon and Anheier 1998; Salamon et al. 2017), these patterns have not emerged by magic. Rather, they are embedded in historically shaped power relationships among various social forces and governmental institutions that retain influence over extended periods due to the phenomenon of "path dependence." Inevitably, therefore, while TSOs all over Europe are unanimously affected by certain changes in their organizational environment, they can be expected to react differently given the path-dependent course they happen to be on. Hence, although there are broad common trends in how TSOs in Europe are hindered to live up to their potentials, there are also nuances and even exceptions from country to country, and country cluster to country cluster, in how TSOs are affected by the circumstances they face, and we will need to be sensitive to these variations even while documenting whatever general patterns are evident.

To achieve this balance between regional specificity and Europe-wide commonality, each country team of the TSI project conducted an in-depth analysis of the country-specific situation of the sector and its organizations. Each team used a mixed-methods approach involving a review of the literature, expert interviews with key stakeholders and an online survey with questions addressed to policy experts and leading third sector practitioners. The findings for each country were summarized in "county reports,"[1] brought to the research team as a whole to identify commonalities as well as regional differences that emerged from the regional inquiries. However, before depicting those barriers and hurdles that are a common problem in almost each of the project countries, we will first provide an assessment of general economic and societal trends that have occurred during the last decades and that have a significant impact on the environment of the sector and its organizations. One of these environmental factors which has to be taken into account is closely related to the European Union and its financial support for the sector in certain regions, as well as to the Union's overall support of a zeitgeist of marketization and competitiveness.

---

[1] See National Reports of the TSI countries: http://thirdsectorimpact.eu/the-project/working-areas/barriers/.

3 Third Sector Environment

3.1 Societal and Economic Trends

Although the sector looks back on a story of remarkable growth, there are some indicators that might hinder further success. One of these is related to the 2008 financial crisis, which still lingers. Although it originated in the business sector, this crisis fixed on the continent a belief in the recuperative potentials of the market as the engine to get Europe out of its economic doldrums. Governmental austerity became the medicine of choice, starving the public sector and cutting heavily into the financial support to TSOs both nationally and at the EU level.

A second development is related to the impact of the worldwide trend commonly referred to as individualization on TSOs. More, perhaps, than in other regions of the world, European societies used to be drawn to concepts of solidarity and belonging that had not only familial, but also religious and political components. For a long time, citizens in Europe considered themselves born not only into a family and a religion, but also into a broad social group with a shared worldview and sense of mutual obligation. In many European countries such as Austria, Germany or Italy, there were either people of the "right" or people of the "left." And these colorations carried over into the structure of the third sector, which functioned as a transmission belt and central carrier of these respective group concepts. Against this background of normatively divided societies, the notion of "membership" emerged as a synonym for belongingness and lifelong commitment to a specific social camp. Now, however, times have changed and citizens are increasingly less inclined to sign up for lifelong membership and commitment to a specific TSO. This trend is particularly pronounced among the younger generations in Europe. They are no longer interested in membership per se; instead, they prefer to volunteer on a temporary basis and to get engaged in short term activities, or "episodic volunteering" (Beck 1997; Brudney 2010: 1525).

Finally, neoliberalism (Steger and Roy 2010) and its more tangible manifestation in the form of market-oriented reform policies, put in place by the public sector (Wijkström 2011; Zimmer 2014; Maier et al.

2016; Salamon 1993), had an impact on the sector. Indeed, the first boost of neoliberal thinking and specifically the privatization of social service production opened windows of opportunity for TSOs. In many European countries, particularly in the UK and in the still-developing welfare states of the Mediterranean and post-socialist countries in the South and East of Europe, TSOs became core partners of governments in social service production (Gidron et al. 1992; Salamon 1995). However, nowadays, in the midst of the second wave of privatization, governments are no longer opting in favor of TSOs; on the contrary, the private commercial provision of public services is increasingly challenging service provision through TSOs (Henriksen et al. 2012; Salamon 1993).

This is not to say that the third sector is of rapidly decreasing importance in Europe. However, the distinctiveness of TSOs might be at risk. Also, the societal function of the sector might increasingly be jeopardized. Because of their organizational culture, governance and revenue sources, TSOs belong neither to the efficiency-driven market nor to the authority-driven state. To be part of this sector is to be different from the market and the state in terms of governance, resources, organizational culture as well as mission and vision. It also means to be based significantly on sentiments of solidarity. If TSOs are losing these very special qualities due to external pressures, Europe would be very different from today, without the broad and encompassing variety of TSOs and their contribution to democratic governance, improved service provision and the quality of everyday life of the European people. Whether and to what extent officials in Brussels are aware that an important cornerstone of Europe's identity might be jeopardized if TSOs are hindered from getting the most out of their potentials is difficult to assess. The findings of our research indicate that there is rather limited awareness of the sector's capacity and its potentials.

3.2 European Union as a Key Actor?

The question whether the European Union constitutes a key actor for the further advancement of the third sector in Europe has to be answered with a straightforward "yes" and "no." In a nutshell, Whenever TSOs are asked about the relevance of Brussels for their daily work, the importance of the European Union is judged as being nonrelevant. But the EU has an impact on the sector and its TSOs in various ways, and the relevance of the EU has been growing over the last decades.

Most obviously, the EU has an impact on the sector in monetary terms through grants and contracts. The relevance for the build-up of the sector in the new member states before accession is without any question. In the accession states, the PHARE program of the EU with its focus on supporting social cohesion paved the way for grassroots initiatives such as small and local TSOs. Currently, in particular TSOs, active in post-socialist countries and in the South of Europe, are profiting from the EU's cohesion policy, specifically from monetary transfers paid out of the European Regional Development Fund (ERDF) and the European Social Fund (ESF) or Structural Fund (Venables 2014). As clearly shown in Chap. 2, public funding continues to be a very important source of revenue for TSOs all over Europe. In structurally deprived areas, such as East Europe, or in regions hit hard by the recession, such as the Mediterranean countries in the South, European money plays a significant role for TSOs, particularly for those that are active in the area of social services, health and education. But, as recent studies also reveal, the EU money goes primarily to larger organizations that are in a position to fulfill the burdensome requirements of EU-grants with respect to application, monitoring and evaluating. This means that EU-funding is heavily biased and supports primarily those TSOs in Europe that are already fairly established. In other words, the EU works in favor of the more business prone TSOs while simultaneously being disadvantageous for small and community oriented ones.[2]

A further impact on the sector is closely related to the EU's overall political agenda of fostering competition between different providers of goods and services within the European Union. In this respect, the EU is indeed a driving force. Since the early beginnings of the Common Market, the EU has pushed into the direction of competiveness and has worked in favor of a primarily market-driven integration process (Boje

---

[2] See National Reports of the TSI countries: http://thirdsectorimpact.eu/the-project/working-areas/barriers/.

and Potucek 2011). A textbook example constitutes the Directive on Services of General Economic Interest that was highly disputed about two decades ago (Zimmer et al. 2009: 33; Kendall et al. 2009: 358). In its original contours, the Directive directly jeopardized the model of third sector embeddedness in the welfare partnership countries. TSOs active in core welfare domains in social and health services were supposed to be treated on equal footing with commercial providers. Furthermore, public grants as well as sponsorships of companies supporting TSOs—most likely in sports—were considered to be subsidies that cause market disruption and therefore should be significantly restricted or totally banned by European law. Hence, the directive designed by the DG for Internal Market originally treated any human service like a commodity that was to become subject to similar regulations than any other marketable good. In the end, the directive was watered down in such a way that the specificity of TSOs active in human services was finally acknowledged. TSOs successfully argued that they are distinct from for-profit providers because they are working close to their communities, which is evidenced by the many volunteers who are engaged locally in the provision of social services delivered by TSOs.

But despite the EU's concession, the majority of European governments enacted the directive in very much the way it was originally intended by the European Union (2012). Hence, the EU's impact on TSOs in Europe is rather implicit but, nevertheless, the EU strongly influences the environment of the sector, specifically, in terms of fostering an overall culture of competiveness that downsizes the relevance of other mechanisms of co-ordination such as solidarity or community orientation. In parallel to the enactment of the Directive, instruments of NPM were introduced in the EU member states that had a deep and lasting influence on third sector government relationships. Key features of NPM instruments such as competitive tendering and contract management go along with encompassing and time-consuming procurement procedures, which are difficult to handle, specifically for small TSOs, since the organizations have to devote a considerable amount of time for administration, reporting and book-keeping. All in all, the decisive change of third sector government relationships, at least partly inaugurated by the EU, resulted in the increased bureaucratization of the TSO governance.

Finally and controversially discussed is the impact of the so-called European third sector community that consists of encompassing third sector umbrella organizations operating in Brussels (Kendall et al. 2009). The so-called European TSOs are working as lobbyists on behalf of the sector in Brussels in close contact with the EU policy machinery, the Commission, the Parliament and the various interdepartmental groups (Kendall et al. 2009). Partly funded and sometimes even founded by EU institutions, the so-called community of European TSOs operating in Brussels is somehow in a position of dependency. It has a low profile and seems to serve a useful function for the EU's policy machine by providing expertise and also legitimacy for selected policies, initiated by the Commission. TSOs active in Brussels are not at all in a position of being able to significantly influence the agenda or addressing major topics that are key concerns of the EU and directly and indirectly impinge TSOs' fortunes in the European member states such as the liberalization of social service provision, the introduction of rigid and highly bureaucratic procurement procedures, the neglect of the added value of TSO activity in terms of community building and civicness, just to name a few (Zimmer and Hoemke 2016).

In sum: Although the EU does not have a direct impact on TSOs in Europe, the EU exercises a remarkable influence on the environment of European TSOs by both neglecting the third sector as a valuable underpinning of the social fabric of Europe and exclusively supporting third sector activities that are business-like and favorable for the economy. Moreover, the "cultural shift" toward marketization in third sector government relationships as well as the increase in bureaucratic control mechanisms, on which we will focus in the following chapter, has been promoted and significantly supported by the European Union. Therefore, the impact of the European Union translates into a homogenization of the barriers TSOs have to cope with; however, these barriers play out very differently in the countries due to the heterogeneity and diversity of TSO embeddedness in the European regions.

In the following, we will draw heavily on the results of country reports of the TSI team.[3] Thanks to the reports, we were able to identify both

---

[3] See National Reports of the TSI countries: http://thirdsectorimpact.eu/the-project/working-areas/barriers/.

common problems with which TSOs in all the European countries are confronted and difficulties that are region- or country-specific. We will firstly depict the common problems and secondly turn to barriers and hurdles that are an outcome of the legacy of history and belongingness of the sector to a particular pattern and/or country cluster.

4 Barriers to Third Sector Development

4.1 Common Barriers

Despite the variety of developmental trajectories of the sector in Europe, we identified common barriers standing in the way of TSOs in almost every project country. Graphs and tables presented in the following are based on the results of online surveys conducted in the project countries. Representatives of TSO umbrellas, high profile managers and experts in the field were invited to fill out an online questionnaire. Our intention was to conduct a "stakeholder survey," the goal of which was to find out what stakeholders working at the organizational level of the sector think about general trends within the sector, indicating which barriers and difficulties they perceive as the most salient regarding the current situation and the development of the sector in the future (see Appendix on the data gathering process).

The results of the surveys show that the sector in Europe is confronted with a serious set of problems that translate into:

- financial barriers,
- human resource/governance barriers, and
- external relation barriers/overload of bureaucratic requirements (Zimmer and Pahl 2016).

As the graphs indicate, the identified barriers play out differently in the project countries, thus reflecting and underlining the embeddedness of TSOs in different environments. Although TSOs are confronted with financial barriers all over Europe, the lack of public funding is perceived as a very serious barrier, particularly in the post-communist countries (Fig. 5.1).

Barriers to Third Sector Development

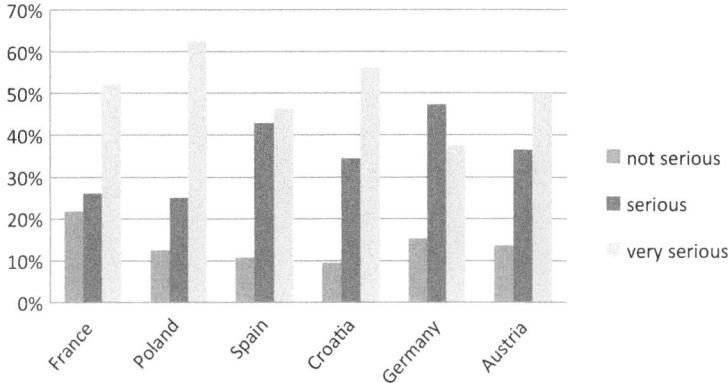

Fig. 5.1 Financial Barrier: Lack of Public Funding. Source: Zimmer and Pahl (2016: 10)

Asked to assess the financial situation of the sector and to indicate the financial difficulties with which TSOs in the country are currently struggling the most, it turned out that "public sector underfunding" constitutes a major barrier and hence a serious or even very serious problem. However, as outlined in the country reports, the reasons why stakeholders are concerned about the lack of public resources are different. In the case of Croatia and Poland, there are hardly any alternative sources of financing available and the countries are significantly hit by the crisis. This is also true for France and Spain. The situation is different in Austria and Germany. Here, the modes of public financing have changed significantly in the last decades. TSOs are working primarily on grant money, which constitutes a "commodity" and not a monetary support for the sector. TSOs, particularly those working in the social domain, are paid on a per capita basis. For each service delivery, TSOs receive a fixed amount of money that is agreed upon in a process of competitive tendering among various service providers—for-profit and nonprofit organizations. Hence, TSOs in these countries are struggling with difficulties in financing their infrastructure because they almost exclusively work with contract money (Fig. 5.2).

Asked to assess which are the most serious difficulties related to human resource management, recruitment of volunteers turned out to be rated

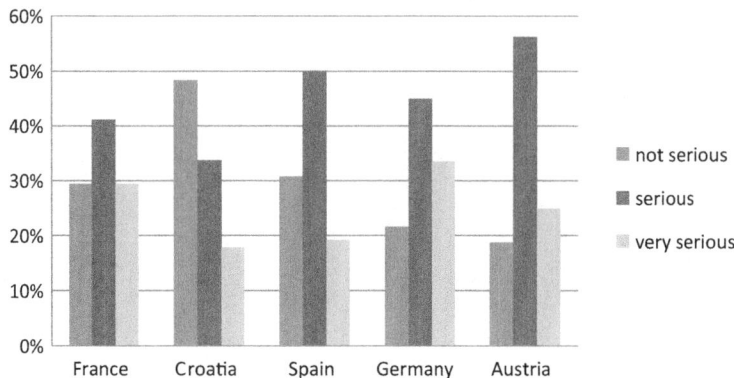

Fig. 5.2 Human Resource Barrier: Difficulties Recruiting Volunteers. Source: Zimmer and Pahl (2016: 6)

as a serious or even very serious problem in particular by stakeholders from Austria and Germany, countries which belong to the welfare partnership cluster. The reasons for this rating might be linked to trends of individualization and societal pluralization that have a deep impact on German and Austrian society, with the effect that volunteer engagement in a specific TSO, either positioned in the conservative or the more liberal camp, does no longer correspond to the Zeitgeist in these countries. In particular, Austria and Germany look back upon a legacy of divided societies, structured into social camps of "the left" and "the right" that carried over into the structure of the sector. In France and Croatia, volunteering has never been very popular. This might be the reason why stakeholders perceive the recruitment problem as less serious than their counterparts in the welfare partnership countries. The reason why, on the contrary, Spanish stakeholders are concerned about volunteer recruitment might mirror the current situation of a sector that is in a state of transition, in which the impact of former state dominance is more and more on the retreat (Fig. 5.3).

Responses to the question concerning the governance of TSOs, specifically, whether there are difficulties in recruiting board members and hence attracting citizens to take on positions of authority on a voluntary basis, turns out to provide a very clear picture. With the only exception of Croatia, recruitment of board members is perceived as a significant or even crucial problem in the majority of the project countries. There are many reasons why this is the case. Serving on a board and being a trustee of a TSO is hard work, time-consuming and demanding in terms of required qualities and responsibilities, which come with the position. As an effect of the generalization of quasi-markets, particularly in the social service domain, managing TSOs has become more demanding. Simultaneously, control mechanisms have been intensified, which translates into a transformation of TSOs in far more bureaucratic organizations with the outcome that expertise in business administration is needed in order to be capable of managing and supervising TSOs today (Fig. 5.4).

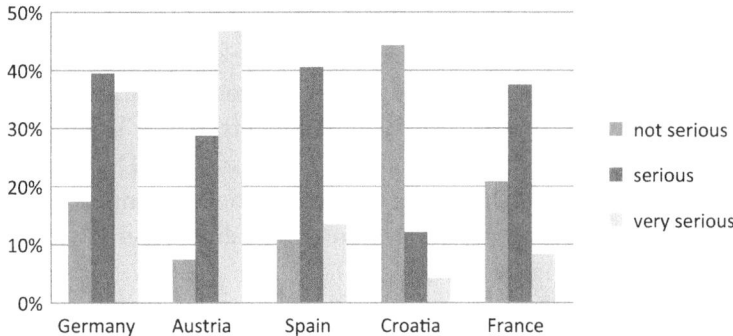

Fig. 5.3 Human Resource Barrier: Difficulties Recruiting Board Members. Source: Zimmer and Pahl (2016: 7)

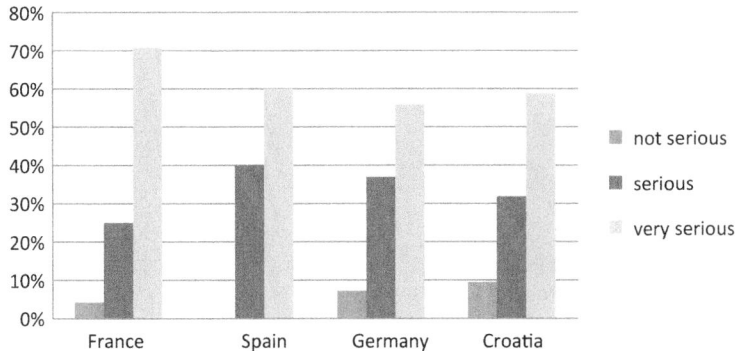

Fig. 5.4 External Relations Barrier: Increasing Bureaucracy. Source: Zimmer and Pahl (2016: 8)

Asked which aspect, from their point of view, constitutes the most pressing problem as regards the external relations of TSOs, "increasing bureaucracy" was named first. Again, the assessment of the stakeholders reflects the significant changes of the sector's environment in Europe. Today, TSOs in the majority of European countries are treated on par with for-profit providers, in particular, in the area of social service provision where they almost exclusively work on contracts. The new policy environment impacts significantly on third sector government relations. These used to be trust based at eye level and changed to a customer-supplier relationship. Nowadays, TSOs have to prove that they are thoroughly in compliance with their contracts. Today, this results in a situation where a significant amount of time, which in former times was available for the "real work," has to be allocated to record keeping and documentation of costs. This is specifically the case in Germany, France and partly also in Spain. In contrast, TSOs in Croatia are still perceived as somehow untrustworthy partners of governments, which simultaneously reflects the statist tradition of the country. The reason why TSOs in Croatia are faced with increased demands for documentation and control are slightly different form the situation in the "welfare partnership countries", as we will outline in the following chapter (Fig. 5.5).

Marketization might come at a price for TSOs. Social service provision is under rigid cost-containment strategies enforced by government. TSOs working in this area are acting in very competitive markets, in which they

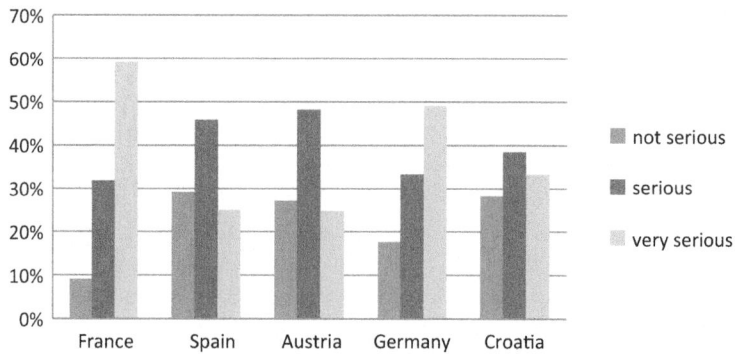

Fig. 5.5 External Relations Barrier: Low Pay of Employees. Source: Zimmer and Pahl (2016: 11)

are challenged by efficiency-driven for-profits. In order not to lose ground, TSOs have to bring production costs down. Reducing the costs of labor might offer a way to be competitive. Against this background, our stakeholders indicated that TSOs in some areas are not able to pay decent wages. Participants in our survey rated "low pay of employees" as a key issue with which TSOs in their countries are struggling. This might not come as a surprise in countries where TSO-government relationships are still in a developmental stage. However, it is worrisome that stakeholders of the welfare partnership countries Germany, Austria and France perceive low pay of employees as a major barrier, which might decrease the attractiveness of TSOs on the labor market in the long run, even if this is not yet the case. As stressed by the TSI teams and clearly underlined by the UK report, "it is noteworthy that very few respondents pointed to problems with their paid workforce, in terms of recruitment, quality, training or motivation" (Kendall et al. 2016a, b). However, the attractiveness of the sector, which up until now has been a central reason for its remarkable growth, might not be durable. Asked to assess how they see the future of the sector, the majority of stakeholders is reluctant and prefers a conservative and careful view into the future, indicating that they strongly or rather disagree (70 percent) with an overall optimistic preview that "the next ten years might be easier for TSOs than the previous ten" (Hoemke et al. 2016: 15). Although skepticism turned out to be a general trend all over Europe, the TSI research team also unfolded variant trajectories of third sector development as well as significant differences between the European countries as they are affected by the afore-described changes of the environment.

4.2 Regional Diversity and Regime-specific Barriers to TSO Development

4.2.1 From Liberal to Welfare Partnership to Liberal Again—The UK

In the UK, TSOs see their environment as increasingly market-driven in terms of resources and governance practices, the result of a shift in the political climate and ideological discourses from an incipient welfare partnership model back to an earlier liberal, now neoliberal, market-oriented model (Kendall et al. 2016a, b; Mohan et al. 2016; Kendall and Knapp 1996).

After moving from a historically liberal pattern of third sector development, until the expansion of the British welfare state in the aftermath of World War II and the adoption of key features of a social-democratic model, the UK third sector became a beneficiary of the Third Way political philosophy of the post-Thatcher Labour government, which adopted key features of the welfare partnership model involving the increased reliance of government on TSOs to deliver social welfare services. The state was assigned a more passive role as an enabler and not as a provider of welfare activities. The third sector policies were meant to be achieved via enabling the emergence of a quasi-market with preferences for standardization and large-scale provision. Thus, large organizations were able to deal with the challenges regarding procurement, commissioning and contracting to the detriment of more specialized responses to needs.

Furthermore, the Labour government made major investments into a third sector infrastructure and into the organizational capacity of TSOs. As one reflection of this, following the advice of a special commission on the third sector created by a group of foundations (the Deakin Commission) a concordat or compact between the government and third sector was initiated. However, against the background of the required marketization and professionalization that was also pursued, many organizations were not able to, or did not wish to, work with government as a partner in such a marketized climate of operations.

With the entry of the Cameron coalition government, the philosophy of "Big Society" provided the ideological backbone for a return to the traditional UK Liberal Model featuring an independently financed third sector and hostility toward state involvement in terms of public spending. In a nutshell, the government program envisaged scaling back public expenses, which were to be replaced by volunteers, or in other words, the "Big Society" substituting for "Big Government." In practice, quasi-markets were extended and welfare services were opened to market forces as far as possible. For-profit agencies were granted (market) access to all policy fields, including voluntarism and work with vulnerable groups.

Besides quasi-market approaches, the UK governments, mostly with the new legislation in 2016, have fostered financing models that follow a social investment logic, such as loan and bond finance initiatives. Hence, these sorts of schemes have gained relevance among British TSOs.

Extensive budgetary cuts went hand-in-hand with market promotion in all areas of welfare spending, with the financial crisis providing the legitimacy to far-reaching austerity policies. In particular, the budgets of local authorities, which are a core source for third sector funding in the UK, were massively reduced. Additionally, the third sector infrastructure, which the Labour government had set up or substantially supported—like the Charity Commission and the Office for Civil Society—was cut back. As the sectoral infrastructure has collapsed and the financial support from local authorities has been cut, TSOs face difficulties to function properly. Especially the capacity to mobilize and encourage volunteer contribution is severely diminished. The case of the UK provides an example that volunteering does not work properly if an appropriate infrastructure is lacking. Furthermore, the Cameron government took a hostile stance toward the campaigning and advocacy work of TSOs, stating that the use of public grants for campaigning activities would be prohibited. Generally, the British Third Sector's ability to perform its multiple roles seems to be increasingly constrained because its organizations are facing the double challenge of reduced public funding (austerity) and intensifying scrutiny through statutory bodies and an increasingly critical national media (Kendall et al. 2016a, b). Summarizing the general picture, the UK report underlines that "significant numbers of organizations experience their environment as increasingly market and quasi-market driven in terms of resource origins and governance practices, and experience the current political climate as unconducive to non-service provision roles" (Kendall et al. 2016).

4.2.2 Welfare Partnership Countries: Adjustment to a Changed Social Policy Environment—Germany, the Netherlands, Austria

Unrivaled welfare partnership in the social domain used to be the central feature of the third sector in these countries (Brandsen and Pape 2016;

Simsa et al. 2015, b; Hoemke et al. 2016). Deeply embedded in the institutional design of the welfare state, TSOs enjoyed a privileged position as providers of social services. However, in response to the neoliberal surge, the policy environment in this cluster of countries has changed significantly in the last decades. The welfare partnership, based on secured public funding for TSOs, which were legally protected from competition of alternative providers, was modified in such a way that today TSOs are treated on par with commercial providers. Secured public funding for TSOs is a story of the past. Alongside the introduction of NPM, competitive tendering and contract management have become ubiquitous in the social domain. Furthermore, commercial providers successfully made inroads into areas of social service provision that used to be core domains of TSOs—such as hospitals or child-care facilities. Indeed, TSOs are nowadays confronted with increased competition from for-profit providers in every field of social service provision. The changed policy environment has a deep impact on the governance and organizational culture of TSOs. In order to survive in these by now highly competitive markets for social and health services, TSOs have to be efficiently managed. Hence, the "marketization" of the social domain translates into a situation in which TSOs turn to "managerialism" as a business-like way of governance and management.

From an economic point of view, many TSOs accomplished the shift toward a professionally managed nonprofit enterprise successfully. Despite the mounting cost and efficiency pressures, TSOs in this cluster of countries have defended their positions as core providers of social services. The market share of TSOs in the social domain is relatively stable compared to the share of for-profit competitors. As TSOs look back upon a long tradition and expertise in service provision in many fields of human service delivery, such as health care or child care, they are able to compete successfully with commercial providers in competitive tendering procedures. Also, TSOs are able to communicate their professionalism to the general public. Compared to the UK, where the media increasingly looks upon TSOs with skepticism, in particular, the religiously affiliated "big players" among the third sector service providers, such as the Caritas in Austria and Germany, enjoy a good reputation among the general public. Against this background, TSOs can rely on an established brand as a social service provider that constitutes an asset compared to new commercial competitors that have to create awareness among customers. Moreover, TSOs can count on good relations with local politicians and administrators, which enable TSOs to improve their position in negotiations for service contracts. However, the successful adaptation of TSOs in competitive markets comes at a price: there are indicators that TSOs might lose some of the specific qualities that are commonly attributed to the sector. The "winds of change," which might endanger the core values of TSOs in Austria, Germany and the Netherlands, are the change of the legal form toward a limited liability company, the preference for professional managers with a background in business administration instead of, for example, social work, and the decreasing attractiveness of TSOs for volunteers.

TSOs are still providing important avenues for civic engagement and volunteering in the countries of this cluster. However, they seem to lose their pole position as the key terrain for volunteer engagement. As outlined earlier, Europeans have long considered themselves born not only into a family and a religion, but also into a broad social group with a shared worldview and a sense of mutual obligation. Being an active member in terms of both volunteering on a regular basis and serving on a board of a TSO used to be key ingredients of the way of life for the majority of citizens in these countries. The reason for the steady volunteer influx into the sector was that the societies of this country cluster used to be highly structured and organized into religious or ideological communities, of which TSOs served as the organizational underpinning and infrastructure. For describing this phenomenon, "pillarization" is used in the Netherlands, while in Germany and Austria, the "social milieu" is referred to frequently (Brandsen 2011; Golbeck 2011: 92; Zimmer 2013). However, both the societal pillars of the Netherlands and the social milieus of Austria and Germany—of which the catholic and the social democratic used to be the most important ones—are no longer strongly in place. Citizens born into these pillars and/or social milieus used to constitute a stable resource base of volunteers for TSOs of a respective pillar or milieu. Since the pillars and milieus are almost gone, the religious and ideological bonds to TSOs have significantly eroded. Citizens are no longer born into a pillar or milieu that used to pave the way for lifelong engagement for a particular TSO. Accordingly, nowadays, TSOs have to actively recruit volunteers. With respect to voluntary contributions, such as donations, volunteering and serving on boards, TSOs are faced with a competitive environment, similar to the one they encounter on the market for government grants and contracts. Additionally, a growing share of volunteering takes place independently and without the framing of TSOs.

As regards the key topic of our inquiry, the Austrian report summarized, "One of the biggest barriers of TSOs stems from the lack of financial resources (Simsa et al. 2015, b)." The combined lack of public funding and private donations as well as the decreasing profit margins from TSOs' market activities result in an ongoing trend toward marketization and professionalization, which will most likely impact negatively on the social and civic mission of the sector. TSOs in the welfare partnership countries are confronted with problems of identity and legitimacy since they are becoming more and more business-like in order to hold their central position in the market domain of social service provision.

4.2.3 The Social-Democratic Model on the Retreat

Scandinavian countries like Norway exhibit a "social-democratic" pattern of third sector development in which the sector is heavily focused on expressive functions such as sports, recreation and culture, with high levels of volunteer involvement and relatively little government support (Lundström and Wijkström 1997; Wijkström and Zimmer 2011). Social service provision is not perceived as a function of TSOs; instead, the social domain is generally acknowledged to be a core area of welfare state activity. For decades, social services used to be government-regulated, generously financed through tax money and, with very few exceptions, delivered by government entities.

However, in line with the trends in other European regions, the Scandinavian countries have begun to implement NPM tools to regulate relations between public contracting authorities and providers of welfare services. Local governments made an internal separation between contracting authorities and providers of services in the beginning of the nineties in Sweden (Erlandsson et al. 2013: 27) and late in the nineties in Denmark and Norway (Vabø et al. 2013: 171). Since then, contract negotiations or competitive tendering have replaced agreements between public purchasers and service providers, which otherwise would have been renewed almost automatically. The reason why this is the case is closely linked to the overall assessment of public policy and, particularly, social policy. In a nutshell, public institutions are no longer perceived to be capable of responding to social needs adequately; instead, in line with neoliberal thinking, the market and hence competition between different providers—for-profit and nonprofit—is supposed to provide social services efficiently, appropriately and in accordance with the needs and preferences of the clients. The roll back of the state in social service provision is still very much in its infancy in Scandinavia. However, at least in Sweden and Denmark, the share of for-profit providers in the welfare domain is slightly increasing, while employment in the public sector has started to decrease. In Norway, with no need for austerity measures because of the income from oil production, all three sectors still grow in real numbers, although the public sector's share is decreasing (Sivesind 2017).

What might work against the sector and in the long run might impact negatively on TSOs is related to the overall image of the sector in the Scandinavian countries. It is reported that in Norway public authorities are not particularly interested in the distinctive profiles of TSOs (Trætteberg and Sivesind 2015). Furthermore, if we look at the expressive TSOs in Norway, there is a decline in formal membership, indicating an erosion of bonds between TSOs and their members. At the same time, surveys report an increase in volunteering. In Norway, 61 percent of the adult population volunteer at least once a year. However, volunteers are not necessarily members of TSOs, and if so, they tend to move from one TSO to another. Very similar to the pluralization of the societies in the "welfare partnership countries," the collective identities on which volunteering in Scandinavia used to be based are no longer strongly in place. These identities were closely connected to the traditional Scandinavian popular movements, such as consumer cooperative movements (Hilson 2010). Today, similar to other European regions in the Scandinavian countries, volunteering is first and foremost connected with conceptions of self-expression and self-realization. This may indicate that the sector's role as part of the democratic infrastructure of the country has diminished with the decline of the traditional popular movements. Simultaneously, TSOs have not managed to make inroads into the markets of social service delivery, which have just started to develop due to the most recent social policy changes.

4.2.4 Struggling with the Past and Catching up on the Edge: Croatia and Poland

Poland and Croatia exemplify the power of path dependence in shaping a pattern of third sector development highly influenced by past realities (Leś et al. 2016; Bežovan et al. 2016). Like other third sectors exhibiting the classic features of the statist pattern of civil society development, Eastern European third sectors were subject to an authoritarian state that pursued modernization and social control from the top, and was eager to avoid disruptive third sector elements raising objections from below. TSOs in the realm of the church, sports and TSOs in the social economy, such as cooperatives, were partly able to survive. In addition, the state organized its own third sector-type entities, particularly in the professions and labor, but these were most likely controlled by the state and therefore outside the kind of definition of the third sector identified in Chap. 2 of this report. Conjointly, support structures for the third sector were brought under state control. Reflecting this, the third sector in Poland and Croatia remains fragmented and relatively small compared to the third sector particularly in the welfare partnership countries. Also, the societal embeddedness of the sector in terms of volunteering and giving is still very limited compared to Western European standards. The majority of TSOs are expressive organizations working in the areas of leisure and sports. In both countries, cooperation with government in the social service domain is still in its infancy. Funding continues to be a difficult issue for TSOs in the region and has deteriorated due to the financial crises and austerity measures put in place by government. If there were no EU-support, many TSOs in Poland and Croatia would probably be forced to stop operating.

Although the two countries share many commonalities, there are also striking differences that again are linked to history. It is worthwhile to stress that Poland was the pioneer among the countries in Eastern Europe to stand up against Soviet rule and to develop under the leadership of a third society organization—the trade union Solidarnosc—a societal and political alternative that facilitated peaceful transition and democratization all over the region. Although the Catholic Church in Poland has always been traditional and quite conservative, the charismatic Pope John Paul II, born as Karol Józef Wojtyła, supported the process of transformation. However, even today, there is a divide between the rural, conservative and very catholic countryside and the more liberal, open-minded and somehow even rebellious urban Poland. In particular, in Warsaw, but also in other major cities, TSOs are very active addressing societal issues and problems that are not taken up by government (Siemieńska et al. 2016). In addition, TSOs are of increasing importance in the field of education (schools) in Poland (Leś et al. 2016: 14). When the government, due to fiscal difficulties, began to close down schools in urban neighborhoods as well as in the country side, TSOs—set up and financed by citizens—stepped in with the goal of providing an educational infrastructure that is easily accessible and nearby (Siemieńska et al. 2011). These examples indicate that TSOs in Poland enjoy the backing of local communities and case-related constituencies.

Compared to Poland, the development of the sector in Croatia did not start from below. Instead, as the authors of the country report outline, third sector activities were activated from "outside" (Bežovan et al. 2016). The atrocities of the civil war resulted in an influx of many TSOs, which were and, partly, still are funded and supported by foreign money. A large part of the sector in Croatia still consists of humanitarian TSOs. This, in turn, has nurtured general skepticism toward the sector as being a product of Western intervention in Croatian society. Lack of trust combined with the low profile of the sector in Croatian society continues to be a significant hurdle, which impacts negatively on the sector's further development. Moreover, in Croatia and partly also in Poland, government was and still is reluctant to partner with TSOs in the provision of social services. It took more than ten years to clarify legal issues and to set up a framework for cooperation between public institutions and TSOs in the two countries (Rymsza 2013; Bežovan et al. 2016). Even today, social service providing TSOs play a very minor role in both countries. A lack of public awareness and a lack of trust on the part of both citizens and state authorities in the professionalism and capacity of TSOs are reported to be crucial barriers for the flourishing of TSOs in the social service domain. Furthermore, contracting with public authorities is troublesome and TSOs are partly discriminated against by public providers by practices of clientelism and the opaque nature of contracting procedures. As already mentioned, the low social anchorage of TSOs is reflected in the limited degree of private giving. Additionally, public funds are increasingly limited due to cost-containment strategies as well as policies of austerity in both countries. On the grounds that alternative financial sources are missing to compensate for the tense situation of the public purse, EU funds are of particular significance for TSOs in Poland and Croatia, as well as all over Eastern Europe. In fact, EU funds have been crucial to the growth of the sector in the region (Zimmer and Hoemke 2016). As EU funds are very complex and bureaucratic, highly professionalized organizations have evolved around EU-funded themes. However, rigid control and an overload of bureaucracy are not restricted to EU funding; public support also increasingly comes with the high prize of intensified control procedures and book-keeping requirements. As the national report of the Croatian TSI team neatly summarized, the key barriers to the development of TSOs in the region are "the path-dependent problem of lacking awareness, the government quasi-monopoly of providing social services, the deficient implementation of policies advancing welfare partnerships between government and TSOs and finally the low levels of citizen engagement in terms of volunteering and private giving" (Bežovan et al. 2016; Leś et al. 2016).

4.2.5 In between Statism and Welfare Partnership: France and Spain

Until the 1970s, with the demise of the Franco regime, Spain had most of the features of the statist model of civil society development, with limited third sector institutions and little government support for them (Chanial and Laville 2014; Petrella et al. 2016; Chaves et al. 2016). During the dictatorship, large parts of the sector were suppressed and the

Spanish third sector is still underdeveloped compared to France or Central Europe. France is a slightly different case, though its historic opposition to third society organizations reflecting Rousseau-ist sentiments born out of the French Revolution and the etatist nature of its social welfare system well into the post-World War II era gave it many of the features of the statist model as well (Archambault 1997). Volunteering is low in both countries. Particularly in Spain, volunteering is more directed toward one's next of kin. Both countries, but particularly Spain, also featured substantial social economy units in the form of cooperatives and mutuals, though these are heavily commercial in orientation and only a small segment of the cooperative sector operates under the binding limitation on the distribution of profits stipulated in the in-scope definition of the TSE sector formulated in this project.

Current scholarly discourse as well as policy development are focusing on the Social and Solidarity Economy (SSE), in particular, in France. Faced with a difficult economic situation, social economy might provide tools for reforming social service delivery in a way that citizens might get the same quantity and quality of services while government spends less. France's welfare state is highly developed and, according to OECD data, ranks among the top spenders (Chabanet 2016). Alongside policies of decentralization, the sector has developed into a prime partner of government with respect to social service delivery. The embracement of the sector by the welfare state resulted in a success story and in the remarkable growth of the third sector in France. In accordance with the welfare partnership mode, France's third sector today constitutes a highly integrated component of the country's welfare state (Archambault et al. 2013). However, similar to Spain, France is severely hit by the crisis. As a reaction, government provides incentives for TSOs to become more business-like and for for-profits to get active in those areas and fields, which used to be earmarked for TSO engagement, such as social services. As a result, relationships between TSOs and public authorities are deeply affected. According to the French national report, TSOs are increasingly perceived just as "service providers" instead of co-producers of public policies. Since French authorities acknowledge the civic values of the sector far less than previously, the advocacy and social integration functions of the sector might be jeopardized.

In this respect, the current state of affairs of the sector in France and the barriers the sector currently is confronted with are quite similar to those that are encountered by the sector in the classical welfare partnership countries Germany, Austria and the Netherlands.

Beginning in the mid-1970s in Spain and in the 1980s in France, significant elements of the welfare partnership model have emerged. In Spain, this transformation has been significantly aided by an influx of EU funds as national funding of social welfare activity remains relatively low and concentrated on old age pensions. Locally financed social services are rather underdeveloped and the extended family still compensates for the lack of welfare institutions. A few privileged "quango" organizations benefited from a moderate welfare expansion since the democratization of Spain in 1978 and the majority of public funds toward the sector concentrate on these organizations. In France, a major shift in social welfare policy in the 1980s helped usher in key elements of the welfare partnership pattern as the state decentralized welfare services and local governments turned extensively toward newly strengthened TSOs to deliver the services. In both counties, however, the sector is fragmented and divided along societal cleavages between secular and religious as well as left wing and right wing organizations. Against this background, the support structure is scattered and underdeveloped. With the financial crisis in Spain, new organizations have emerged in the course of the anti-austerity protests in 2008. These new organizations are not linked to the established "quango" organizations.

Particularly Spain was hit hard by the financial crisis. Public funding was cut due to vast austerity measures. Additionally, private donations decreased mostly due to the collapse of savings banks. Likewise, the social needs of the population escalated due to mass unemployment and social deprivation. Thus, TSOs in Spain have to survive in a particularly hostile environment "having to address more needs with fewer resources" (Chaves et al. 2016).

TSOs have reacted to the crisis by lowering the working hours and extending part time work. Despite the fact that it is difficult for TSOs to recruit volunteers in light of a relatively low social embeddedness of the sector and the increasingly resource-intensive management of volunteers, paid employment is substituted by volunteers. Thus, working hours per volunteer have been rising. Furthermore, since TSOs have to manage an increasing deficit, debts are increasing (Chaves et al. 2016; Petrella et al. 2016). TSOs are struggling in Spain to make ends meet; however, compared to Poland and particularly Croatia, the sector enjoys a favorable public image, TSOs active in the social domain are linked to powerful umbrellas, specifically, to ONCE, Red Cross and Caritas (Chaves et al. 2016), and recently, a major support infrastructure was set up—the Spanish Social Third Sector Platform. On the other hand, the sector in Spain is also confronted with significant difficulties in developing further into the direction of the welfare partnership model. There is a lack of awareness of the social and economic impact of the sector; politicians and government officials tend to overlook the sector while designing public policies. Finally, clearly indicated in the Spanish national report on the sector are the difficulties firstly to assess and secondly to work with EU funds. Also, in Spain, working with public funds comes along with increased requirements for control, and hence bureaucracy.

In summary, the third sector struggles with a scarcity of resources and increasing difficulties to cope with those administrative demands that are most likely a side effect of the introduction of NPM instruments in Europe. It seems that TSOs have to invest time and organizational capacity to comply with administrative and monitoring requirements of funders and/or contracting partners. Furthermore, due to changes in their environment, TSOs are forced to act more and more business-like. If we perceive working with volunteers as a special ingredient of TSOs, during the last decades, it has become more difficult for TSOs to be volunteer-based in terms of both their labor force and their governance structures. In order to be competitive, TSOs tend to reduce the cost of their labor force. However, the organizations are aware that in the future this might cause problems, since the low-pay jobs offered by TSOs might be less attractive for highly qualified personnel. "To get the right person for the job" also constitutes a big problem for the governance of TSOs that look upon a tradition of being managed and/or supervised by board members serving in honorary positions. Nowadays, there is a decreasing interest in taking over these positions. In the next chapter, we will turn to the topic of how to address the identified barriers appropriately and to develop a policy agenda that indicates "the way ahead" for the third sector in Europe.

Appendix

Stakeholder Survey

An online survey was conducted with the aim of prioritizing the barriers, which were identified through interviews and focus groups realized with stakeholders in the project countries. With a special eye on the identified barriers, the design of the survey (items) paralleled the manual for the interviews. It is noteworthy to underline that the outcome of the survey is not representative. Instead, it constitutes an evaluation and personal assessment of those who participated in the survey. We addressed stakeholders, such as managers, heads of departments, and board members of TSOs, to take part in the survey. The number of respondents was 250 in Germany, 171 in Croatia and 102 in Austria. The response rate was very low in Spain (28 responses), France (24) and Poland (8). For these countries, the results of the survey are merely illustrative.

In the UK and the Netherlands, the questionnaire of the online survey was adapted to better reflect the national situations. Therefore, the results of the surveys conducted in these two countries are not included in the analysis. However, the outcome of the surveys in the UK and the Netherlands point in the same direction, that is, indicating the same barriers. The response rate was 1200 in the UK, 372 in the Netherlands.

The outcome of the online survey reflects the priorization of the respondents as to which barriers and hurdles they perceive as the most important and salient ones for the TSOs they are either representing (board members) or working for. The results of the survey and the interviews were published in individual working papers per project country and made available on the website of the project.

References

Archambault, E. (1997). *The nonprofit sector in France*. Manchester: Manchester University Press.

Archambault, E., Priller, E., & Zimmer, A. (2013). European civil societies compared: Typically German—Typically French? *Voluntas: International Journal of Voluntary and Non-profit Organisations, 24*(1), 1–24.

Beck, U. (Ed.). (1997). *Kinder der Freiheit*. (Edition Zweite Moderne). Frankfurt: Suhrkamp Verlag.

Bežovan, G., Matančević, J., & Baturina, D. (2016). Identifying external and internal barriers to third sector development—Croatia. *TSI National Report No. 5*, Seventh Framework Programme (grant agreement 613034), European Union. Brussels: Third Sector Impact. Retrieved from http://thirdsectorimpact.eu/documentation/tsi-national-report-no-5-identifying-external-internal-barriers-third-sector-development-croatia/

Boje, T. P., & Potucek, M. (Eds.). (2011). *Social rights, active citizenship, and governance in the European Union*. Baden-Baden: Nomos Verlag.

Brandsen, T. (2011). Social services in the Netherlands—Position and authority of non-profit sector organizations. In A. Zimmer (Ed.), *Jenseits von Bier und Tulpen* (pp. 75–86). Münster: Waxmann Verlag.

Brandsen, T., & Pape, U. (2016). Barriers to third sector development in the Netherlands. *TSI National Report No. 2*. Retrieved from http://thirdsectorimpact.eu/documentation/tsi-national-report-no-2-barriers-to-third-sector-development-in-the-netherlands/

Brudney, J. L. (2010). Volunteers. In H. Anheier, S. Toepler, & R. A. List (Eds.), *International encyclopedia of civil society* (pp. 1620–1627). New York: Springer.

Chabanet, D. (2016). Between traditions and changes: Institutional support to social economy in France. *Arnova Conference 2016* in Washington, DC.

Chanial, P., & Laville, J.-L. (2014). L'économie sociale et solidaire en France. In J.-L. Laville, J.-P. Magnen, G. Carvalho da Franca, & A. Medeiros (Eds.), *Action publique et économie solidaire* (pp. 47–73). Paris: Erès.

Chaves, R., Alguacil-Mari, P., Fajardor-Garcia, I. G., & Savall-Morera, T. (2016). Third sector barriers in Spain. *TSI National Report No. 8*. Retrieved from http://thirdsectorimpact.eu/documentation/tsi-national-report-no-8-third-sector-barriers-spain/

Dedman, M. (2010). *The origins and development of the European Union 1945–2008: A history of European integration*. London: Routledge.

Defourny, J. (2014). From third sector to social enterprise: A European research trajectory. In J. Defourny, L. Hulgard, & V. Pesthoff (Eds.), *Social enterprises and the third sector* (pp. 17–41). London and New York: Routledge.

Delors, J. (2004). The European Union and the third sector. In A. Evers & J. L. Laville (Eds.), *The third sector in Europe* (pp. 206–215). Cheltenham: Edward Elgar.

Erlandsson, S., Storm, P., Strantz, A., Szebehely, M., & Trydegård, G.-B. (2013). Marketising trends in Swedish eldercare: Competition, choice and calls for stricter regulation. In G. Meagher & M. Szebehely (Eds.), *Marketisation in Nordic eldercare: A research report on legislation, oversight, extent and consequences* (pp. 23–84). Stockholm: Department of Social Work, Stockholm University.

European Commission. (2001). European Governance—A White Paper. COM(2001)428final.

European Commission. (2014). *A map of social enterprises and their eco-systems in Europe; (Country reports)*. European Union, 2014. Retrieved from http://ec.europa.eu/social/keyDocuments.jsp?pager.offset=0&&langId=en&mode=advancedSubmit&year=0&country=0&type=0&advSearchKey=socentcntryrepts&orderBy=docOrder

Freise, M., & Zimmer, A. (2004). Der Dritte Sektor im wohlfahrtsstaatlichen Arrangement der post- sozialistischen Visegrád-Staaten. In A. Croissant, G. Erdmann, & F. W. Rüb (Eds.), *Wohlfahrtsstaatliche Politik in jungen Demokratien* (pp. 153–172). Wiesbaden: VS-Verlag.

Gidron, B., Kramer, R., & Salamon, L. M. (Eds.). (1992). *Government and the third sector: Emerging relationships in welfare states*. San Francisco: Jossey-Bass.

Golbeck, C. (2011). Auf der Suche nach produktiven Kompromissen—Wohlfahrtsverbände zwischen sozialem Anspruch und wirtschaftlicher Effizienz. In A. Zimmer (Ed.), *Jenseits von Bier und Tulpen* (pp. 87–109). Münster: Waxmann.

Havel, V., & Keane, J. (Eds.). (1985). *The power of the powerless: Citizens against the state in Central Eastern Europe*. London: Taylor and Francis.

Henriksen, L. S., Smith, S. R., & Zimmer, A. (2012). At the eve of convergence? Transformation of social service provision in Denmark, Germany, and the United States. *Voluntas, 23*(2), 458–501.

Hilson, M. (2010). The Nordic consumer co-operative movements. In R. Alapuro & H. Stenius (Eds.), *Nordic associations in a European perspective* (pp. 215–240). Baden-Baden: Nomos.

Hoemke, P., Pahl, B., Rentzsch, C., & Zimmer, A. (2016). External and internal barriers to third sector development in Germany. *TSI National Report No. 6*. Retrieved from http://thirdsectorimpact.eu/documentation/tsi-national-report-no-6-external-internal-barriers-third-sector-development-germany/

Huntington, S. P. (1991). *The Third Wave: Democratization in the late 20th century*. Oklahoma: Oklahoma University Press.

Johnston, H., & Noakes, J. A. (2005). *Frames of protest: Social movements and the framing perspective*. Lanham: Rowman & Littlefield Publishers.

Keane, J. (1998). *Civil society: Old images, new visions*. Stanford: Stanford University Press.

Kendall, J., Brookes, N., & Mohan, J. (2016a). Identifying external and internal barriers to third sector development in the UK. *TSI Working Paper Series No. 1*, Seventh Framework Programme (grant agreement 613034), European Union. Brussels: Third Sector Impact.

Kendall, J., Brookes, N., & Mohan, J. (2016b). The English third sector policy in 2015: An overview of perceived barriers to realizing impact potential, Summary of research findings for Work Package 5. *TSI Policy Brief No. 3*. Retrieved from http://thirdsectorimpact.eu/documentation/tsi-barriers-briefing-no-1-english-third-sector-policy-in-2015/

Kendall, J., & Knapp, M. (1996). *The voluntary sector in the UK*. Manchester: Manchester University Press.

Kendall, J., Will, C., & Brandsen, T. (2009). The third sector and the Brussels dimension: Trans-EU governance work in progress. In J. Kendall (Ed.), *Handbook on third sector policy in Europe. Multi-level processes and organized civil society* (pp. 341–381). Cheltenham: Edward Elgar.

Leś, E., Nałęcz, S., & Pieliński, B. (2016). Third sector barriers in Poland. *TSI National Report No. 7*. Retrieved from http://thirdsectorimpact.eu/documentation/tsi-national-report-no-7-third-sector-barriers-poland/

Lundström, T., & Wijkström, F. (1997). *The nonprofit sector in Sweden*. Manchester: Manchester University Press.

Maier, F., Meyer, M., & Steinbereithner, M. (2016). Nonprofit organizations becoming business-like: A systematic review. *Nonprofit and Voluntary Sector Quarterly, 45*(1), 64–86.

Mansfeldova, Z., Nałęcz, S., Priller, E., & Zimmer, A. (2004). Civil society in transition: Civic engagement and nonprofit organisations in Central and Eastern Europe after 1989. In A. Zimmer & E. Priller (Eds.), *Future of civil society: Making Central European nonprofit- organizations work* (pp. 99–127). Wiesbaden: VS Verlag.

Mohan, J., Kendall, J., & Brookes, N. (2016). Third sector impact: Towards a more nuanced understanding of barriers and constraints. *TSI National Report No. 1*. Retrieved from http://thirdsectorimpact.eu/documentation/tsi-barriers-briefing-no-2-towards-a-more-nuanced-understanding-of-barriers-and-constraints/

Osborne, D., & Gaebler, T. (1992). *Reinventing government: How the entrepreneurial spirit is transforming the public sector*. Reading, MA: Addison-Wesley.

Petrella, F., Richez-Battesti, N., Bruis, L., Maisonnasse, J., & Meunier, N. (2016). Challenges for the third sector in France. *TSI National Report No. 4*. Retrieved from http://thirdsectorimpact.eu/documentation/tsi-narional-report-on-challenges-for-the-third-sector-in-france/

Roth, R., & Rucht, D. (Eds.). (2008). *Die sozialen Bewegungen in Deutschland seit 1945: Ein Handbuch*. Frankfurt: Campus-Verlag.

Rymsza, M. (2013). The two decades of social policy in Poland: From protection to activation of citizens. In A. Evers & A.-M. Guillemard (Eds.), *Social policy and citizenship: The changing landscape* (pp. 305–334). Oxford: Oxford University Press.

Salamon, L. M. (1993). The marketization of welfare: Changing nonprofit and for-profit roles in the American welfare state. *Social Service Review, 67*(1), 16–39.

Salamon, L. M. (1994, July/August). The rise of the nonprofit sector. *Foreign Affairs*. Retrieved from https://www.foreignaffairs.com/articles/1994-07-01/rise-nonprofit-sector

Salamon, L. M. (1995). *Partners in public service: Government-nonprofit relations in the modern welfare state*. Baltimore, MD: Johns Hopkins University Press.

Salamon, L. M., & Anheier, H. K. (1998). Social origins of civil society: Explaining the non-profit sector cross-nationally. *Voluntas, 9*(3), 213–248.

Salamon, L. M., Anheier, H. K., List, R., Toepler, S., & Sokolowski, S. W. (1999). *Global civil society: Dimensions of the nonprofit sector, Volume I*. Baltimore, MD: The Johns Hopkins Center for Civil Society Studies.

Salamon, L. M., Sokolowski, S. W., & Haddock, M. A. (2017). *Explaining civil society development: A social origins approach*. Baltimore: Johns Hopkins University Press.

Siemieńska, R., Domaradzka, A., & Matysiak, I. (2011). Local welfare in Poland from a historical and institutional perspective, Warsaw. *WILCO Publication No. 2*. Retrieved from http://www.wilcoproject.eu/national-reports-on-local-welfare-systems-focused-on-housing-employment-and-child-care/

Siemieńska, R., Domaradzka, A., & Matysiak, I. (2016). Warsaw: Paving new ways for participation of mothers, fathers, and children in local public and social life—The MaMa Foundation. In T. Brandsen, S. Cattacin, A. Evers, & A. Zimmer (Eds.), *Social innovations in the urban context* (pp. 181–188). New York: Springer (Open Access).

Simsa, R., Herndler, M., & Simic, Z. (2015). Third sector barriers in Austria. *TSI National Report No. 3*. Retrieved from http://thirdsectorimpact.eu/documentation/tsi-national-report-no-3-third-sector-barriers-in-austria/

Simsa, R., Herndler, M., & Totter, M. (2015). Meta-analysis of SROI studies—Indicators and proxies. *TSI Working Paper Series No. 6*, Seventh Framework Programme (grant agreement 613034), European Union. Brussels: Third Sector Impact.

Sivesind, K.-H. (2017). The changing roles of for-profit and nonprofit welfare provision in Norway, Sweden and Denmark. In K.-H. Sivesind & J. Saglie (Eds.), *Promoting active citizenship? Markets and choice in Scandinavian welfare*. London: Palgrave Macmillan.

Staggenborg, S. (2013). Institutionalization of social movements. In D. Snow, D. della Porta, B. Klandermans, & D. McAdam (Eds.), *The Wiley-Blackwell encyclopedia of social and political movements*. Oxford, UK: Wiley-Blackwell.

Steger, M. B., & Roy, R. K. (2010). *Neoliberalism: A very short introduction*. Oxford: Oxford University Press.

Trætteberg, H. S., & Sivesind, K.-H. (2015). Ideelle organisasjoners særtrekk og merverdi på helse- og omsorgsfeltet (Rapport 2015:2). Oslo: Senter for forskning på sivilsamfunn og frivillig sektor. Retrieved from http://sivilsamfunn.no/content/download/108121/1857028/file/VR_2015_2_V4_nett.pdf

Vabø, M., Christensen, K., Jacobsen, F. F., & Trætteberg, H. D. (2013). Marketisation in Norwegian eldercare: Preconditions, trends and resistance. In G. Meagher & M. Szebehely (Eds.), *Marketisation in Nordic eldercare: A research report on legislation, oversight, extent and consequences* (pp. 163–202). Stockholm: Department of Social Work, Stockholm University.

Venables, T. (2014). Panoramic view of the funding problems of the third sector and the social economy in the European Union. *Revista Espanola del Tercer Sector, 27*.

Wijkström, F. (2011). Charity speak and business talk: The on-going (re)hybridization of civil society. In F. Wijkström & A. Zimmer (Eds.), *Nordic civil societies at a cross-roads* (pp. 27–54). Baden-Baden: Nomos.

Wijkström, F., & Zimmer, A. (2011). *Nordic civil societies at a cross-roads. Transforming the popular movement tradition*. Baden-Baden: Nomos.

Zimmer, A. (Ed.). (2013). *Civil societies compared: Germany and the Netherlands*. Baden-Baden: Nomos.

Zimmer, A. (2014). Money makes the world go round! Ökonomisierung und die Folgen für NPOs. In A. Zimmer & R. Simsa (Eds.), *Forschung zu Zivilgesellschaft, NPOs und Engagement* (pp. 163–180). Wiesbaden: Springer VS-Verlag.

Zimmer, A., Appel, A., Dittrich, C., Lange, C., Sitterman, B., Stallmann, F., et al. (2009). Germany: On the social policy centrality of the Free Welfare Associations. In J. Kendall (Ed.), *Handbook on third sector policy in Europe: Multi-level processes and organized civil society* (pp. 21–42). Aldershot: Edward Elgar.

Zimmer, A., & Hoemke, P. (2016). Riders on the storm. TSOs and the European Level of Government—A contested terrain. *TSI Working Paper No. 11*.

Retrieved from http://thirdsectorimpact.eu/documentation/tsi-working-paper-no-11-riders-storm/

Zimmer, A., & Pahl, B. (2016). Comparative report: Learning from Europe—Report on third sector enabling and disabling factors. *TSI Comparative Report No. 1*. Retrieved from http://thirdsectorimpact.eu/documentation/comparative-report-learning-europe/

Open Access This chapter is distributed under the terms of the Creative Commons Attribution 4.0 International License (http://creativecommons.org/licenses/by/4.0/), which permits use, duplication, adaptation, distribution and reproduction in any medium or format, as long as you give appropriate credit to the original author(s) and the source, a link is provided to the Creative Commons license and any changes made are indicated.

The images or other third party material in this chapter are included in the work's Creative Commons license, unless indicated otherwise in the credit line; if such material is not included in the work's Creative Commons license and the respective action is not permitted by statutory regulation, users will need to obtain permission from the license holder to duplicate, adapt or reproduce the material.

6

The Road Ahead: A Policy Agenda for the Third Sector in Europe

Bernard Enjolras

As the previous chapters made clear, the third sector in Europe is under the strain of various forces—individualization, bureaucratization and marketization—endangering third sector organizations' (TSOs') distinctive features and sustainability. The third sector has the third largest workforce in Europe and yet is invisible and lacks recognition as an economic and social force and as an interlocutor in policymaking at the European level. Our research shows that changes in the social, economic and political environment in which TSOs operate—mostly due to increased financial pressures and the introduction of market-based financing and regulatory mechanisms—are jeopardizing the sustainability of the third sector in Europe and, more importantly, increasingly undermining the distinctiveness and civic character of TSOs. Our comparative research has also uncovered innovative strategies of resilience that have enabled TSOs to tackle and cope with these challenges, though often

B. Enjolras (✉)
Institute for Social Research (ISF), Oslo, Norway
e-mail: bernard.enjolras@socialresearch.no

© The Author(s) 2018
B. Enjolras et al., *The Third Sector As A Renewable Resource for Europe*,
https://doi.org/10.1007/978-3-319-71473-8_6

with consequences that threaten the distinctiveness that has long made the third sector a positive force on the continent.

The market and bureaucratic impulses appear to be gaining the upper hand across Europe—and significantly displacing the voluntaristic and civic ones that have historically characterized this sector. Although there are significant differences across countries and civil society models depending on their institutional arrangements and public policies, this developmental trend is evident to some extent everywhere and is of importance since it puts TSOs under a survival watch, privileging adaptation strategies that pay primary attention to what has to be done in order to survive. Survival strategies may be detrimental to these organizations' distinctiveness and civic character, that is, what makes TSOs special. To be sure, these two orientations, survival and distinctiveness, are not necessarily in conflict, as illustrated by innovative resilience strategies developed by TSOs that have managed to adapt to a more competitive and market-oriented environment while retaining their distinctiveness and civic orientation. Whether such innovative resilience strategies will prevail is, to a large extent, dependent on the political environment of the third sector.[1]

1 Three Scenarios

Given the tendencies and the changes characterizing the environment of TSOs in Europe, how should the sector and its stakeholders respond and what supports will be needed? Fundamentally, three main scenarios are possible.

In the first scenario—*the return to the golden age scenario*—TSOs would prioritize the imperative of maintaining their distinctiveness and civic character when facing financial pressures and the increased marketization of the fields in which they operate. They would turn their backs on the government funding that is pulling them away from their distinctive character and rely more heavily on volunteering and philanthropic giving to sustain and protect their civic orientation. However, TSOs may lose

---

[1] This paragraph, and the section that follows, draw heavily on a similar diagnostic set of scenarios outlined in Lester M. Salamon, *The Resilient Sector Revisited: The New Challenge to Nonprofit America*. Washington: Brookings Institution Press, 2015.

ground and be increasingly out-performed by for-profit actors delivering public services in a market-based regulatory environment.

In a second scenario—*the drift or commercialization of the third sector scenario*—TSOs would prioritize the survival imperative, adapting to their increasingly marketized environment, even if this costs losing their distinctiveness and civic character. They may rely increasingly on market resources and redesign their activities in order to serve the profitable part of the market and secure public procurement contracts in competition with for-profit actors. By doing so, they may become increasingly isomorphic with their for-profit competitors and abandon their mission-critical functions, acting as any other commercial actors.

In a third scenario, *the civic economy scenario*, TSOs would adapt to their transformed environment without losing their distinctiveness. They would strive to balance the imperatives of survival and distinctiveness by finding innovative solutions. In this scenario, TSOs would rethink and redesign their roles and activities in light of the economic and institutional transformations of their environment, sustaining their economic sustainability without sacrificing their mission orientation.

2 The Civic Economy Strategy: A Policy Agenda for Europe

Which of these scenarios will prevail depends to a great extent on the nature of the policy environment created by the EU, the national governments and the regional and local authorities in each European country. A strategy for fostering the development of a *civic economy* that is adapted to the realities of public finances in Europe and preserves the distinctiveness and socioeconomic contribution of the third sector in Europe needs to act on the following dimensions.

2.1 Improving the Legitimacy and Visibility of the Third Sector in Europe

Despite the third sector's remarkable contribution to the well-being of European citizens in terms of social service provision, opportunities and space for leisure activities, and despite the sector's voice function and its significant importance as a transmitter of interests and needs of the citizens, the third sector in Europe is still an unknown entity, almost invisible in the national statistics and hardly acknowledged by Eurostat. What is needed throughout Europe and in Brussels is to get the third sector out of the shadows and into the limelight of public awareness. TSOs and the sector have to be appreciated as a vital element of Europe's cultural heritage and diversity. Also, the sector's impact as a growing economic force outdistancing most major European industries in the scale of its workforce has finally to be appreciated. And the sector's political and communicative potentials, its voice function as well as its capacity to serve as an activator and incubator of citizens' engagement and volunteering, have to finally to be put up front.

However, how is this to be accomplished? How is the awareness for the achievements and potentials of the sector and its organizations to be increased? We put forward the following policy recommendations with the aim of structurally enhancing the visibility of the third sector and its organizations all over Europe and in Brussels.

2.1.1 Improvement of the Sector's Knowledge Base

As a crucial first step, a solid database of European third sector activity is necessary for assessing the societal, economic and political impact of the sector within the European Union. There is a decisive lack of solid statistical information on the sector and its organizations at the European level and throughout Europe. In some countries, there has been significant progress in this respect over the last decades. However, there is no concerted action across Europe. Fortunately, the United Nations Statistics Division, which oversees the System of National Accounts, the guidance system for economic data gathering around the world, has just completed work on a new handbook designed to stimulate precisely this—a comprehensive, official body of comparative statistical data on the third sector as conceptualized by this project, embracing carefully defined in-scope nonprofit organizations, cooperatives, mutuals, social enterprises and volunteer activities. We need a European task force working with the aim of convincing the national statistical offices and Eurostat to implement this *Satellite Account on Nonprofit and Related Institutions and Volunteer Work* on a priority basis to bring the European third sector out of the shadows. And we need the European Commission to provide the resources needed to underwrite the costs of the initial integration of this handbook into the statistical systems of member states. Furthermore, there are some areas of TSO activity that are worse off than others. One of these is the area of arts and culture that is also closely linked to identity building and hence to the spirit or soul of Europe. As the results of the third sector impact (TSI) project reveal, research on the impact of the third sector and its organizations is still in its infancy, and some areas of third sector activity, most prominently arts and culture, are thoroughly neglected and overlooked. To make the impact of the sector visible, the European Community has to invest in research and data gathering with a focus on third sector activities. It might be advisable for the European Commission to establish a Third Sector Research Fund to finance a robust program of research as a follow-up to the Third Sector Impact Project.

2.1.2 Enhance Visibility through European Statutes for TSOs

European legal stipulations for third sector activities would significantly contribute to the growth of the sector in Europe. Currently, there is not a commonly shared understanding of the third sector in Europe. In some countries, reflecting the Mediterranean and French social economy tradition, third sector activities are perceived as being commensurate with business endeavors; in other European regions, the third sector is looked upon as a synonym for voluntary activity based on the principle of reciprocity. Still today, legal stipulations strongly reflect the regional traditions and legacies of history of the various European countries. But diversity and variation with respect to the legal forms definitely stand in the way of the development of a European third sector identity. In addition, the variety of legal forms translates into a significant hurdle for data gathering. Finally, umbrellas of TSOs working in Brussels are faced with significant difficulties in speaking with just one voice when they stand for legally very different constituencies. Introducing European Statutes for third sector service providers, voluntary associations and foundations would definitely be a big step ahead in the direction of the Europeanization of the sector.

2.1.3 Make the Voice of the Sector Heard

A decisive lack of infrastructural backing in terms of support organizations as well as "umbrellas" that are able to give a voice to the needs of TSOs and volunteers at the various levels of European governance, in Brussels and in the capitals of Europe, turned out to be a significant deficiency of the sector throughout Europe. There are many reasons why it is necessary to facilitate the establishment of third sector support infrastructures. In countries without a long tradition of third sector social service provision, TSOs operating in close cooperation with the government are perceived as semi-public organizations that sometimes are prone to clientelism or even corruption. Umbrellas of the sector are necessary to help TSOs in these countries escape the legitimacy gap. In countries looking back upon a long tradition of partnership with the government, it is increasingly necessary to draw attention to the distinctiveness of TSOs. These organizations are major employers; they speak to the needs of increasingly heterogeneous communities, and due to their economic strength, they are in a position to voice the negative side of neoliberal marketization. However, even the big players of the third sector need umbrellas, in particular in Brussels, in order to make their claims heard. Therefore, beyond setting up and supporting "umbrellas," stakeholders suggested establishing ombudsmen and/or ombudswomen for the third sector and its organizations inside key political institutions, such as the European and National Parliaments. Furthermore, public awareness nowadays constitutes an outcome of media coverage. Here, the sector and its organizations are significantly overlooked. There is some notice of the sector and its achievements when major humanitarian or ecological disasters happen throughout the world. However, the media thoroughly falls short in providing a realistic and simultaneously appealing picture of the sector and its organizations. Instead, the media looks out for cases of embezzlement and cases of corruption. If there is no broker in terms of umbrella organizations working on behalf of the sector, there is little chance that lack of awareness of the sector does not change into skepticism or even mistrust.

2.1.4 Help TSOs to Market Themselves

TSOs not only need "umbrellas" to make their voice heard in the wider public and in the political arena; they also need support to adapt to a significantly changed environment. They need help to modernize themselves, particularly with respect to both public relations and marketing. Although new web-based technologies carry enormous potentials, TSOs are limited in their capacity to adapt to technological change. Particularly small- and medium-sized TSOs embedded in local communities and working primarily with volunteers face difficulties in addressing the public with the help of new technology. They are, as our stakeholders indicate, simply not accustomed and also not well equipped to address all these new publics that are of increasing importance for both the visibility of the organization and the new modes of acquiring resources or organizing constituencies. For sure, civic actions are increasingly organized on the net (e.g. flash mobs); with the support of the net, citizens also increasingly arrange ad-hoc sporting activities; additionally, campaigns are progressively formed within social media, and volunteers gather on social platforms for joint community action. The success story of crowd funding was primarily made possible by the World Wide Web. Furthermore, many of the activities organized via the web take place outside formal organizations. This trend might result in a situation in which TSOs are losing relevance to European citizens. Doubtlessly, modern communication technology is providing new ways of organizing support and of informing and empowering people and therefore constitutes a valuable asset for the third sector. Consequently, TSOs should increasingly make use of technological and communication tools in order to develop their potential as social impact generators. However, the technological know-how of TSOs is by and large rather limited, primarily used by larger TSOs and furthermore restrained by either the nonexistence of or limited access to TSO-support organizations. The need for help and assistance is particularly prominent in areas of TSO activity beyond social service provision, such as the arts and culture. There is urgency for building up infrastructural support organizations and *intermediaries* to facilitate access to modern communication technology. Philanthropy, but also public funders, should invest in infrastructural support organizations that address the needs of TSOs active in certain fields and areas. This could serve as a structural backbone for those new demands that come with technological change.

2.1.5 Get the Public Back In—Provide Space for Third Sector Activities

Small TSOs engaged in sports, arts and culture or other community-based areas are increasingly facing the difficulty of finding "space" and facilities for their activities all over Europe. In metropolitan areas with rising shortages of residential space, it also has become increasingly difficult for TSOs that are active in interest representation to find places for encounters and gatherings. Due to gentrification, areas and locations that used to be public spaces are converted into upscale real estate or commercial centers. In municipalities under austerity regimes, public facilities such as gyms, auditoriums, exhibitions or concert halls are often in very poor condition and in urgent need of renovation. Since municipalities have to make money, renting these spaces has turned into a costly affair. On the other hand, the majority of small and middle-sized TSOs are not able to afford operating their own venues and facilities. Consequently, compared with commercial providers, many TSOs, in particular, sport clubs, but also those who are active in the arts and culture, have lost attractiveness, and they are limited in pursuing their specific activities. This has a decisive effect on local community life, as arts and culture, as well as sports, are the most popular areas of volunteer commitment; the venues of these TSOs serve as points of crystallization for social life in neighborhoods. Local governments should be aware that there is an urgent need for public spaces and facilities in order to enrich and sustain community life. Simultaneously, national governments and the European Union should finally recognize that the provision and maintenance of public facilities and public spaces constitute a solid investment into the future of Europe. And finally, TSOs could also help get the public back by pooling their resources and cooperating in acquiring and maintaining facilities.

2.2 Improving Third Sector Finances and Government-Third Sector Partnership

In addition to improving TSO legitimacy and visibility, a second broad set of strategies is needed to address third sector finances and government-third sector partnerships. All over Europe, TSOs are struggling to make ends meet. The reasons why TSOs are facing a hard time are manifold. As the results of the TSI project indicate, acquisition of resources, finances and personnel, has changed significantly for TSOs during the last decades. Partly, this constitutes an outcome of modified TSO-government relations caused by the neoliberal-inspired introduction of competitive markets for social services and instruments of new public management (NPM), such as competitive tendering or contract management. But other factors are also at work, and several steps will be needed to address this strategic priority.

2.2.1 Get Structural Funds Back In

In the first place, there is an urgent need for structural funds all over Europe in order to safeguard the durability and sustainability of both TSOs and government-third sector cooperation. All over Europe, public funding nowadays is by and large based on temporary contracts. Furthermore, governments have generally shifted from so-called institutional or structural funding to temporary funding related to specified projects. Therefore, TSOs that bounce from one project to another have less and less capacity for building up and maintaining an organizational infrastructure that safeguards stability and allows quick responses to new challenges. The need for more sustainable funding is very acute in those regions where TSOs are not accepted partners of public service delivery, such as in Eastern Europe and the Mediterranean region. Furthermore,

TSOs that are active in leisure and community-oriented areas such as arts and culture or sports, where the sector consists of myriads of small organizations, small structural funds would significantly contribute to a more sustainable development of the sector. European foundations also have a role to play in providing such core support. There is no way that those TSOs can exclusively live on so-called project money. They are in need of long-term structural public and private support that constitutes a bottom-up approach and an investment into sustainable community development.

2.2.2 Lift up the Burden of Procurement Procedures

The introduction of NPM has had a decisive impact on third sector-government relations, and particularly on the modes of financing. Funding for TSOs is increasingly acquired through competitive grants and contracts. As a result of the new funding environment, third sector bureaucratization has developed into a major obstacle impacting negatively on TSOs. The accountability requirements accompanying procurement have increased significantly during the last decades all over Europe. This translates into a situation in which TSOs have to allocate more and more resources to complying with the administrative requirements of applying, reporting and evaluating grants and contracts instead of devoting time and energy for "doing the right thing" and supporting the community. Urgently needed at every level of governance in Europe are new modes of procurement that take the specificity of TSOs into account. Again, TSOs are not proxies for commercial enterprises. Modes of procurement have to be reevaluated and ideally homogenized throughout Europe. They should also incorporate a so-called social clause—giving priority in public procurement to TSOs having a social impact—that will ease competition between TSOs and for-profits; they should provide modes for cooperation between governments and TSOs that are tailored toward the needs of TSOs; they should specify tasks and functions for both sides in order to enhance cooperation instead of creating a culture of surveillance; and finally, without losing attention to accountability, they should simplify monitoring and evaluation procedures. The need to reduce the complexity of procurement procedures is especially necessary at the European level. EU-procurement and funding procedures are far too complicated for the majority of European TSOs. There is a decisive need to adapt the European directive on public procurement to the needs of TSOs and, in particular, to those active in interest representation and lobbying. In addition, the European directive on VAT needs to be altered. A more favorable tax framework has to be introduced that envisages a reduction of VAT for TSOs and that makes tax reimbursement for TSOs possible. Moreover, the policies of matching funds for EU-grants have to be changed. It should be made possible to use specific third sector resources, for example, voluntary work, as an equivalent to money, in order to pave the way for smaller organizations to get access to EU-support.

2.2.3 Facilitate Access to Capital Markets and to Alternative Sources of Financing

As the results of the TSI project clearly show, public money is no longer the prime source of income for TSOs in several fields of activities. Despite increasingly competitive environments, the economic success story of the sector has been impressive in Europe. Nevertheless, TSOs are not yet treated on an equal footing with for-profit enterprises. This is particularly the case with respect to their access to capital markets. Banks and other financing institutions are very reluctant to do business with TSOs. Additionally, most TSOs cannot access equity finance due to their non-profit distribution constraint and legal inability to share ownership with shareholders. A change of culture is needed as well as an empowerment strategy for TSOs supporting them in getting access to capital markets and in experimenting with new modes of financing such as crowd funding, social loans and cooperation with ethical banks.[2]

---

[2] For a discussion of how this can be done, see Lester M. Salamon, *Leverage for Good: An Introduction to the New Frontiers of Philanthropy and Social Investment*. New York: Oxford University Press, 2014a; and Lester M. Salamon, ed. *The New Frontiers of Philanthropy: A Guide to the New Actos and Tools Reshaping Global Philanthropy and Social Investment*. Oxford: Oxford University Press, 2014b.

3 Fostering Foundations' Supportive Role of the Third Sector in Europe

Philanthropic institutions and especially foundations have the potential to become the backbone of the third sector; they should play a critical role in canalizing private funds to value-oriented projects emanating from third sector initiatives and as supporters of the entire European third sector by helping building up its visibility and capacity. As of now, most foundations in Europe assume no responsibility for the sector as a whole. Yet, they are the only source of alternative funding (to public funding) for these sector-wide objectives.

Because foundations have limited resources, they need to act strategically orienting the use of their limited funds to activities to maximize leverage and impact. Paul Brest and Hal Harvey capture the basic issues and motivation of strategic philanthropy: "Accomplishing philanthropic goals requires having great clarity about what those goals are and specifying indicators of success before beginning a philanthropic project. (…) This, in turn, requires an empirical, evidence-based understanding of the external world in which the plan will operate" (Brest and Harvey 2008: 7). Supporting the third sector as a whole by helping TSOs to build their capacity constitutes a prioritized avenue for European foundations to maximize their impact. By helping build the capacity of the third sector as a whole, they will generate broader socioeconomic impacts than by just focusing on particular projects.

4 Improving the Attractiveness of TSOs

A third broad strategy needed to sustain the core capabilities and values of the third sector in Europe is to improve the overall attractiveness of TSOs to their fundamental constituencies. The new culture of volunteering, which is characterized by a high degree of volatility, significantly affects membership affiliation and the concept of the voluntary association that used to be the nucleus and core concept of European TSOs. Indeed, there is a real danger that the third sector in its current contours and how it has developed in Europe over the years will not be capable of continuing to be a thriving societal force in Europe that gives people a voice, provides opportunities for community and leisure activities and, last but not least, constitutes an important provider of social services, contributing to the community life and well-being of European citizens. The environment of TSOs needs to be enhanced in order to increase the attractiveness of these organizations for volunteers and paid staff. However, TSOs need to improve awareness of their values and distinctive features.

4.1 Renewing the Third Sector's Values

At the center of the civic economy scenario must be a clarification of the third sector's values, the distinctive qualities and attributes that TSOs bring to society in Europe. The third sector's distinctive contribution is closely related to a set of values such as equity, openness, empowerment, participation, responsiveness and commitment to the enrichment of human life. The marketization of the sector, accompanied by an emphasis on metrics that privileges the service function of TSOs, contributes to the downplaying of these values. Making these values visible and clearly articulated for the sector as a whole and for particular organizations will be crucial for the success of the civic economy renewal of the third sector and the sustainability of its specific contribution to society in Europe.

4.2 Increase the Attractiveness of TSOs as Employers

Despite high qualifications and outstanding commitment, TSO-employees are faced with deteriorating working conditions. Low salaries, which are not comparable with those paid in the commercial sector, constitute a further outcome of the changed environment and funding situation of TSOs in several parts of the third sector. Consequently, working in the third sector becomes increasingly unattractive. Particularly in areas where the mental and physical stress is high, TSOs face serious problems to recruit highly qualified personnel. Hence, it is most likely that in the near future the quality of services will deteriorate as TSOs have to employ less professional personnel and reduce personnel costs per service unit. Women are particularly hit hard by the degraded working conditions in the sector, as they account for the largest part of the sector's labor force. Introduction of collective wage agreements in prominent areas of the sector, for example, social services, provide an effective tool for stopping the ruinous competition for contracts. TSOs are called upon to agree with their employees on fair labor standards throughout the sector. In addition, the specificity of third sector management and governance has hardly been recognized by institutions of higher education throughout Europe. Our stakeholders time and again indicated that there is a decisive lack of training facilities and courses tailored to the needs of third sector managers who have to get along with a broad spectrum of very different constituencies and who also should never lose track of the mission and vision of the respective TSO.

4.3   Increase the Attractiveness of TSOs for Volunteers

Volunteers are a pivotal source of legitimacy, community orientation and embeddedness for TSOs. However, volunteer engagement is not free. All over Europe, there is a trend for more flexible, fluid and tailor-made forms of volunteering. Life-long commitment to a specific TSO, as used to be the case in former times, no longer reflects the reality of volunteering in Europe today. The modernized culture of volunteering is also characterized by a new expressiveness of volunteers. They have become more vocal about their voluntary commitment. Nowadays, volunteers want to decide how they become active, how long they volunteer and where they specifically get engaged. This new voluntarism forces TSOs to install procedures of continuing infrastructural support, indeed, volunteer management. It also requires further training of volunteers as well as of the TSO-personnel who are in charge of coordinating and monitoring volunteer work.

4.4   Increase the Attractiveness of TSOs for Honorary Board Members

A dual governance structure that encompasses honorary board members or trustees and full-time professional managers still seems to be an appropriate governance model for many TSOs in Europe. However, as indicated by our research and by many of our stakeholders, there are escalating problems around recruitment for governance roles, particularly with respect to the honorary positions of board members. Again, the reasons for this development are manifold and closely related to the increased responsibilities of board members, which are partly a result of the changed procurement procedures. In addition, in local communities, there nowadays are many opportunities to get involved and to serve in prestigious positions without being responsible for hundreds of employees or millions of Euros. In order to safeguard the local embeddedness of TSOs through community trusteeship and honorary board members, those who are willing to be engaged have to be supported and provided with task- oriented training programs and courses that indeed speak to their needs.

5 Conclusion

In a time when Europe faces economic and social developments characterized by accelerated technological changes, increased globalization of world markets, increased migration flows and a shift in the economic opportunity structure creating rising inequalities among individuals and national communities, the collective capacity embedded in the third sector constitutes a major factor of social resilience (Hall and Lamont 2013) of Europe.

Indeed, when facing the challenges posed by rapid socioeconomic transformations, entailing economic reorganization, social dislocation and redistributive effects, the capacity of groups and communities to adapt to transformations and to secure their well-being in spite of these transformations—their degree of resilience—is dependent upon their collective capacities. Individuals' social resilience, their capacity to mobilize resources and solidarities, is enhanced by social organization. TSOs and the third sector in its entirety, in interplay with the state, play a crucial role in enhancing social resilience by fostering social solidarities, social capital, capacities for collective action, and the provision of collective goods.

The third sector and volunteering truly represent a unique "renewable resource for social and environmental problem-solving" for Europe. The results of our research have provided evidence supporting this claim. They have also shown that the third sector in Europe is subject to major changes and challenges. The future developmental path of Europe depends not only on its economy and polity, but also on the dynamism of its third sector. Policy adjustments are needed in order to support a dynamic third sector in Europe and preserve the distinctiveness of the organizations that compose it. However, these policy adjustments will not take place without a better public understanding of the state of the third sector in Europe. Hopefully, the analysis developed in this report will contribute to such an understanding.

References

Brest, P., & Harvey, H. (2008). *Money well spent: A strategic plan for smart philanthropy*. New York: Bloomberg Press.
Hall, P. A., & Lamont, M. (2013). *Social resilience in the neoliberal era*. New York: Cambridge University Press.
Salamon, L. M. (2014a). *Leverage for good: An introduction to the new frontiers of philanthropy and social investment*. New York: Oxford University Press.
Salamon, L. M. (2014b). *The new frontiers of philanthropy: A guide to the new actos and tools reshaping global philanthropy and social investment*. Oxford: Oxford University Press.
Salamon, L. M. (2015). *The resilient sector revisited: The future of nonprofit America* (2nd ed.). Washington, DC: Brookings Institution.

Open Access This chapter is distributed under the terms of the Creative Commons Attribution 4.0 International License (http://creativecommons.org/licenses/by/4.0/), which permits use, duplication, adaptation, distribution and reproduction in any medium or format, as long as you give appropriate credit to the original author(s) and the source, a link is provided to the Creative Commons license and any changes made are indicated.

The images or other third party material in this chapter are included in the work's Creative Commons license, unless indicated otherwise in the credit line; if such material is not included in the work's Creative Commons license and the respective action is not permitted by statutory regulation, users will need to obtain permission from the license holder to duplicate, adapt or reproduce the material.

References

Alcock, P., & Kendall, J. (2011). Constituting the third sector: Processes of decontestation and contention under the UK Labour governments in England. *Voluntas: International Journal of Voluntary and Non-profit Organisations, 22*(3), 450.

Almond, G. A., & Verba, S. (1963). *The civic culture: Political attitudes and democracy in five nations.* Boston: Little, Brown and Company.

Amin, A., Cameron, A., & Hudson, R. (2002). *Placing the social economy.* London: Routledge.

Angrist, J. D., & Pischke, J. S. (2009). *Mostly harmless econometrics.* Princeton, NJ: Princeton University Press.

Archambault, E. (1997). *The nonprofit sector in France.* Manchester: Manchester University Press.

Archambault, E., Priller, E., & Zimmer, A. (2013). European civil societies compared: Typically German—Typically French? *Voluntas: International Journal of Voluntary and Non-profit Organisations, 24*(1), 1–24.

Armingeon, K. (2007). Political participation and associational involvement. In J. W. van Depth, J. R. Montero, & A. Westhilm (Eds.), *Citizenship and involvement in European democracies.* London: Routledge.

Bandura, A. (2000). Exercise of human agency through collective efficacy. *Current Directions in Psychological Science, 9*(3), 75–78.

Banfield, E. (1958). *The moral basis of a backward society.* New York: Free Press.

Barea, J., & Monzón, J. L. (2006). *Manual for drawing up the satellite accounts of companies in the social economy: Co-operatives and mutual societies.* Liege: CIRIEC.
Baturina, D., & Bežovan, G. (2015). Social innovation impact-review. *TSI Working Paper No. 9*, Seventh Framework Programme (grant agreement 613034), European Union. Brussels: Third Sector Impact.
Beck, U. (Ed.). (1997). *Kinder der Freiheit.* (Edition Zweite Moderne). Frankfurt: Suhrkamp Verlag.
Benz, M. (2005). Not for the profit, but for the satisfaction? Evidence on worker well-being in non-profit firms. *Kyklos, 58*(2), 155–176.
Bežovan, G. (2004). *Civilno društvo.* Zagreb: Nakladni zavod Globus.
Bežovan, G. (2016). The role and impact of the Third Sector in transformative process: A comparison of post-socialist countries Slovenia, Czech Republic and Croatia. *TSI Working Paper Series No. 13*, Seventh Framework Programme (grant agreement 613034), European Union. Brussels: Third Sector Impact.
Bežovan, G., Matančević, J., & Baturina, D. (2016). Identifying external and internal barriers to third sector development—CROATIA. *TSI National Report No. 5.* Retrieved from http://thirdsectorimpact.eu/documentation/tsi-national-report-no-5-identifying-external-internal-barriers-thirdsector-development-croatia/.
Bjørnskov, C. (2006). Determinants of generalized trust: A cross-country comparison. *Public Choice, 130*, 1–21.
Boje, T. P., Fridberg, T., & Ibsen, B. (2006). Den frivillige sektor i Danmark. Omfang og betydning (Rapport 06:19). København: Socialforskningsinstituttet. Retrieved from http://www.sfi.dk/Admin/Public/DWSDownload.aspx?File=%2fFiles%2fFiler%2fSFI%2fPdf%2fRapporter%2f2006%2f0619_Den_frivillige_sektor.pdf
Boje, T. P., & Potucek, M. (Eds.). (2011). *Social rights, active citizenship, and governance in the European Union.* Baden-Baden: Nomos Verlag.
Borgonovi, F. (2008). Doing well by doing good. The relationship between formal volunteering and self-reported health and happiness. *Social Science & Medicine, 66*, 2321–2334.
Bornstein, D. (2004). *How to change the world: Social entrepreneurs and the power of new ideas.* New York: Oxford University Press.
Borzaga, C., & Defourny, J. (Eds.). (2001). *The emergence of social enterprise.* London and New York: Routledge.
Borzaga, C., & Tortia, E. (2006). Worker motivations, job satisfaction, and loyalty in public and nonprofit social services. *Nonprofit and Voluntary Sector Quarterly, 35*(2), 225–248.

Brandsen, T. (2011). Social services in the Netherlands—Position and authority of non-profit sector organizations. In A. Zimmer (Ed.), *Jenseits von Bier und Tulpen* (pp. 75–86). Münster: Waxmann Verlag.

Brandsen, T., & Pape, U. (2016). Barriers to third sector development in the Netherlands. *TSI National Report No. 2*. Retrieved from http://thirdsectorimpact.eu/documentation/tsi-national-report-no-2-barriers-to-third-sector-development-in-the-netherlands/

Brest, P., & Harvey, H. (2008). *Money well spent: A strategic plan for smart philanthropy*. New York: Bloomberg Press.

Brooks, A. C. (2006). *Who really cares? The surprising truth about compassionate conservatism*. New York: Basic Books.

Brudney, J. L. (2010). Volunteers. In H. Anheier, S. Toepler, & R. A. List (Eds.), *International encyclopedia of civil society* (pp. 1620–1627). New York: Springer.

Caliendo, M., & Kopeinig, S. (2008). Some practical guidance for the implementation of propensity score matching. *Journal of Economic Surveys, 22*(1), 31–72.

Chabanet, D. (2016). Between traditions and changes: Institutional support to social economy in France. *Arnova Conference 2016* in Washington, DC.

Chambers, S., & Kopstein, J. (2001). Bad civil society. *Political Theory, 29*(6), 837–865.

Chambers, S., & Kymlicka, W. (Eds.). (2002). *Alternative conceptions of civil society*. Princeton: Princeton University Press.

Chandhoke, N. (2001). The 'civil' and the 'political' in civil society. *Democratization, 8*(2), 1–24.

Chanial, P., & Laville, J.-L. (2014). L'économie sociale et solidaire en France. In J.-L. Laville, J.-P. Magnen, G. Carvalho da Franca, & A. Medeiros (Eds.), *Action publique et économie solidaire* (pp. 47–73). Paris: Erès.

Chaves, R., Alguacil-Mari, P., Fajardor-Garcia, I. G., & Savall-Morera, T. (2016). Third sector barriers in Spain. *TSI National Report No. 8*. Retrieved from http://thirdsectorimpact.eu/documentation/tsi-national-report-no-8-third-sector-barriers-spain/

Chaves, R., & Monzón, J. L. (2012). Beyond the crisis: The social economy, prop of a new model of sustainable economic development. *Service Business: An international Journal, 6*(1), 5–26.

Claibourn, M., & Martin, P. (2000). Trusting and joining? An empirical test of the reciprocal nature of social capital. *Political Behavior, 22*(4), 269–291.

Cohen, J. L., & Arato, A. (1994). *Civil society and political theory*. Cambridge, MA: MIT Press.

Costa, L. P., & Andreaus, M. (Eds.). (2014). *Accountability and social accounting for social and non-profit organizations: Advances in social accounting* (Vol. 17). Bingley, UK: Emerald Group Publishing Limited.

Cummins, R. A. (2000). Objective and subjective quality of life: An interactive model. *Social Indicators Research, 52*, 55–72.

Davister, C., Defourny, J., & Grégoire, O. (2004). Work integration social enterprises in the European Union: An overview of existing models. *EMES Working Paper*. Retrieved from http://www.emes.net

Dedman, M. (2010). *The origins and development of the European Union 1945–2008: A history of European integration*. London: Routledge.

Defourny, J. (2001). From third sector to social enterprise. In C. Borzaga & J. Defourny (Eds.), *The emergence of social enterprise* (pp. 1–28). London and New York: Routledge.

Defourny, J. (2014). From third sector to social enterprise: A European research trajectory. In J. Defourny, L. Hulgard, & V. Pesthoff (Eds.), *Social enterprises and the third sector* (pp. 17–41). London and New York: Routledge.

Defourny, J., & Develtere, P. (1999). Social economy: North and South. In J. Defourny, P. Develtere, & B. Fonteneau (Eds.), *Social economy: The worldwide making of a third sector* (pp. 25–56). Brussels: De Boeck.

Defourny, J., Develtere, P., & Fonteneau, B. (Eds.). (1999). *L'économie sociale au Nord et au Sud*. Brussels and Paris: De Boeck.

Defourny, J., & Pestoff, V. (2014). Toward a European conceptualization of the third sector. In L. P. Costa & M. Andreaus (Eds.), *Accountability and social accounting for social and non-profit organizations: Advances in social accounting* (Vol. 17, pp. 1–61). Bingley, UK: Emerald Group Publishing Limited.

Dekker, P. (2004). The Netherlands. From private initiatives to non-profit hybrids and back? In A. Evers & J.-L. Laville (Eds.), *The third sector in Europe* (pp. 144–165). Cheltenham: Edward Elgar.

Delhey, J., & Newton, K. (2005). Predicting cross-national levels of social trust: Global pattern or Nordic exceptionalism? *European Sociological Review, 21*(4), 311–328.

Delors, J. (2004). The European Union and the third sector. In A. Evers & J. L. Laville (Eds.), *The third sector in Europe* (pp. 206–215). Cheltenham: Edward Elgar.

Deutsch, K. (1962). *The nerves of government: Models of political communication and control*. New York: Free Press.

Ebrahim, A., & Rangan, V. K. (2010). The limits of nonprofit impact: A contingency framework for measuring social performance. *Working Paper 10-099*, Harvard Business Scholl.

Edwards, M. (2004). *Civil society*. Cambridge: Polity Press.
Edwards, M. (2009). *Civil society*. Cambridge: Polity Press.
Edwards, M. (2011). *The Oxford handbook of civil society*. New York: Oxford University Press.
Elliot, C. M. (Ed.). (2003). *Civil society and democracy: A reader*. Oxford: Oxford University Press.
Elliott, C. M. (2003). Civil society and democracy: A comparative review essay. In C. M. Elliot (Ed.), *Civil society and democracy: A reader* (pp. 1–39). Oxford: Oxford University Press.
Enjolras, B. (2009). A governance-structure approach to voluntary organizations. *Nonprofit and Voluntary Sector Quarterly, 38*(5), 761–783.
Enjolras, B. (2015a). Measuring the impact of the third sector: From concept to metrics. *TSI Working Paper No. 5*, Seventh Framework Programme (grant agreement 613034), European Union. Brussels: Third Sector Impact.
Enjolras, B. (2015b). The impact of volunteering on volunteers in 23 European countries. *Third Sector Working Paper No. 4*, Seventh Framework Programme (grant agreement 613034), European Union. Brussels: Third Sector Impact.
Enjolras, B. (2016). Assessing the macro socio-economic impact of the third sector in Europe: Theoretical considerations and some empirical evidences. *TSI Working Paper Series No. 10*, Seventh Framework Programme (grant agreement 613034), European Union. Brussels: Third Sector Impact.
Erlandsson, S., Storm, P., Strantz, A., Szebehely, M., & Trydegård, G.-B. (2013). Marketising trends in Swedish eldercare: Competition, choice and calls for stricter regulation. In G. Meagher & M. Szebehely (Eds.), *Marketisation in Nordic eldercare: A research report on legislation, oversight, extent and consequences* (pp. 23–84). Stockholm: Department of Social Work, Stockholm University.
Erstellt vom Institut für interdisziplinäre Nonprofit Forschung an der Wirtschaftsuniversität Wien (NPO-Institut), Freiwilliges engagement in österreich. (2009). Wien. Retrieved from http://www.bmask.gv.at
European Commission. (2001). European Governance—A White Paper. COM(2001)428final.
European Commission. (2014). *A map of social enterprises and their eco-systems in Europe; (Country reports)*. European Union, 2014. Retrieved from http://ec.europa.eu/social/keyDocuments.jsp?pager.offset=0&&langId=en&mode=advancedSubmit&year=0&country=0&type=0&advSearchKey=socentcntryrepts&orderBy=docOrder
European Social Survey. (2012). Retrieved from http://www.europeansocialsurvey.org/data/download.html?r=6

Evers, A., & Laville, J.-L. (Eds.). (2004). *The third sector in Europe*. Cheltenham: Edward Elgar.
Fowler, A. (2002). Civil society research funding from a global perspective: A case for redressing bias, asymmetry and bifurcation. *Voluntas, 13*(3), 287–300.
Freise, M., & Zimmer, A. (2004). Der Dritte Sektor im wohlfahrtsstaatlichen Arrangement der post- sozialistischen Visegrád-Staaten. In A. Croissant, G. Erdmann, & F. W. Rüb (Eds.), *Wohlfahrtsstaatliche Politik in jungen Demokratien* (pp. 153–172). Wiesbaden: VS-Verlag.
Freitag, M. (2003). Social capital in (dis)similar democracies: The development of generalised trust in Japan and Switzerland. *Comparative Political Studies, 36*(8), 936–966.
Frič, P. (2009). The third sector and the policy process in the Czech Republic: Self-limited dynamics. In J. Kendal (Ed.), *Handbook on third sector policy in Europe-multi-level processes and organized civil society* (pp. 184–206). Cheltenham: Edward Elgar.
Fukuyama, F. (1995). *Trust: The social virtues and the creation of prosperity*. New York: Free Press.
Garton, J. (2009). *The regulation of organised civil society*. Oxford: Hart Publishing.
General Secretariat of the Council of the European Union. (2015, December). *The promotion of the social economy as a key driver of economic and social development in Europe* (Paras. 8,18, and 19. Doc No. 15071/15). Brussels.
Gidron, B., Kramer, R., & Salamon, L. M. (Eds.). (1992). *Government and the third sector: Emerging relationships in welfare states*. San Francisco: Jossey-Bass.
Główny Urząd Statystyczny, Wolontariat W Organizacjach I Inne Formy Pracy Niezarobkowej Poza Gospodarstwem Domowym. (2011). Volunteering through organizations and other types of unpaid work outside own household, 2011, Warszawa, 2012.
Golbeck, C. (2011). Auf der Suche nach produktiven Kompromissen—Wohlfahrtsverbände zwischen sozialem Anspruch und wirtschaftlicher Effizienz. In A. Zimmer (Ed.), *Jenseits von Bier und Tulpen* (pp. 87–109). Münster: Waxmann.
Golbeck, C. (2012). *Soziale Dienste in Europa zwischen Kooperation und Konkurrenz*. Freiburg: Lambertus.
Granovetter, M. (1973). The strength of weak ties. *American Journal of Sociology, 78*(6), 1360–1380.
Greffe, X. (2003). Innovation, value added and evaluation in the third system: A European perspective. In *The Non-profit Sector in a Changing Economy* (pp. 189–220). Paris: OECD.

Guo, S., & Fraser, M. W. (2015). *Propensity score analysis*. London: Sage.
Habermas, J. (1989). *The structural transformation of the public sphere: An inquiry into a category of bourgeois society*. Cambridge, MA: MIT Press.
Habermas, J. (1996). *Between facts and norms*. Cambridge: MIT Press.
Habermas, J. (1998). *Between facts and norms*. Cambridge: The MIT Press.
Hall, P. A., & Lamont, M. (2013). *Social resilience in the neoliberal era*. New York: Cambridge University Press.
Hansmann, H. (1980). The role of non profit enterprise. *Yale Law Journal, 89*(2), 835–898.
Hansmann, H. (1987). Economic theories of nonprofit organizations. In W. W. Powell (Ed.), *The nonprofit sector: A research handbook* (pp. 27–42). New Haven: Yale University Press.
Hatry, H. P. (1999). *Performance measurement: Getting results*. Washington, DC: The Urban Institute.
Havel, V., & Keane, J. (Eds.). (1985). *The power of the powerless: Citizens against the state in Central Eastern Europe*. London: Taylor and Francis.
Hegel, G. W. F. (1967). *The philosophy of rights*. Oxford: Oxford University Press.
Hegel, G. W. F. (1977). *The phenomenology of spirit*. Oxford: Oxford University Press.
Heinrich, V. F. (2005). Studying civil society across the world: Exploring the thorny issues of conceptualization and measurement. *Journal of Civil Society, 1*(3), 211–228.
Heins, V. (2002). *Das Andere der Zivilgesellschaft. Zur Archäologie eines Begriffs*. Bielefeld: Transcript.
Henriksen, L. S., Smith, S. R., & Zimmer, A. (2012). At the eve of convergence? Transformation of social service provision in Denmark, Germany, and the United States. *Voluntas, 23*(2), 458–501.
Hilson, M. (2010). The Nordic consumer co-operative movements. In R. Alapuro & H. Stenius (Eds.), *Nordic associations in a European perspective* (pp. 215–240). Baden-Baden: Nomos.
Hoemke, P., Pahl, B., Rentzsch, C., & Zimmer, A. (2016). External and internal barriers to third sector development in Germany. *TSI National Report No. 6*. Retrieved from http://thirdsectorimpact.eu/documentation/tsi-national-report-no-6-external-internal-barriers-third-sector-development-germany/
Howard, M., & Gilbert, L. (2008). A cross-national comparison of the internal effect of participation in voluntary organizations. *Political Studies, 56*, 12–32.
Howell, J., & Pearce, J. (2001). *Civil society and development: A critical exploration*. Denver: Lynne Rienner.

Howlett, S. (2011). *Volunteering and society in the 21st century*. Paper presented at the 21st IAVE World Volunteer Conference, January 24–27, Singapore.

Huntington, S. P. (1991). *The Third Wave: Democratization in the late 20th century*. Oklahoma: Oklahoma University Press.

International Labour Organization. (2011). *Manual on the measurement of volunteer work*. Geneva: International Labour Organization.

ISTAT. (2014). *Nonprofit institution profile based on 2011 census results*. Rome: Istituto nazionale di statistica. Retrieved from http://www.istat.it/en/files/2014/10/Nonprofit-Institution-Profile-based-on-2011-Census-results_EN_definitivo.pdf?title=Nonprofit+institutions+profile+-+9+Oct+2014+-+Full+text.pdf

Jacobs, J. (1961). *The death and life of great American cities*. New York: Random House.

Johnston, H., & Noakes, J. A. (2005). *Frames of protest: Social movements and the framing perspective*. Lanham: Rowman & Littlefield Publishers.

Julià, J. F., & Chaves, R. (2012). Introduction: Social economy, a third sector in a plural people- oriented economy. *Service Business: An International Journal*, 6(1), 1–4.

Kamerāde, D. (2015). Third sector impacts on human resources and community: A critical review. *Third Sector Impact Working Paper No. 3*, Seventh Framework Programme (grant agreement 613034), European Union. Brussels: Third Sector Impact.

Kamerāde, D., & Bennett, M. (2015). Unemployment, volunteering, subjective well-being and mental health. *TSI Working Paper Series No. 7*, Seventh Framework Programme (grant agreement 613034), European Union. Brussels: Third Sector Impact.

Kamerāde, D., Crotty, J., & Ljubownikow, S. (2016). Civil liberties and volunteering in six former Soviet Union countries. *Nonprofit and Voluntary Sector Quarterly*, 45(6), 1150–1168. https://doi.org/10.1177/0899764016649689.

Kaminski, P. (2005). Table1. The NPS in France, 2002 (version INSEE). Le compte des Institutions Sans But Lucratif (ISBL) en France (Année 2002). Paris: l'Institut National de la Statistique et des Études Économiques (INSEE).

Kawachi, I., Ichida, Y., Tampubolon, G., & Fujiwara, T. (2013). Causal inference in social capital research. in Kawachi, I, Takao, S., Subramian, S.V., (eds.), *Global perspective on social capital and health*. New York: Springer.

Kawashi, I., & Berkman, L. F. (2014). Social capital, social cohesion, and health. In L. F. Berkman, I. Kawachi, & M. M. Glymour (Eds.), *Social epidemiology* (pp. 290–319). Oxford: Oxford University Press.

Keane, J. (1998). *Civil society: Old images, new visions.* Stanford: Stanford University Press.
Kendall, J., Brookes, N., & Mohan, J. (2016a). Identifying external and internal barriers to third sector development in the UK. *TSI Working Paper Series No. 1,* Seventh Framework Programme (grant agreement 613034), European Union. Brussels: Third Sector Impact.
Kendall, J., Brookes, N., & Mohan, J. (2016b). The English third sector policy in 2015: An overview of perceived barriers to realizing impact potential, Summary of research findings for Work Package 5. *TSI Policy Brief No. 3.* Retrieved from http://thirdsectorimpact.eu/documentation/tsi-barriers-briefing-no-1-english-third-sector-policy-in-2015/
Kendall, J., & Knapp, M. (1996). *The voluntary sector in the UK.* Manchester: Manchester University Press.
Kendall, J., & Thomas, G. (1996). The legal position of the voluntary sector in the UK. In J. Kendall & M. Knapp (Eds.), *The voluntary sector in the UK.* Manchester: Manchester University Press.
Kendall, J., Will, C., & Brandsen, T. (2009). The third sector and the Brussels dimension: Trans-EU governance work in progress. In J. Kendall (Ed.), *Handbook on third sector policy in Europe. Multi-level processes and organized civil society* (pp. 341–381). Cheltenham: Edward Elgar.
Klein, A., Kern, K., Geißel, B., & Berer, M. (Eds.). (2004). *Zivilgesellschaft und Sozialkapital. Herausforderungen politischer und sozialer Integration.* Wiesbaden: VS Verlag für Sozialwissenschaften.
Lane, M. J. (2011). *Social enterprise: Empowering mission-driven entrepreneurs.* Chicago: American Bar Association.
Leete, L. (2000). Wage equity and employee motivation in nonprofit and for-profit organizations. *Journal of Economic Behavior & Organization, 43,* 423–446.
Leete, L. (2006). Work in the nonprofit sector. In W. W. Powell & R. Steinberg (Eds.), *The nonprofit sector: A research handbook* (2nd ed., pp. 159–179). New Haven, CT: Yale University Press.
Leś, E., Nałęcz, S., & Pieliński, B. (2016). Third sector barriers in Poland. *TSI National Report No. 7.* Retrieved from http://thirdsectorimpact.eu/documentation/tsi-national-report-no-7-third-sector-barriers-poland/
Lijphart, A. (1999). *Patterns of democracy: Government forms and performance in thirty six countries.* New Haven: Yale University Press.
Lundström, T., & Wijkström, F. (1997). *The nonprofit sector in Sweden.* Manchester: Manchester University Press.

Maier, F., Meyer, M., & Steinbereithner, M. (2016). Nonprofit organizations becoming business-like: A systematic review. *Nonprofit and Voluntary Sector Quarterly, 45*(1), 64–86.

Mansfeldova, Z., Nałęcz, S., Priller, E., & Zimmer, A. (2004). Civil society in transition: Civic engagement and nonprofit organisations in Central and Eastern Europe after 1989. In A. Zimmer & E. Priller (Eds.), *Future of civil society: Making Central European nonprofit- organizations work* (pp. 99–127). Wiesbaden: VS Verlag.

Miranda, V. (2011). Cooking, caring and volunteering: Unpaid work around the world. OECD social, employment and migration *Working Papers, No. 116.* OECD Publishing. https://doi.org/10.1787/5kghrjm8s142-en

Moen, P., Dempster-McCain, D., & Williams, R. M. (1993). Successful aging. *American Journal of Sociology, 97*, 1612–1632.

Mogrovejo, R., Mora, A., & Vanhuynegem, P. (Eds.). (2012). *El cooperativismo en América Latina. Una diversidad de contribuciones al desarrollo sostenible.* La Paz: OIT, Oficina de la OIT para los Países Andinos.

Mohan, J., & Bennett, M. R. (2015). Community-level impacts of the third sector: Linking indicators of the local distribution of third sector resources to survey data on the likelihood of volunteering. *TSI Working Paper Series No. 7,* Seventh Framework Programme (grant agreement 613034), European Union. Brussels: Third Sector Impact.

Mohan, J., & Bennett, M. R. (2016). Community-level impacts of the third sector: Does the local distribution of voluntary organisations influence the likelihood of volunteering? *TSI Working Paper Series No. 7,* Seventh Framework Programme (grant agreement 613034), European Union. Brussels: Third Sector Impact.

Mohan, J., Kendall, J., & Brookes, N. (2016). Third sector impact: Towards a more nuanced understanding of barriers and constraints. *TSI National Report No. 1.* Retrieved from http://thirdsectorimpact.eu/documentation/tsi-barriers-briefing-no-2-towards-a-more-nuanced-understanding-of-barriers-and-constraints/

Monzón Campos, J. L., & Ávila, R. C. (2012). *The social economy in the European Union.* Brussels: European Economic and Social Committee.

Monzón, J. L., & Chaves, R. (2008a). The European social economy: Concept and dimensions of the third sector. *Annals of Public and Cooperative Economics, 79*(3/4), 549–577.

Monzón, J. L., & Chaves, R. (2008b). *The social economy in the European Union* (CIRIEC Report for the European Economic and Social Committee). Retrieved from http://www.eesc.europa.eu/resources/docs/qe-30-12-790-en-c.pdf

Monzón, J. L., & Chaves, R. (2009). The European social economy: Concept and dimensions of the third sector. *Annals of Public and Cooperative Economics, 79*(3/4), 560–561.

Musick, M. A., Herzog, A. R., & House, J. S. (1999). Volunteering and mortality among older adults: Findings from a national sample. *Journals of Gerontology Series B, 54*(3), 173–180.

Musick, M. A., & Wilson, J. (2003). Volunteering and depression: The role of psychological and social resources in different age groups. *Social Science & Medicine, 56*, 259–269.

Musick, M. A., & Wilson, J. (2008). *Volunteers, a social profile*. Bloomington and Indianapolis: Indiana University Press.

Nagy, R., & Sebestény, I. (2009). Table A 10 in methodological practice and practical methodology: Fifteen years in nonprofit statistics (Hungarian Statistical Review Special Number 12). Budapest: Hungarian Central Statistical Office. Retrieved from http://www.ksh.hu/statreview

Nicholls, A. (2004). Social entrepreneurship: The emerging landscape. In S. Crainer & D. Dearlove (Eds.), *Financial times handbook of management* (3rd ed., pp. 636–643). Prentice Hall/Financial Times.

Nicholls, A. (2006). *Social entrepreneurship: New models of sustainable social change*. Oxford: Oxford University Press.

Nicholls, A., Paton, R., & Emerson, J. (Eds.). (2010). *Social finance*. Oxford: Oxford University Press.

Nickel, P. M., & Eikenberry, A. M. (2016). Knowing and governing: The mapping of the nonprofit and voluntary sector as statecraft. *Voluntas: International Journal of Voluntary and Non-profit Organisations, 27*(1), 392–408.

Offe, C. (2005). *Reflections on America*. Cambridge: Polity Press.

Olson, M. (1965). *The logic of collective action*. Cambridge, MA: Harvard University Press.

Oman, D., Thoresen, C. E., & McMahon, K. (1999). Volunteerism and mortality among the community-dwelling elderly. *Journal of Health Psychology, 4*, 301–316.

Osborne, D., & Gaebler, T. (1992). *Reinventing government: How the entrepreneurial spirit is transforming the public sector*. Reading, MA: Addison-Wesley.

Pennerstorfer, A., Schneider, U., & Badelt, C. (2013). Der Nonprofit Sektor in Österreich. In R. Simsa, M. Meyer, & C. Badelt (Eds.), *Handbuch der nonprofit-organisation Strukturen und Management*. (5. überarbeitete Auflage) (pp. 55–75). Stuttgart: Handbuch der Nonprofit-Organisation.

Petrella, F., Richez-Battesti, N., Bruis, L., Maisonnasse, J., & Meunier, N. (2016). Challenges for the third sector in France. *TSI National Report No. 4*. Retrieved from http://thirdsectorimpact.eu/documentation/tsi-narional-report-on-challenges-for-the-third-sector-in-france/

Pollack, D. (2004). Zivilgesellschaft und Staat in der Demokratie. In A. Klein, K. Kern, B. Geißel, & M. Berer (Eds.), *Zivilgesellschaft und Sozialkapital. Herausforderungen politischer und sozialer Integration* (p. 23). Wiesbaden: VS Verlag für Sozialwissenschaften.
Post, S. G. (2005). Altruism, happiness, and health: It's good to be good. *International Journal of Behavioral Medicine, 12*(2), 66–77.
Putnam, R. D. (1993). *Making democracy work: Civic traditions in modern Italy*. Princeton, NJ: Princeton University Press.
Putnam, R. D. (2000). *Bowling alone*. New York: Touchstone.
Rhodes, R. A. W. (1997). *Understanding governance: Policy networks, governance, reflexivity, and accountability*. Buckingham: Open University Press.
Richez-Battesti, N., Petrella, F., & Enjolras, B. (2013). Economie sociale et solidaire et politiques publiques en France: Entre fragmentation et institutionnalisation. In R. Chaves-Avila & D. Demoustier (Eds.), *L'émergence de l'économie sociale dans les politiques publiques* (pp. 239–260). Brussels: Peter Lang.
Rochester, C., Ellis Paine, A., Howlett, S., & Zimmeck, M. (2010). *Volunteering and society in the 21st century*. Basingstoke: Palgrave Macmillan.
Rose-Ackerman. (1996). Altruism, nonprofits, and economic theory. *Journal of Economic Literature, XXXIV*, 701–728.
Rosemblum, N. (2003). Civil societies: Liberalism and the moral use of pluralism. In C. M. Elliot (Ed.), *Civil society and democracy: A reader*. Oxford: Oxford University Press.
Roth, R., & Rucht, D. (Eds.). (2008). *Die sozialen Bewegungen in Deutschland seit 1945: Ein Handbuch*. Frankfurt: Campus-Verlag.
Rothstein, B. (1998). *Just institutions matter: The moral and political logic of the universal welfare state*. Cambridge: Cambridge University Press.
Rothstein, B. (2001). Social capital in the social democratic welfare state. *Politics & Society, 29*(2), 207–241.
Rothstein, B. (2005). *Social traps and the problem of trust*. Cambridge: Cambridge University Press.
Rothstein, B., & Stolle, D. (2008). The state and social capital—An institutional theory of generalized trust. *Comparative Politics, 40*(4), 441.
Rymsza, M. (2013). The two decades of social policy in Poland: From protection to activation of citizens. In A. Evers & A.-M. Guillemard (Eds.), *Social policy and citizenship: The changing landscape* (pp. 305–334). Oxford: Oxford University Press.
Sabatier, P. A. (1998). The advocacy coalition framework: Revisions and relevance for Europe. *Journal of European Public Policy, 5*(1), 98–130.

Salamon, L. M. (1970). Comparative history and the theory of modernization. *World Politics, 23*(1), 83–103.

Salamon, L. M. (1987). Of market failure, voluntary failure, and third party government: Toward a theory of government -nonprofit relations in the modern welfare state. *Journal of Volontary Reaserch, 16*, 1.

Salamon, L. M. (1993). The marketization of welfare: Changing nonprofit and for-profit roles in the American welfare state. *Social Service Review, 67*(1), 16–39.

Salamon, L. M. (1994, July/August). The rise of the nonprofit sector. *Foreign Affairs*. Retrieved from https://www.foreignaffairs.com/articles/1994-07-01/rise-nonprofit-sector

Salamon, L. M. (1995). *Partners in public service: Government-nonprofit relations in the modern welfare state*. Baltimore, MD: Johns Hopkins University Press.

Salamon, L. M. (1996). *Partners in public service: Government-nonprofit relations in the modern welfare state*. Baltimore: Johns Hopkins University Press.

Salamon, L. M. (2010). Putting civil society on the economic map of the world. *Annals of Public and Cooperative Economics, 81*(2), 167–210.

Salamon, L. M. (2014a). *Leverage for good: An introduction to the new frontiers of philanthropy and social investment*. New York: Oxford University Press.

Salamon, L. M. (2014b). *The new frontiers of philanthropy: A guide to the new actos and tools reshaping global philanthropy and social investment*. Oxford: Oxford University Press.

Salamon, L. M. (2015). *The resilient sector revisited: The future of nonprofit America* (2nd ed.). Washington, DC: Brookings Institution.

Salamon, L. M., & Anheier, H. K. (Eds.). (1997a). *Defining the non-profit sector: A cross-national analysis*. Manchester: Manchester University Press.

Salamon, L. M., & Anheier, H. K. (1997b). In search of the nonprofit sector: The question of definition. In L. M. Salamon & H. K. Anheier (Eds.), *Defining the nonprofit sector: A crossnational analysis*. Manchester: Manchester University Press.

Salamon, L. M., & Anheier, H. K. (1998). Social origins of civil society: Explaining the non-profit sector cross-nationally. *Voluntas, 9*(3), 213–248.

Salamon, L. M., Anheier, H. K., List, R., Toepler, S., & Sokolowski, S. W. (1999). *Global civil society: Dimensions of the nonprofit sector, Volume I*. Baltimore, MD: The Johns Hopkins Center for Civil Society Studies.

Salamon, L. M., & Sokolowski, S. W. (2014). The third sector in Europe: Towards a consensus conceptualization. Third Sector Impact Project *Working Paper 02/2014*.

Salamon, L. M., & Sokolowski, S. W. (2016). Beyond nonprofits: Reconceptualizing the third sector. *Voluntas, 27*, 1515–1545.
Salamon, L. M., Sokolowski, S. W., & Associates (Eds.). (2004). *Global civil society: Dimensions of the nonprofit sector* (Vol. II). Bloomfield, CT: Kumarian Press.
Salamon, L. M., Sokolowski, S. W., & Haddock, M. (2011). Measuring the economic value of volunteer work globally: Concepts, estimates, and a roadmap to the future. *Annals of Public and Cooperative Economics, 82*(3), 217–252.
Salamon, L. M., Sokolowski, S. W., & Haddock, M. A. (2017). *Explaining civil society development: A social origins approach*. Baltimore: Johns Hopkins University Press.
Salamon, L. M., & Toepler, S. (2015). Government–nonprofit cooperation: Anomaly or necessity? *Voluntas: International Journal of Voluntary and Nonprofit Organizations, 26*(6), 2155–2177. https://doi.org/10.1007/s11266-015-9651-6.
Scheuregger, D. (2011). *Individualisierung im internationalen Vergleich*. Hamburg: Verlag Verlag Dr. Kovač.
Seligman, A. (1992). *The idea of civil society*. New York: Free Press.
Shils, E. (1991). The virtue of civil society. *Government and Opposition, 26*(1), 3–20.
Shils, E. (1997). *The virtue of civility*. Indianapolis: Liberty Fund.
Siemieńska, R., Domaradzka, A., & Matysiak, I. (2011). Local welfare in Poland from a historical and institutional perspective, Warsaw. *WILCO Publication No. 2*. Retrieved from http://www.wilcoproject.eu/national-reports-on-local-welfare-systems-focused-on-housing-employment-and-child-care/
Siemieńska, R., Domaradzka, A., & Matysiak, I. (2016). Warsaw: Paving new ways for participation of mothers, fathers, and children in local public and social life—The MaMa Foundation. In T. Brandsen, S. Cattacin, A. Evers, & A. Zimmer (Eds.), *Social innovations in the urban context* (pp. 181–188). New York: Springer (Open Access).
Sills, D. (1968). Voluntary associations: Sociological aspects. In D. Sills (Ed.), *International encyclopedia of the social sciences*. New York: Macmillan and Free Press.
Simsa, R. (2013). Gesellschaftliche Restgröße oder treibende Kraft? Soziologische Perspektiven auf NPOs. In R. Simsa, M. Meyer, & C. Badelt (Eds.), *Handbuch der Non-profit-Organisation: Strukturen und Management* (pp. 125–145). Stuttgart: Schäffer & Poeschel.
Simsa, R., Herndler, M., & Simic, Z. (2015). Third sector barriers in Austria. *TSI National Report No. 3*. Retrieved from http://thirdsectorimpact.eu/documentation/tsi-national-report-no-3-third-sector-barriers-in-austria/

Simsa, R., Herndler, M., & Totter, M. (2015). Meta-analysis of SROI studies—Indicators and proxies. *TSI Working Paper Series No. 6*, Seventh Framework Programme (grant agreement 613034), European Union. Brussels: Third Sector Impact.

Simsa, R., Meyer, M., & Badelt, C. (Eds.). (2013). *Handbuch der Non-profit-Organisation: Strukturen und Management*. Stuttgart: Schäffer & Poeschel.

Simsa, R., Rausher, O., Schober, C., & Moder, C. (2014). Methodological guidelines for impact assessment. Third Sector Impact *Working Paper No. 1*, Seventh Framework Programme (grant agreement 613034), European Union. Brussels: Third Sector Impact.

Sivesind, K. H. (2016). Developmental trends of the third sector in EU—Growth in paid employment and volunteering. *TSI Working Paper Series*, Seventh Framework Programme (grant agreement 613034), European Union. Brussels: Third Sector Impact.

Sivesind, K.-H. (2017). The changing roles of for-profit and nonprofit welfare provision in Norway, Sweden and Denmark. In K.-H. Sivesind & J. Saglie (Eds.), *Promoting active citizenship? Markets and choice in Scandinavian welfare*. London: Palgrave Macmillan.

Sivesind, K.-H., & Selle, P. (2010). Civil society in the Nordic countries: Between displacement and vitality. In R. Alapuro & H. Stenius (Eds.), *Nordic associations in a European perspective* (pp. 89–120). Baden-Baden: Nomos.

Six 6, P., & Leat, D. (1997). Inventing the British voluntary sector by committee: From Wolfenden to Deakin. *Non-profit Studies, 1*(2), 33–46.

Smith, A. (1759). *The theory of moral sentiments*. London: A. Millar.

Staggenborg, S. (2013). Institutionalization of social movements. In D. Snow, D. della Porta, B. Klandermans, & D. McAdam (Eds.), *The Wiley-Blackwell encyclopedia of social and political movements*. Oxford, UK: Wiley-Blackwell.

Steger, M. B., & Roy, R. K. (2010). *Neoliberalism: A very short introduction*. Oxford: Oxford University Press.

Stiglitz, J. E., Sen, A., & Fitoussi, J.-P. (2009). Report by the commission on the measurement of economic performance and social progress. Retrieved from www.stiglitz-sen-fitoussi.fr

Teasdale, S. (2010). What's in a name? The construction of social enterprise. *TSRC Working Paper 46*, Birmingham and Southampton: Third Sector Research Centre.

Teune, S. (2008). Rechtsradikale Zivilgesellschaft—contradictio in adiecto? *Forschungsjournal Soziale Bewegungen, 25*(4), 17–22.

Thoits, P. A., & Hewitt, L. N. (2001). Volunteer work and well-being. *Journal of Health and Social Behavior, 42*(2), 115–131.

Thräghardh, L. (Ed.). (2007). *State and civil society in Northern Europe: The Swedish model reconsidered*. New York and Oxford: Berghahn Books.

Tocqueville, A. (1955/2000). *Democracy in America*. New York: Vintage Books.

Tortia, E. (2008). Worker well-being and perceived fairness: Survey-based findings from Italy. *The Journal of Socio-Economics, 37*, 2020-2094.

Trætteberg, H. S., & Sivesind, K.-H. (2015). Ideelle organisasjoners særtrekk og merverdi på helse- og omsorgsfeltet (Rapport 2015:2). Oslo: Senter for forskning på sivilsamfunn og frivillig sektor. Retrieved from http://sivilsamfunn.no/content/download/108121/1857028/file/VR_2015_2_V4_nett.pdf

U.K., Office for the Third Sector. (2006). *Partnership in public services: An action plan for third sector involvement*. London: Office for the Third Sector, Cabinet Office.

United Nations. (2008). *System of national accounts 2008*. New York: United Nations.

United Nations Statistics Division. (2003). *Handbook on non-profit institutions in the system of national accounts*. New York: United Nations.

Uslaner, E. M. (2002). *The moral foundations of trust*. Cambridge: Cambridge University Press.

Uslaner, E. M. (2003). *Trust, democracy and governance: Can government politics influence generalised trust?* New York: Palgrave Macmillan.

Vabø, M., Christensen, K., Jacobsen, F. F., & Trætteberg, H. D. (2013). Marketisation in Norwegian eldercare: Preconditions, trends and resistance. In G. Meagher & M. Szebehely (Eds.), *Marketisation in Nordic eldercare: A research report on legislation, oversight, extent and consequences* (pp. 163-202). Stockholm: Department of Social Work, Stockholm University.

Van Til, J. (1988). *Mapping the third sector: Voluntarism in a changing social economy*. New York: The Foundation Center.

Venables, T. (2014). Panoramic view of the funding problems of the third sector and the social economy in the European Union. *Revista Espanola del Tercer Sector, 27*.

Walzer, M. (Ed.). (1995). *Toward a global civil society*. New York: Berghahn Books.

Walzer, M. (2003). The idea of civil society. In C. M. Elliot (Ed.), *Civil society and democracy: A reader*. Oxford: Oxford University Press.

Weisbrod, B. A. (1977). *The voluntary nonprofit sector*. Lexington, MA: D.C. Heath.

Weisbrod, B. A. (2001). An agenda for quantitative evaluation of the nonprofit sector: Needs, obstacles and approaches. In P. Flynn & V. A. Hodgkinson

(Eds.), *Measuring the impact of the Nonprofit sector* (pp. 273–290). New York: Kluwer Academic.

Wheeler, J. A., Gorey, K. M., & Greenblatt, B. (1998). The beneficial effects of volunteering for older volunteers and the people they serve: A meta-analysis. *International Journal of Aging and Human Development, 47*, 69–79.

Whiteley, P. (2004). *The art of happiness: Is volunteering the blueprint for bliss?* London: Economic and Social Research Council.

Wijkström, F. (2011). Charity speak and business talk: The on-going (re)hybridization of civil society. In F. Wijkström & A. Zimmer (Eds.), *Nordic civil societies at a cross-roads* (pp. 27–54). Baden-Baden: Nomos.

Wijkström, F., & Zimmer, A. (2011). *Nordic civil societies at a cross-roads. Transforming the popular movement tradition.* Baden-Baden: Nomos.

Wilson, J. (2000). Volunteering. *Annual Review of Sociology, 26*, 215–240.

Zimmer, A. (Ed.). (2013). *Civil societies compared: Germany and the Netherlands.* Baden-Baden: Nomos.

Zimmer, A. (2014). Money makes the world go round! Ökonomisierung und die Folgen für NPOs. In A. Zimmer & R. Simsa (Eds.), *Forschung zu Zivilgesellschaft, NPOs und Engagement* (pp. 163–180). Wiesbaden: Springer VS-Verlag.

Zimmer, A., Appel, A., Dittrich, C., Lange, C., Sitterman, B., Stallmann, F., et al. (2009). Germany: On the social policy centrality of the Free Welfare Associations. In J. Kendall (Ed.), *Handbook on third sector policy in Europe: Multi-level processes and organized civil society* (pp. 21–42). Aldershot: Edward Elgar.

Zimmer, A., & Hoemke, P. (2016). Riders on the storm. TSOs and the European Level of Government—A contested terrain. *TSI Working Paper No. 11.* Retrieved from http://thirdsectorimpact.eu/documentation/tsi-working-paper-no-11-riders-storm/

Zimmer, A., & Pahl, B. (2016). Comparative report: Learning from Europe—Report on third sector enabling and disabling factors. *TSI Comparative Report No. 1.* Retrieved from http://thirdsectorimpact.eu/documentation/comparative-report-learning-europe/

Zimmer, A., & Priller, E. (2007). *Gemeinnützige Organisationen im gesellschaftlichen Wandel. Ergebnisse der Dritte-Sektor-Forschung.* Wiesbaden: VS Verlag für Sozialwissenschaften.

Index

B
Barriers, 136–141
    external relation barriers, 136
    financial barrier, 136
    governance barrier, 136
    human resource, 136

C
Civil society, 96

E
European Union (EU), 133

F
Financial crisis, 131

I
Impact, 96
    social impact, 95
Individualization, 131

M
Marketization, 140

N
Neoliberalism, 131

Q
Quasi-market, 142

S

Satellite Account, 120
Social-democratic model, 146–148
Social enterprises, 95
Social finance, 95
Social investment, 95
Social origins theory, 74
Social value, 95

T

Third sector impact project's study, 114
Third sector organizations (TSO), 100, 101
TSE sector activities, 50
TSE sector revenue source, 50

U

Umbrella organizations, 135

V

Volunteering
 direct volunteering, 84–85

W

Welfare partnership, 70, 143–146
Workforce composition, 50
Workforce size, 50

The manufacturer's authorised representative in the EU is Springer Nature Customer Service Centre GmbH, Europaplatz 3, 69115 Heidelberg, Germany. If you have any concerns regarding our products, please contact ProductSafety@springernature.com

Printed and bound by CPI Group (UK) Ltd, Croydon, CR0 4YY
23/03/2026
02076739-0001